THE
Covenant
PATH

FINDING *the* TEMPLE *in*
the BOOK OF MORMON

THE
Covenant
PATH

FINDING *the* TEMPLE *in* *the* BOOK OF MORMON

VALIANT K. JONES

CFI
An imprint of Cedar Fort, Inc.
Springville, Utah

ISBN 13: 978-1-4621-3706-0

Published by CFI, an imprint of Cedar Fort, Inc.
2373 W. 700 S., Springville, UT 84663
Distributed by Cedar Fort, Inc., www.cedarfort.com

Library of Congress Control Number: 2019956118

Cover design by Shawnda T. Craig
Cover design © 2020 Cedar Fort, Inc.
Edited by Allyson Jones and Heather Holm
Typeset by Heather Holm

Printed in the United States of America

10 9 8 7 6 5 4 3 2 1

Printed on acid-free paper

To my late father, Merlyn Paul Jones Sr., who spent his life studying and teaching the restored gospel of Jesus Christ, which was one of the great loves of his heart. And to the other love of his heart, my mother, Rosemary Wright Jones, who has exemplified the pure love of Christ and a commitment to her temple covenants in everything she has ever done. She personifies the gospel, and everyone who interacts with her can feel it. My father once said that he didn't know which he loved more—the gospel of Jesus Christ or his wife, Rosemary. Then he realized that they were one and the same. These two saints made me who I am.

CONTENTS

PREFACE

In 1996, the Sunday School curriculum for the Gospel Doctrine class in The Church of Jesus Christ of Latter-day Saints was the Book of Mormon. That year my ward in Midland, Michigan, was blessed to have our class taught by one of the most insightful and interesting gospel teachers I have ever known, Brother Howard W. Clark. As we began the year of Book of Mormon study, Brother Clark said something close to this:

> Nephi was a great example of obedience, and he and his family made great personal sacrifices as they traveled through the wilderness and across oceans to reach their new promised land. Lehi taught his family the gospel, and Jacob taught the importance of chastity. I also expect that when they arrived in the promised land, they probably had a special prayer and consecrated themselves to God.

The topics in Brother Clark's description caught my attention: obedience, sacrifice, the gospel, chastity, and consecration. I recognized a covenant pattern there. While the presence of some of these topics in the early part of the Book of Mormon was not immediately apparent to me, others were so clearly noticeable that I thought there might be something deeper in this sacred text than I had realized. His comments were a spark that ignited years of scripture study, note taking, and pondering in the temple, which eventually resulted in this book. I am grateful for his embryonic insight.

I hope that the discussion presented in this book will add a new dimension of understanding for those who study the Book of Mormon without detracting from other insights already gained through study of that marvelous volume of scripture. Temple themes in the Small Plates of

Nephi will be presented. Seeing these themes makes the Book of Mormon appear even more sacred to me than it did before discovering them; however, I do not propose that the themes and teachings presented here are any more significant than any interpretations that others might discover in the book. The most important teachings and applications from the Book of Mormon are those that the Holy Ghost impresses upon our minds at any particular time. Nevertheless, I believe that the connections between the temple and themes taught in the early part of the Book of Mormon are so striking that they are worthy of special study and prayerful thought.

I want to make it clear that I alone am responsible for the ideas and conclusions presented in this book. While they do reflect Latter-day Saint doctrine and include many quotes of scriptures and statements by Church leaders, the context, organization, and conclusions drawn are my own. This book is not a product of The Church of Jesus Christ of Latter-day Saints, its leaders, or the publisher. I, alone, am responsible for this book, including any errors or flaws.

ACKNOWLEDGMENTS

I am grateful for the contributions of Howard W. Clark whom I mentioned in the preface. I must also acknowledge the Book of Mormon studies of my sister, Sandra L. Name, because they also contributed to this work. Sandra has spent many years compiling quotes and commentaries on every chapter of the Book of Mormon, and she uses these to teach a weekly Book of Mormon study class for her stake in Alpine, Utah. Her unpublished compilation was a valuable resource for me as I worked on this volume.

In addition, I am grateful for the many doctrinal discussions that my siblings and I shared through the years: Sandra and my other sisters, Anne Sloat and Christine Cole, as well as my brothers, Paul, Creed, Maurice, and Wesley Jones. They and their spouses have helped fortify my faith through their words and actions.

Sandra and our dear mother, Rosemary Wright Jones, read early drafts of this work and provided helpful comments and encouragement to move forward. Sandy's input was especially helpful. Readers can thank her for suggesting that I add a few personal stories to illustrate what started out as a purely doctrinal treatise. My only regret is that our father, Merlyn Paul Jones Sr., was not around to review and critique this work, but his influence is present on every page.

My treasured wife, Lori Ransom Jones, has been a great support throughout my many long hours of writing. I am especially grateful for the work that she and our daughter Allyson put into later reviews and edits of this book. Both are trained in literary skills, unlike their engineer husband and father, so their suggestions and finishing touches were greatly appreciated.

I am grateful for all my children—Allyson, Bradley, Craig, Camilla, and Dallin—and the crucible of learning that my wife and I have experienced in raising them. I am grateful for the faith they exhibit in the Book of Mormon and the restored gospel of Jesus Christ as they face the challenges of today's world. I hope that this book will fortify them and their children as they continue along the covenant path.

Finally, I am grateful to Cedar Fort for publishing this work, and especially for the input of editor Heather Holm and the beautiful cover by Shawnda T. Craig.

CHAPTER 1

INTRODUCTION:
A WISE PURPOSE

Every member of The Church of Jesus Christ of Latter-day Saints knows how the Book of Mormon begins: "I, Nephi, having been born of goodly parents" (1 Nephi 1:1). This is the story of a family, led by their prophet father, Lehi, and documented by his prophet son, Nephi. It is a family history. They left Jerusalem six hundred years before Christ was born and traveled to the new world where they established a new civilization. After arriving in their promised land, Nephi was commanded of the Lord to start a record of his people, which Nephi did, engraving it on metal plates. This record was to be a secular history of his people (see 1 Nephi 9:2–4; 2 Nephi 5:33), although Nephi, in addition, included "the prophecies of my father; and also many of mine own prophecies" (1 Nephi 19:1).

Later, Nephi was commanded of God to write a second record of "the ministry and the prophecies, the more plain and precious parts of them" (1 Nephi 19:3), and "things which are good in my sight, for the profit of thy people" (2 Nephi 5:30). This, he stated, was for a "wise purpose" known only to the Lord (see 1 Nephi 9:5–6; 19:3; Words of Mormon 1:7). Nephi's second record was written on a set of metal plates smaller than the first and has therefore become known as the Small Plates of Nephi. They comprise the books of 1 Nephi through Omni in the Book of Mormon.

Of course, the primary wise purpose for Nephi's second record was to prepare for the day when Joseph Smith's translation of the first part of Nephi's record would be lost. After the loss of the 116-page manuscript translation from the Large Plates of Nephi, Joseph was told not to retranslate the text (see headings to D&C chapters 3 and 10). The Lord explained that evil people had modified the transcript and that Joseph should not repeat the work he had done: "For, behold, if you should bring forth the same words they will say that you have lied and that you have pretended to translate, but that you have contradicted yourself" (D&C 10:31). The Lord told Joseph to translate the separate, independent history of Nephi and his family instead, which was contained on the Small Plates of Nephi (see D&C 10:30, 41).

It is a marvel that the Lord foresaw this deception so many centuries earlier and had prepared for it by directing Nephi to engrave a second record that covered the same time period. This is truly a wise purpose for the existence of the Small Plates of Nephi. However, Elder Jeffrey R. Holland has pointed out that the Lord had more than one wise purpose for preparing the Small Plates of Nephi. Chief among these purposes is the triad of witnesses given by Nephi, Jacob, and Isaiah regarding two important truths. Elder Holland stated, "After reading Nephi, Jacob, and Isaiah, we know two things in bold, powerful strokes—(1) that Jesus is the Christ, the Son of the living God, and (2) that God will keep his covenant promises with the remnants of the house of Israel. These two themes constitute the very purpose of the Book of Mormon."[1]

These two themes—testifying of Jesus Christ and testifying that God fulfills His covenant promises—are specified on the title page of the Book of Mormon. They not only constitute the purpose of the Book of Mormon, but they also are the two most prominent and repeated themes in the Small Plates of Nephi. The focus on Jesus Christ stands out from Lehi's vision in chapter 1 of 1 Nephi, wherein "he saw One descending out of the midst of heaven" (1 Nephi 1:9), to Amaleki's plea in the final verses of Omni to "come unto Christ, who is the Holy One of Israel" (Omni 1:26). The focus on God's covenant promises to Israel is equally prominent throughout the Small Plates.

Both themes are taught repeatedly in the words of Nephi and Jacob and in their quotations of Isaiah. Explaining one reason why he quoted Isaiah, Jacob declared, "I have read these things that ye might *know concerning the covenants of the Lord* that he has covenanted with all the house of Israel" (2 Nephi 9:1; emphasis added). Jacob then proceeded to give one of the most beautiful dissertations on the Atonement of Christ in all of recorded scripture. He ended by stating, "How great are the *covenants of the Lord*, and how great his condescensions unto the children of men" (2 Nephi 9:53; emphasis added). After recording Jacob's speech, Nephi added, "Behold, my soul delighteth in the *covenants of the Lord* which he hath made to our fathers. . . . And my soul delighteth in proving unto my people that save *Christ should come* all men must perish" (2 Nephi 11:5–6; emphasis added).

If Christ and covenants are the primary themes of the Small Plates, is it possible that this portion of scripture might also contain direction on the specific covenants that God would have us enter into as we seek to come unto Christ?

As I have studied the Small Plates of Nephi, I have come to recognize that, underlying the two main themes of Christ and covenants, there is, indeed, a sacred pattern of subthemes that I believe outline the instructions and covenants that the Lord would have us commit to follow as we become, like the Nephites of old, a covenant people. I call these the covenant path themes of the Small Plates of Nephi. These covenant topics present themselves as subthemes within the Small Plates, one for each book, and they are the topics that will be discussed in subsequent chapters. They include the following:

1 Nephi:	Obedience and Sacrifice
2 Nephi:	The Gospel
Jacob:	Chastity
Enos:	Prayer
Jarom:	Family History Research
Omni (and King Benjamin):	Consecration

These topics outline a covenant path that we should follow as covenant children of God. Studying these subthemes in the sacred Small Plates portion of the Book of Mormon will help us incorporate the book's primary themes of Christ and covenants into our lives and help us return to live eternally in God's presence.

Nephi explained that the writings on his Small Plates were used to instruct his people, this being one of the wise purposes for which they were prepared. He wrote,

> And after I had made these [large] plates by way of commandment, I Nephi, received a commandment that the ministry and prophecies, the more plain and precious parts of them, should be written upon these [small] plates; and that the things which were written should be kept *for the instruction of my people*, who should possess the land, and also for *other wise purposes*, which purposes are known unto the Lord.

. . . Nevertheless, I do not write anything upon plates save it be that I think *it be sacred.* (1 Nephi 19:3, 6; emphasis added)

The key principles recorded in the Small Plates were foundational topics of instruction for the Nephite people, and they were considered sacred. King Benjamin verified this, stating, "And behold, also the plates of Nephi, which contain the records and sayings of our fathers from the time they left Jerusalem until now, and they are true. . . . And now, my sons, I would that ye should remember to search them diligently, that ye may profit thereby" (Mosiah 1:6–7). Clearly, the spiritual leaders of the Nephites used the sacred teachings on the plates of Nephi to instruct and bless their people.

We will likewise be blessed if we will incorporate these covenant path teachings from the Small Plates of Nephi into our own lives. As with all scripture, the key principles and themes are not always presented as doctrinal sermons on those topics. Many are lessons from the life experiences of the people who lived them. Following the path outlined by these principles will help us to come unto Christ as a covenant people so that we can fulfill the promises of the Lord given unto the house of Israel.

A SACRED TEMPLE CONNECTION

Many endowed Latter-day Saints will recognize that the covenant path themes described above are reflected in the covenants, rites, and focus of the temple endowment. We do not often see or hear a list of the endowment covenants presented outside of the temple. They are considered sacred and, like the Lord said regarding the original name of the Melchizedek Priesthood, "out of respect or reverence" and "to avoid the too frequent repetition" (D&C 107:4), we do not often speak directly of these covenants and their association with the temple endowment. However, avoiding too frequent repetition does not mean they are never mentioned. Just as we know that the original name of the Melchizedek Priesthood is "the Holy Priesthood, after the Order of the Son of God" (D&C 107:3), so it is that several prophets and apostles have, on occasion, named some or all of the covenants we make in the temple endowment. In the April 2019 general conference, Elder David A. Bednar said,

We may discuss the basic purposes of and the doctrine and principles associated with temple ordinances and covenants. . . . Across the generations, . . . the doctrinal purposes of temple ordinances and covenants have been taught extensively by Church leaders. . . . Information . . . is available about following the Savior by receiving and honoring covenants to keep the law of obedience, the law of sacrifice, the law of the gospel, the law of chastity, and the law of consecration.[2]

In addition, President Ezra Taft Benson gave the following description of the covenants of the temple endowment at a BYU devotional in 1977 while he was President of the Quorum of the Twelve Apostles:

Celestial laws, embodied in certain ordinances belonging to the Church of Jesus Christ, are complied with by voluntary covenants. The laws are spiritual. Thus, our Father in Heaven has ordained certain holy sanctuaries, called temples, in which these laws may be fully explained, the laws include the law of obedience and sacrifice, the law of the gospel, the law of chastity, and the law of consecration.[3]

Numerous other Church leaders or Church-related publications have presented statements that specify one or more of the covenants of the temple endowment. Many are included in an appendix at the end of this chapter.

If the subthemes that have been proposed for the books of the Small Plates of Nephi truly exist therein—and this book will seek to demonstrate that they do—then the parallels between these subthemes and the temple covenants are striking. In fact, they are more than striking; they are remarkable. They are sacred and inspired. Their presence is a divine witness that the covenants of the temple are eternal, that the Book of Mormon is true, and that Joseph Smith was truly a prophet of God, for such an integration of the Book of Mormon and the temple endowment could only have been designed by God.

It should not come as a surprise that there would be a strong connection between temple worship and the scriptures. My wife and I once watched a movie that had a scene inside a Jewish synagogue where the congregants were preparing for worship. Into the hall walked the Rabbi, carrying a scroll, the Torah. People reached out from the aisles and from the balcony above, trying to touch the holy scriptures as he walked by. They did this with great awe and respect for their holy word. The Rabbi moved through the aisle to the front of the sanctuary where there was an altar. He stood behind the altar, raised the scriptures high above his head, and then laid them respectfully on the altar.

When I saw that dramatic depiction, I knew the roots from whence it came. The scriptures are treated with similar attention and respect (albeit with much less drama) when we make covenants in our temples today. The covenants there are repeatedly characterized as being taught in the holy scriptures. The obvious lesson is that the Lord intends that we should use the scriptures to understand the temple and, in particular, to understand the covenants of the temple. The remainder of this book will attempt do to this through an analysis of the Small Plates of Nephi. However, in keeping with the sacredness of the temple, the proposed subthemes of each book will be discussed as principles and covenants, independent of direct references to temple ceremonies and instruction.

Sharing insights on these sacred covenant topics carries some risks. One of the great strengths of temple worship is that it is individual. By using the Holy Ghost as our personal guide for understanding the covenants of the temple, we receive customized insights to fit our individual circumstances and needs. Elder John A. Widtsoe said, "The endowment which was given by revelation can best be understood by revelation; and to those who seek most vigorously, with pure hearts, will the revelation be greatest."[4]

When the Lord appeared to the Nephites, He spent a full day teaching and ministering to them at the temple in Bountiful. Then He told them, "I perceive that ye are weak, that ye cannot understand all my words which I am commanded of the Father to speak unto you at this time. Therefore, go ye unto your homes, and ponder upon the things which I have said, and ask of the Father, in my name, that ye may understand, and prepare your minds for the morrow, and I come unto you again" (3 Nephi 17:2–3).

Benefits come from having to wrestle through the spirit to gain understanding and revelation directly from God. Spiritual growth is more permanent when we discover insights on our own. This cannot easily happen when everything is spoon-fed to us. Joseph Smith said, "The things of God are of deep import; and time, and experience, and careful and ponderous and solemn thoughts can only find them out. Thy mind, O man! if thou wilt lead a soul unto salvation, must stretch as high as the utmost heavens, and search into and contemplate the darkest abyss, and the broad expanse of eternity—thou must commune with God."[5]

So we don't typically discuss the temple ceremonies and covenants outside of the temple. Rather, we are instructed to go to the temple often and think about what is taught. We should use our own "time and experience and careful and ponderous and solemn thoughts" to discover the things of God. This requires us to develop our minds and strengthen our spirits so that we can understand the ways of God. The thing that separates man from animals is that we can reason. We have advanced brains and self-awareness and can develop our minds further. That is part of our potential to become like God. In the temple, our minds and spirits are stretched as we pray and think about the ceremonies and symbols presented therein.

However, the personal, revelatory experiences we seek inside the temple should be supplemented by scripture study outside of the temple. The scriptures will not only help us better understand the stories presented in the temple, but they will also help us better understand our temple covenants. For example, we can learn about obedience and sacrifice from stories in the Old Testament and from the great example recorded in the New Testament of Christ's obedience to His Father and of His great atoning sacrifice. And the gospel is taught so clearly throughout the entire Book of Mormon—especially in the teachings of Christ during his personal visit to the Nephites. Also, in the New Testament, the Apostle Paul wrote frequently about the need to follow the law of chastity. And finally, there are specific instructions on the law of consecration in the Doctrine and Covenants. Indeed, all of the books of scripture are worthy of study as resources for understanding our temple covenants.

The Book of Mormon is an especially strong witness that God's ancient covenants continue with us today. In a compelling article on covenants, Elder Lance B. Wickman of the Seventy wrote the following:

> The Book of Mormon provides an unparalleled perspective on covenants. . . . Indeed, one of the principal purposes of the Book of Mormon is to restore knowledge and understanding concerning God's covenants with man. The title page itself contains this statement by Moroni regarding the purposes of the book: ". . . to show unto the remnant of the House of Israel what great things the Lord hath done for their fathers; *and that they may know the covenants of the Lord, that they are not cast off forever*" (emphasis added). . . . Thus, the Book of Mormon reestablishes truths associated with the sacred covenants of the Lord. Many of these truths we find reflected in the writings of Nephi. He delighted in the Lord's covenant with the patriarchs Abraham, Isaac, and Jacob.[6]

Elder Wickman supported his declaration with this statement by Nephi: "My soul delighteth in the covenants of the Lord which he hath made to our fathers; yea, my soul delighteth in his grace, and in his justice, and power, and mercy in the great and eternal plan of deliverance from death" (2 Nephi 11:5).

It is clear that the entire Book of Mormon is a powerful witness of God's covenants, and I propose that one of the wise purposes for which the Lord has given us the Small Plates of Nephi is to help us better understand and keep our temple covenants. In support of this purpose, each book of the Small Plates will be analyzed through the lens of its associated covenant path theme.

This analysis will reach a little beyond the Small Plates of Nephi to include, alongside the book of Omni, King Benjamin's farewell address as recorded in Mosiah 1–6. This inclusion is explained in that chapter. Suffice it to say here that King Benjamin and Amaleki, the final author of the book of Omni, were contemporaries and that the works of both combine to establish the theme of consecration.

Many readers will recognize that prayer, the proposed theme of the book of Enos, is not among the list of temple covenants given in the earlier quotes and references. However, it is openly acknowledged in the Church that temple worship includes prayer circles [7, 8, 9] and prayer rolls. [10, 11] Knowing this, and seeing prayer as the obvious theme of the book of Enos, it seems appropriate to include a discussion of prayer as part of the covenant path.

Also, family history research, the proposed theme of the book of Jarom, is another topic not included in the list of temple covenants. However, there is no question about the importance of family history research to temple work, so it can certainly be considered a covenant path theme. As will be shown, the book of Jarom has some things to teach us about this theme.

I hope that this study of the sacred pattern outlined by the Small Plates of Nephi will help all of us be more determined to stay on the covenant path. May we all follow the counsel of President Russell M. Nelson who encouraged, "To each member of the Church I say, keep on the covenant path. Your commitment to follow the Savior by making covenants with Him and then keeping those covenants will open the door to every spiritual blessing and privilege available to men, women, and children everywhere." [12]

Appendix to Chapter 1
Public Descriptions of Temple Covenants

The following quotes supplement others given earlier in this chapter.

James E. Talmage

The ordinances of the endowment embody certain obligations on the part of the individual, such as covenant and promise to observe the law of strict virtue and chastity, to be charitable, benevolent, tolerant and pure; to devote both talent and material means to the spread of truth and the uplifting of the race; to maintain devotion to the cause of truth; and to seek in every way to contribute to the great preparation that the earth may be made ready to receive her King—the Lord Jesus Christ. With the taking of each covenant and the assuming of each obligation a promised blessing is pronounced, contingent upon the faithful observance of the conditions.[13]

Gordon B. Hinckley

We are a covenant people. I have had the feeling that if we could just encourage our people to live by three or four covenants everything else would take care of itself. . . . The first of these is the covenant of the sacrament. . . . Second, the covenant of tithing. . . . Three, the covenants of the temple: Sacrifice, the willingness to sacrifice for this the Lord's work—and inherent in that law of sacrifice is the very essence of the Atonement. . . . Consecration, which is associated with it, a willingness to give everything, if need be, to help in the on-rolling of this great work. And a covenant of love and loyalty one to another in the bonds of marriage, fidelity, chastity, morality. If our people could only learn to live by these covenants, everything else would take care of itself, I am satisfied.[14]

Bruce R. McConkie

We are commanded to live in harmony with the Lord's laws, to keep all his commandments, to sacrifice all things if need be for his name's sake, to conform to the terms and conditions of the law of consecration. We have made covenants so to do—solemn, sacred, holy covenants, pledging ourselves before gods and angels. We are under covenant to live the law of obedience. We are under covenant to live the law of sacrifice. We are under covenant to live the law of consecration. . . . It is our privilege to consecrate our time, talents, and means to build up his kingdom. We are called upon to sacrifice, in one degree or another, for the furtherance of his work. Obedience is essential to salvation; so, also, is service; and so, also, are consecration and sacrifice.[15]

ROBERT D. HALES

As endowed temple recommend holders, we establish patterns of Christlike living. These include obedience, making sacrifices to keep the commandments, loving one another, being chaste in thought and action, and giving of ourselves to build the kingdom of God. Through the Savior's Atonement and by following these basic patterns of faithfulness, we receive "power from on high" (D&C 95:8) to face the challenges of life. We need this divine power today more than ever. It is power we receive only through temple ordinances.[16]

JEFFREY R. HOLLAND

That is what God does for us every time we make a covenant with Him. He endows us. We promise to do certain things, depending on the ordinance, and He promises special gifts in return. . . . So . . . if we want to have the door of heaven thrown open to us that we might receive the powers of godliness, we must keep our covenants! . . . We need every divine power to enhance our effort and move the Church steadily forward. The key to that for us as individuals is the covenant we make in the temple—our promise to obey and sacrifice, to consecrate unto the Father, and His promise to empower us with a great endowment.[17]

JAMES E. FAUST

In the temples of the Lord, we learn obedience. We learn sacrifice. We make the vows of chastity and have our lives consecrated to holy purposes.[18]

BOYD K. PACKER

We are a covenant people. We covenant to give of our resources in time and money and talent—all we are and all we possess—to the interest of the kingdom of God upon the earth. In simple terms, we covenant to do good. We are a covenant people, and the temple is the center of our covenants. It is the source of the covenant.[19]

D. TODD CHRISTOFFERSON

The law of the celestial kingdom is, of course, the gospel law and covenants, which include our constant remembrance of the Savior and our pledge of obedience, sacrifice, consecration, and fidelity.[20]

BONNIE D. PARKIN

So often we talk of making and keeping covenants, but exactly what are they? . . . In the temple, we . . . covenant to be obedient, to sacrifice, to keep ourselves worthily pure, to contribute to the spreading of truth, to be chaste, to pray, to live the gospel, and to be forever faithful.[21]

DALLIN H. OAKS

A willingness to sacrifice all we possess in the work of the Lord is surely a strength. In fact, it is a covenant we make in sacred places.[22]

ENSIGN

The temple endowment is a gift that provides perspective and power. During the temple endowment we receive instructions and make covenants related to our eternal exaltation. . . . You can learn more about the principles behind the covenants we make in the endowment by studying the following:

- "Obedience," *Gospel Principles* (2009), 200–206.
- M. Russell Ballard, "The Law of Sacrifice," *Ensign*, Oct. 1998, 6.
- On "the law of [the] gospel" (D&C 104:18), see D&C 42.
- "The Law of Chastity," *Gospel Principles* (2009), 224–32.
- D. Todd Christofferson, "Reflections on a Consecrated Life," *Ensign*, Nov. 2010, 16.[23]

ENCYCLOPEDIA OF MORMONISM

Covenants involving obligations of faithfulness, magnifying one's calling, sacrifice, obedience, righteousness, chastity, and consecration are made when one is ordained to the Melchizedek Priesthood, when one receives the temple endowment, and when a man and woman enter into eternal marriage.[24]

Chapter 2

1 Nephi:
Obedience and Sacrifice

Obedience and sacrifice are clear subthemes of the book of 1 Nephi. Early in the book, we read Nephi's faithful declaration of obedience: "I will go and do the things which the Lord hath commanded, for I know that the Lord giveth no commandments unto the children of men, save he shall prepare a way for them that they may accomplish the thing which he commandeth them" (1 Nephi 3:7). Nephi's example of obedience without fear or hesitation was constant from the day his family left Jerusalem. Alongside this, his family experienced sacrifice of epic proportions as the entire group abandoned their riches and the comforts of their home in Jerusalem, traveled through the desert wilderness of the Arabian Peninsula while subsisting mostly on raw meat, and then braved a fierce ocean voyage in ships of their own making before finally arriving in their new promised land. In addition, Nephi experienced a lot of personal sacrifice as he suffered extensive abuse and assaults on his life at the hands of his older brothers. Truly, sacrifice defined much of the family's journey, and obedience was a standard of Nephi's life.

God and His prophets have emphasized obedience and sacrifice since the days of Adam (see Moses 5:5–8). Ritual animal sacrifices foreshadowed the sacrifice of Jesus Christ, the Son of God; however, after His Crucifixion, the nature of the law of sacrifice changed: Today we are required to sacrifice whatever is necessary in our personal lives in order to obey God. The book of 1 Nephi shows many examples of this type of sacrifice. Nephi and other members of his family were willing to make these sacrifices because they first chose to be obedient to God. On the other hand, his older brothers exhibited counter-examples of rebellion and disobedience.

Obedience has been called "the first law of heaven,"ᵃ and sacrifice could be called the second law of heaven.ᵇ In fact, President Benson linked them together as one law: "the law of obedience and sacrifice."[26] Our covenants include commitments to keep these laws. This chapter will examine what we can learn about the principles of obedience and sacrifice from the teachings and experiences chronicled in 1 Nephi.

NEPHI CHOOSES THE PATH OF OBEDIENCE

The start of Nephi's record does not reveal much about his early childhood; he summarized his entire upbringing in one sentence, declaring, "I, Nephi, having been born of goodly parents" (1 Nephi 1:1). After a brief introduction, Nephi shifted attention to his father, Lehi, whose prophecies in Jerusalem resulted in people trying to kill him. Nephi then told of their family's departure after his father was commanded in a dream to leave. They camped near a river that Lehi called Laman, in a valley that he called Lemuel. While there, sharp words ensued between Lehi and his two oldest sons. These older brothers "did murmur in many things against their father, because he was a visionary man" (1 Nephi 2:11). Lehi responded to them "with power, being filled with the Spirit, until their frames did shake before him. And he did confound them, that they durst not utter against him; wherefore, they did as he commanded them" (1 Nephi 2:14).

After observing all of this drama, Nephi made a decision on where he stood. He wrote,

---

a Joseph F. Smith called obedience "the first law of heaven" in a general conference address on October 7, 1873.[25] Consider also D&C 130:20–21.

b The first and second "laws of heaven" are, of course, different from the first and second "great commandments" that Christ declared to be love of God and love of neighbor (see Matthew 22:36–39). The covenant laws of obedience and sacrifice are subordinate to the commandments to love. Indeed, speaking of the commandments to love God and our neighbor, Christ said, "On these two commandments hang all the law and the prophets" (Matthew 22:40). The laws of obedience and sacrifice were given as expressions of God's love in order to bless us and help us avoid anguish and sorrow. Likewise, our love of God should be the motivating force behind our commitments to the laws of obedience and sacrifice. Love reigns supreme.

And it came to pass that I, Nephi, being exceedingly young, nevertheless being large in stature, and also having great desires to know of the mysteries of God, wherefore, I did cry unto the Lord; and behold *he did visit me, and did soften my heart* that I did believe all the words which had been spoken by my father; wherefore, I did not rebel against him like unto my brothers. (1 Nephi 2:16; emphasis added)

What a remarkable experience: The Lord visited Nephi and softened his heart. It is hard to think of Nephi as one who ever needed to have his heart softened. This gives hope to the rest of us. It shows that Nephi had to obtain his own witness that the words of his father were from God, and more important, it gives us insights into the personal conversion process that Nephi went through to attain the level of obedience and sacrifice that defined his identity ever after.

Nephi had been observing the examples of those around him. He listened to his father's prophecies in Jerusalem. He watched his rebellious brothers complain, and he saw his father respond with great power. All of this family tension instilled "great desires" in Nephi to know the mysteries of God, motivating him to pray. He turned to the Lord, but his prayer was not a routine ritual of rote requests. He was so filled with desire that he "did cry unto the Lord." His prayer was one of faith, for he states that he "did not rebel against him like unto my brothers."

Nephi summarized his experience:

And it came to pass that the Lord spake unto me, saying: Blessed art thou, Nephi, because of thy faith, for thou hast sought me diligently, with lowliness of heart. And inasmuch as ye shall keep my commandments, ye shall prosper, and shall be led to a land of promise; yea, even a land which I have prepared for you; yea, a land which is choice above all other lands. (1 Nephi 2:19–20)

During this time of family stress and turmoil, Nephi sought the Lord, and he did so humbly. This shows that his commitment to obedience, which he was soon to declare to his father, was an outgrowth of his faith in Christ. We, likewise, should build our commitment to obey upon a foundation of faith in Christ.

Immediately after his interview with the Lord, Nephi went to the tent of his father. He likely shared his sacred experience with his prophet father. Lehi then explained to Nephi that the Lord had told him in a dream that Nephi and his brothers should return to Jerusalem and obtain "the record of the Jews and also a genealogy of my forefathers [which were] engraven upon plates of brass" (1 Nephi 3:3), which were in the possession of their caretaker, a man called Laban.

Lehi had already made this request of Nephi's older brothers, for he said, "And now, behold thy brothers murmur, saying it is a hard thing which I have required of them; but behold I have not required it of them, but it is a commandment of the Lord" (1 Nephi 3:5). Lehi then expressed his confidence in Nephi, adding, "Therefore go, my son, and thou shalt be favored of the Lord, because thou hast not murmured" (1 Nephi 3:6).

And how did Nephi respond? It is a declaration that has become iconic for Latter-day Saints: "I will go and do the things which the Lord hath commanded, for I know that the Lord giveth no commandments unto the children of men, save he shall prepare a way for them that they may accomplish the thing which he commandeth them" (1 Nephi 3:7).

Nephi's example of obedience has become an anthem for Primary children throughout the world. Singing of Nephi's courage, they proudly declare, "I will go; I will do the things the Lord commands. I know the Lord provides a way; he wants me to obey."[27] Nephi's courage to obey the Lord in all circumstances became the foundation of all his later experiences and teachings. Whether the command was to go and get the plates, or to depart into the unknown wilderness with limited provisions, or to build a ship and embark upon the deep and unknown sea, Nephi obeyed with unquestioning faith that he could accomplish what the Lord had commanded.

Nephi's obedience was an echo of the example he had seen in his father, Lehi. Although quoted less often, we read of Lehi's example of faithful obedience one chapter earlier: "And it came to pass that the Lord commanded my father, even in a dream, that he should take his family and depart into the wilderness. And it came to pass that *he was obedient* unto the word of the Lord, wherefore *he did as the Lord commanded him*" (1 Nephi 2:2–3; emphasis added). Lehi was willing to obey the Lord even in the face of great personal difficulty and sacrifice.

Following in his father's footsteps, Nephi did not hesitate when charged with the difficult task of obtaining the brass plates. He responded with faith and confidence that he would go and do what the Lord had commanded. From that point onward, every effort Nephi made to obtain the plates was a reflection of his commitment to obey. After their first failed attempt, he said to his brothers, "As the Lord liveth, and as we live, we will not go down unto our father in the wilderness until we have accomplished the thing which the Lord hath commanded us. Wherefore, let us be faithful in keeping the commandments of the Lord" (1 Nephi 3:15–16). Again, after the second failed attempt, Nephi said to his brothers, "Let us go up again unto Jerusalem, and let us be faithful in keeping the commandments of the Lord" (1 Nephi 4:1). And later, when Nephi was trying to convince Laban's servant, Zoram, to join them, he declared, "Surely the Lord hath commanded us to do this thing; and shall we not be diligent in keeping the commandments of the Lord?" (1 Nephi 4:34). Repeatedly, he declared his commitment to obey the Lord's commands.

What a remarkable role model for obedience Nephi is! We can see that it was a conscious choice on his part to be obedient, based on his faith in Christ. He observed the good and bad examples around him, and he allowed the Lord to soften his heart. From that time forth, he never wavered in his commitment to obey. We should all follow his example.

Obedience in Adversity

Nephi showed us that even though it is not always obvious how we will be able to follow the commandments and direction from the Lord, we should diligently try. When Nephi and his brothers went to get the brass plates, they had to try three times before succeeding. First, they tried simply asking Laban for the plates. Then they tried purchasing the plates. And finally, as a last resort, Nephi was told by the Spirit that he had to take the plates by force. Nephi and his brothers were obviously discouraged after the first two attempts, but Laman and Lemuel let their frustration turn to anger, insomuch that they beat Nephi and Sam with a rod until an angel intervened and halted the abuse.

After suffering a beating and two failed attempts to get the brass plates, perhaps Nephi was discouraged and wondered why they had not been able to accomplish what the Lord had commanded. Certainly the Lord could have orchestrated some other way for Nephi to obtain the plates. Since in the end God had to inspire Nephi to slay Laban, why had He not inspired Nephi to do so during their first attempt to get the plates? Maybe the timing wasn't right. Or maybe Nephi was neither ready nor willing to take such drastic measures at that time. Discouraging as they were, the first two failures prepared Nephi for his eventual success in obeying the Lord.

Sometimes we, too, seek diligently to obey commandments of the Lord, only to be faced with hardships and opposition. This can make us question the Lord's commandments. Nevertheless, we will be blessed if we will follow Nephi's example and continue to be diligent in keeping the commands even after initial failures. Often there is as much benefit in the process we follow in obeying the Lord as there is in attaining the apparent final objective. Sometimes the means are part of the end. In Nephi's case, the brass plates themselves were vital to the future of his people, but there were also lessons in the process that occurred to secure them. Perhaps Nephi became the great prophet he was by struggling with this issue of obedience under such difficult circumstances.

Elder Jeffrey R. Holland said that he believes that this story of obtaining the plates was told in such detail at the beginning of the Book of Mormon "in order to focus every reader of that record on the absolutely fundamental gospel issue of obedience and submission to the communicated will of the Lord. If Nephi cannot yield to this terribly painful command, if he cannot bring himself to obey, then it is entirely probable that he can never succeed or survive in the tasks that lie just ahead."[28] Sometimes we, too, need to go through our own struggles with obedience in order to prepare us to succeed, or at least survive, in the customized challenges and personal sacrifices that lie ahead for us.

QUESTIONING AND OBEDIENCE

Nephi's commitment to obey did not mean that he had no questions about God's commands. He obviously struggled when he "was constrained by the Spirit that [he] should kill Laban" (1 Nephi 4:10). He declared, "But I said in my heart: Never at any time have I shed the blood of man. And I shrunk and would that I might not slay him" (1 Nephi 4:10). This command went contrary to everything he had ever been taught. From his childhood, he had been taught the commandment, "Thou shalt not kill." How could he now kill Laban as he lay helpless on the ground, "drunken with wine" (1 Nephi 4:7)?

Nephi struggled to obey. For eight verses he recounted the internal turmoil he went through. He wrestled with mental anguish, considering all the reasons he should do this, even though he said, "I shrunk and would that I might not slay him" (1 Nephi 4:10). As we read his mental arguments, we sense that he was trying to talk himself into doing something that in his heart he did not want to do. And yet, it was his heart that was moved when thoughts of his posterity gave him the courage to reconcile the thoughts of his mind with the feelings of his heart.

Nephi knew that if his descendants were to be obedient to the commandments of God, they would need a record of those commandments. He wrote, "I remembered the words of the Lord which he spake unto me in the wilderness, saying that: Inasmuch as thy seed shall keep my commandments, they shall prosper in the land of promise. Yea, and I also thought that they could not keep the commandments of the Lord according to the law of Moses, save they should have the law. And I also knew that the law was engraven upon the plates of brass" (1 Nephi 4:14–16). Nephi realized that the future ability of his descendants to obey depended upon his current willingness to obey the Lord's direction and slay Laban. Nephi's continued focus on the principle of obedience determined his actions.

Obeying the commandment to slay Laban was probably the most difficult instruction Nephi ever had to follow. This was clearly a rare exception to God's commandment not to kill and can probably only be understood by soldiers who have felt similar inspiration in times of war. This personalized commandment was given only to Nephi directly from God for the specific circumstances he was in.

It is doubtful that we will ever face a moral dilemma so severe; however, sometimes we may struggle with direction from God, whether it be given in the scriptures, received from Church leaders, or inspired through the Spirit. Such struggles are to be expected. We should not think less of ourselves or of others for questioning such things. Nephi had questions, and he had to work through his questions and mental struggles.

I have had my own struggles along these lines. I once struggled with a new Church policy. I got really worked up inside and was filled with anxiety, fears, and questions. I shared my concerns in an email to my brother-in-law who was a stake president. He gave me some counsel and then added, "Thanks for sharing. As I've told others, questioning is okay. There is a difference between questioning and criticizing—or questioning and complaining. Nephi questioned. Laman criticized and complained!" Soon after, the Church clarified the policy in a way that resolved my concerns and brought me peace.

Coming to terms with our questions is part of the process of obedience. Like me, Nephi had questions about what he was commanded to do, but he did not complain and murmur; rather, he sought answers from the Lord. Questioning is acceptable to God, and He will help us work through our questions and struggles, just as He did with Nephi. Even if some questions are not answered, He will give us peace. However, murmuring, complaining, and criticizing, like Laman and Lemuel did, will withdraw the Holy Ghost. Personally, I can live without every question being answered, but I cannot live without the presence of the Spirit in my life. That Spirit comes through continued obedience as we work through our questions.

SACRIFICE IN THE BOOK OF 1 NEPHI

A natural outcome of obedience is the principle of sacrifice. As described earlier, the two go hand in hand: Anyone who commits to obey God will face personal sacrifice. As President Russell M. Nelson taught, "Our highest sense of sacrifice is achieved as we make ourselves more sacred or holy. This we do by our obedience to the commandments of God. Thus, the laws of obedience and sacrifice are indelibly intertwined."[29]

The interconnection between obedience and sacrifice is dramatically displayed in the experience of Lehi and his family as they left all their personal belongings behind and traveled through the wilderness to the promised land. After describing his father's obedience, Nephi wrote, "And it came to pass that he departed into the wilderness. And he left his house, and the land of his inheritance, and his gold, and his silver, and his precious things, and took nothing with him, save it were his family, and provisions, and tents, and departed into the wilderness" (1 Nephi 2:4). This is a great scriptural example of the type of sacrifice required by those who choose to obey God.

Lehi's family began their journey by offering ritual animal sacrifices. Nephi recorded that Lehi first offered sacrifice after their initial departure from Jerusalem (see 1 Nephi 2:7), a second time after the return of the sons with the plates (see 1 Nephi 5:9), and again after Ishmael's family joined them (see 1 Nephi 7:22). Their animal sacrifices were not only important in their worship of God; they were also symbolic of the extensive personal sacrifices that lay ahead.

These pilgrims of the Arabian Peninsula were not allowed to have much fire and thus had to subsist on raw meat, and that meat was difficult to obtain at times, like when Nephi's bow broke. Yet throughout this eight-year ordeal, the women bore and raised children. After the death of their father, the daughters of Ishmael complained, saying, "We have wandered much in the wilderness, and we have suffered much affliction, hunger, thirst, and fatigue; and after all these sufferings we must perish in the wilderness with hunger" (1 Nephi 16:35).

Even though Laman and Lemuel were known to be murmurers and complainers, they described the sacrifices their families endured in a way that does not sound exaggerated. They said, "Our father . . . hath led us out of the land of Jerusalem, and we have wandered in the wilderness for these many years; and our women have toiled, being big with child; and they have borne children in the wilderness and suffered all things, save it were death" (1 Nephi 17:20). Nephi confirmed their sacrifices, saying, "We had suffered many afflictions and much difficulty, yea, even so much that we cannot write them all" (1 Nephi 17:6). Considering that this statement came from Nephi, who always accepted his sufferings with faith, we can only imagine the level of difficulty his family faced.

The sacrifices that Lehi's family endured to obtain their promised land show us that a willingness to make personal sacrifice is an important step along the covenant path to God. Joseph Smith said,

> A religion that does not require the sacrifice of all things, never has power sufficient to produce the faith necessary unto life and salvation. . . . When a man has offered in sacrifice all that he has, for the truth's sake, not even withholding his life, and believing before God that he has been called to make this sacrifice, because he seeks to do his will, he does know most assuredly, that God does and will accept his sacrifice and offering, and that he has not nor will not seek his face in vain. Under these circumstances, then, he can obtain the faith necessary for him to lay hold on eternal life.[30]

Nephi seemed to understand this. He sacrificed a lot personally, suffering physical abuse at the hands of his older brothers. They beat Nephi with a rod and bound him with cords (see 1 Nephi 3:28, 7:16, 18:12), and at least three times they sought to take his life (see 1 Nephi 7:16, 16:37, 17:48). Yet Nephi endured all of this. He was willing to sacrifice his own life, if necessary, rather than disobey God.

We should realize that the Lord requires very few people to carry out the ultimate sacrifice of giving their lives for the building up of His kingdom. In the end, it was not required of Nephi, but God may ask that we *be willing* to do so, because then we will obey and sacrifice other things when called to do so. If we are willing to sacrifice everything we possess, including the possibility of giving up our lives in the service of God, then we will do what He asks of us and leave the consequences in His merciful hands. This is what Nephi did.

Such commitment requires spiritual fortification from God. Nephi knew this, and he prayed for strength to deal with his troubles rather than simply asking God to take them away. Even though an angel had intervened in an earlier beating, Nephi did not ask God to intercede when Nephi's brothers tied him up and threatened to leave him to be killed by wild beasts. Instead, Nephi prayed, "Give me strength that I may burst these bands with which I am bound" (1 Nephi 7:17). In this case, God responded in a miraculous way, causing the bands to fall loose from Nephi's hands and feet. But Nephi was ready to deal with the burden himself if necessary, only praying for strength to do so.

Nephi and his family also learned that the sacrifices they made on their journey through the wilderness saved them from a worse fate. The Lord told Nephi, "After ye have arrived in the promised land, ye shall know that I, the Lord, am God; and that I, the Lord did deliver you from destruction; yea, that I did bring you out of the land of Jerusalem" (1 Nephi 17:14).

Similar lessons came to my family when I was a boy. In 1961, we moved from Utah, where we felt safe and secure, to Kokomo, Indiana, where our religion and large family were seen as strange curiosities. My dad accepted an opportunity to lease a fast-food restaurant, and he hoped that the move would not only bring financial security but also provide fertile ground where his children could establish firm testimonies of the gospel by living "in the mission field."

Our first year there brought many challenges. A giant tree came down in our yard in one storm, and lightning struck our house in another, damaging the wiring and causing an electrician to express surprise that the house didn't burn down. There were challenges with Dad's new employment, lots of church work to be done in the small branch, an illness and hospitalization of my baby brother, and home sickness for Utah. It seemed like we were passing through our own trek in the wilderness, but my parents believed we were where the Lord wanted us to be. Dad was soon made branch president, and he focused the Saints on growth and the construction of a new meetinghouse.

After four years, the owners of the restaurant told my father they would not renew his lease. It was a hard blow to our family, but Dad soon found other work. Then, just six weeks later, a destructive tornado hit the city. It occurred on Palm Sunday, and our branch was meeting in its new church building for the first time. The meetinghouse was spared, but the restaurant and many other businesses were demolished. We counted our blessings.

Our family lived in Indiana for nearly thirteen years before returning to the mountain west. We always struggled financially, but the hope of my parents that this experience would strengthen their children paid off, and it prepared us all for future challenges in life. Like Nephi's family, my family faced many sacrifices, but we moved forward with faith and came out stronger and feeling blessed.

Faithful Obedience and Sacrifice

Nephi's approach to obedience and sacrifice was one of total and complete faith. His was not blind obedience. It was faithful obedience, and it brought him the guidance of the Holy Ghost as he took action to obey. It can do the same for us.

Upon departing a third time to seek to obtain the brass plates, Nephi said, "And I was led by the Spirit, not knowing beforehand the thing which I should do" (1 Nephi 4:6). Nephi went forth with this faithful attitude after he and his brothers had exhausted all their ideas and resources in trying to fulfill the Lord's command. Nephi never challenged God as to the purpose of His commands. He didn't ask, "Are You sure we really need the brass plates?" or "Can't You get someone else to do this?" Either he moved forward in faith, being "led by the Spirit, not knowing beforehand the things which [he] should do" (1 Nephi 4:6), or he inquired how to carry out the Lord's commands, such as when he asked his father, "Whither shall I go to obtain food?" (1 Nephi 16:23) and Heavenly Father, "Whither shall I go that I may find ore?" (1 Nephi 17:9).

Nephi also never questioned his ability to do what the Lord had commanded, for he knew "that the Lord giveth no commandments unto the children of men, save he shall prepare a way for them that they may accomplish that which he commandeth them" (1 Nephi 3:7). When he was instructed of the Lord to build a ship, he did not doubt that he could do it, even though he had never built a ship before. His brothers thought the idea was foolish and mocked him, saying, "Our brother is a fool, for he thinketh that he can build a ship; yea, and he also thinketh that he can cross these great waters" (1 Nephi 17:17). In spite of this, Nephi moved forward with confidence. He rehearsed to his brothers the miracles the Lord had performed for the Israelites and added,

> If God had commanded me to do all things I could do them. If he should command me that I should say unto this water, be thou earth, it should be earth; and if I should say it, it would be done. And now, if the Lord has such great power, and has wrought so many miracles among the children of men, how is it that he cannot instruct me, that I should build a ship? (1 Nephi 17:50–51)

So with faith that God would guide him in how to do it, and with his brothers' reluctant assistance, Nephi did "go forth" and build a ship. This does not mean that there were not challenges to be solved along the way. Nephi said, "And the Lord did show me from time to time after what manner I should work the timbers of the ship. . . . And I, Nephi, did go into the mount oft, and I did pray oft unto the Lord; wherefore the Lord showed unto me great things" (1 Nephi 18:1, 3).

We likewise demonstrate our faith in God when we "go forth" and obey His directions even though the path ahead is uncertain. This is what my missionary companions and I did as we boarded a jet in Los Angeles bound for Cordoba, Argentina, in 1976. Like thousands of other missionaries, we barely knew the language of the country we were headed to. We were unsure how to manage all of the connections that lay ahead, and we had no idea how we were going to eat or where we were going to sleep during our two-day trip to Cordoba.

After stops in Columbia and Peru, we arrived in Buenos Aires, Argentina, late at night, seventeen hours after our departure. We were shepherded to a hotel by a Church agent and then put on another plane the next morning, bound for Cordoba. We were taken to the mission home where we had a nice meal and simple interviews with our new mission president who spoke no English. The next day, I was walking the streets of a strange neighborhood, hearing words I barely understood, and experiencing foods and culture that were all new to me.

Yet, in spite of all the changes and unknowns, I was excited. I did not let my fears and uncertainties hinder me from "going forth" in faith, with confidence that I would be blessed and guided. That guidance came repeatedly throughout my mission, sometimes with powerful, spiritual manifestations, and other times more subtly. I learned that the more often we take action to obey God's commandments and directions, the more prepared we become to receive additional help and inspiration when we need it.

Nephi and his family learned this same lesson through their interactions with the Liahona. It appeared outside Lehi's tent door before his family left their first campsite and was described by Nephi as "a round ball of curious workmanship; and it was of fine brass. And within the ball were two spindles; and the one pointed the way whither we should go into the wilderness" (1 Nephi 16:10). This sounds like a compass, but the power moving the spindles was not the earth's magnetism. Nephi learned that "the pointers which were in the ball . . . did work according to *the faith and diligence and heed* which we did give unto them" (1 Nephi 16:28; emphasis added).

The Liahona is a "type" or a symbol for guidance from the Holy Ghost. Like the Liahona, the Holy Ghost works "according to the faith and diligence and heed which we did give unto it," or, in other words, according to our faithful obedience and willingness to sacrifice.

Nephi wrote of the pointers on the Liahona, "And there was also written upon them a new writing, which was plain to be read, which did give us understanding concerning the ways of the Lord; and it was written and changed from time to time, according to the faith and diligence which we gave unto it" (1 Nephi 16:29). That is the way the Holy Ghost directs us. Inspiration from the Holy Ghost will change from time to time according to our needs and circumstances as well as our faith and diligence. Our Liahona, the Holy Ghost, is our source of ongoing revelation, customized for each one of us, as we move along the covenant path.

However, the Holy Ghost is not our only guide. The scriptures and words of modern prophets and apostles are other Liahonas for us. If we give heed to them with faith and diligence, they will guide us. These also change from time to time. The words we read in the scriptures often evoke new insights and new understanding for us as our life circumstances change. Also, the words of our living prophets and apostles give us new direction in general conference every six months. We will be guided in all our covenant commitments, including obedience and sacrifice, if we give heed with faith and diligence to all our modern Liahonas: the Holy Ghost, the scriptures, and the words of modern prophets and apostles.

Earlier, when the Lord visited Nephi, He said, "Blessed art thou, Nephi, because of thy *faith*, for thou hast sought me *diligently*, with low-liness of heart" (1 Nephi 2:19; emphasis added). Faith and diligence—these are the same principles that gave function to the Liahona. It is only through our faithfulness and diligence that we qualify for God's promises of guidance and blessings in our lives. Like Nephi, we show our faith and diligence through obedience and sacrifice. If we are "faithful and true in all things" (D&C 124:13), we, like Nephi, will eventually be ushered into the presence of the Lord.

LESSONS FROM LEHI AND SARIAH: WHEN FAITH FALTERS

Nephi's parents were also faithful and true. It is remarkable how will-ing they were to leave their comforts and wealth behind in Jerusalem and to depart into the wilderness. However, they did experience occasions of sacrifice that caused them to falter and murmur. Nevertheless, their strug-gles were temporary. They did not let a crisis of faith permanently separate them from God, for they were quick to humble themselves and obey once they saw the error of their ways.

As Lehi's party journeyed through the wilderness, they depended on hunting to obtain food. After traveling for many days, the hunting bows of the older sons lost their spring, and Nephi's steel bow broke, making everyone angry with him. Nephi wrote, "And it came to pass that we did return without food to our families, and being much fatigued, because of their journeying, they did suffer much for the want of food" (1 Nephi 16:19). Stressed by hunger and fatigue, not only did Laman and Lemuel and the sons of Ishmael mummer, but even Lehi "began to mummer against the Lord his God" (1 Nephi 16:20).

Faithful and obedient Nephi finally resolved the situation. He made a new bow and arrow from materials available in the area, and, arming himself with these and a sling with stones, he approached his wavering father, the patriarch, and asked, "Whither shall I go to obtain food?" (1 Nephi 16:23). Seeing the faithful initiative of his son, Lehi humbled him-self and inquired of the Lord. The Lord answered, first chastening Lehi and then telling him, "Look upon the ball, and behold the things which are written" (1 Nephi 16:26). On the Liahona, Lehi found instructions to go to the top of a certain mountain. Nephi did so, and there he "did slay wild beasts, insomuch that I did obtain food for our families" (1 Nephi 16:31). Lehi was a wonderful example of one who temporarily struggled with obedience and sacrifice but then humbled himself, repented, and again received direction from the Lord.

A similar thing happened with Sariah when she worried about her sons while they were gone so long to obtain the brass plates. Nephi wrote, "And she also had complained against my father, telling him that he was a visionary man; saying: Behold thou hast led us forth from the land of our inheritance, and my sons are no more, and we perish in the wilderness" (1 Nephi 5:2). Sariah's maternal concerns for the safe return of her sons are understandable, but her claim that Lehi was a "visionary man," words also used by Laman and Lemuel, was apparently a phrase of derision in their day. Lehi responded to her with words of faith and comfort, saying, "I know that I am a visionary man; . . . yea, and I know that the Lord will deliver my sons out of the hands of Laban, and bring them down again unto us in the wilderness" (1 Nephi 5:4–5).

Their sons did indeed return, and a joyful reunion ensued. Sariah then exclaimed with renewed faith, "Now I know of a surety that the Lord hath commanded my husband to flee into the wilderness; yea, and I also know of a surety that the Lord hath protected my sons, and delivered them out of the hands of Laban, and given them power whereby they could accomplish the thing which the Lord hath commanded them" (1 Nephi 5:8).

Like Lehi, Sariah's murmurings were a temporary wavering, for she appears to have used her crisis of faith as a developmental experience. Sariah's use of the phrase "that they could accomplish the thing which the Lord hath commanded them" echoes with strong familiarity Nephi's own earlier statement that the Lord "shall prepare a way for them that they may accomplish the thing which he commandeth them" (1 Nephi 3:7). However, when we remember that children usually learn language patterns and phrases from their parents, we recognize that Nephi probably borrowed this phrase from earlier, similar statements by his mother, and that her influence was one of the foundations of his great faith and obedience.

Later, Nephi used the same phrase again: "And thus we see that the commandments of God must be fulfilled. And if it so be that the children of men keep the commandments of God he doth nourish them, and strengthen them, and provide means whereby *they can accomplish the thing which he has commanded them*" (1 Nephi 17:3; emphasis added). This third use of this phrase underlines obedience as a theme of 1 Nephi.

Like Lehi and Sariah, sometimes the sacrifices we face can stress us to the point where we question the Lord and complain. When those times come, it can be helpful to remember not only the struggles of Lehi and Sariah but also their recommitment and determination to sacrifice whatever was necessary to accomplish the things that the Lord had commanded them.

LAMAN AND LEMUEL: MURMURING MODELS OF DISOBEDIENCE

In contrast to the humble change of heart that their parents showed after temporary murmurings, the examples of Laman and Lemuel serve as warnings of what can happen with those who follow a path of constant complaining, hardened hearts, and disbelief. They repeatedly refused to obey God and resented the sacrifices required of them. At least five times before reaching the promised land, they rebelled to the point of trying to kill or otherwise abuse their younger brother. Consider the following:

1. After their second attempt to obtain the brass plates failed, Laman and Lemuel beat Nephi and Sam with a rod. An angel intervened. (See 1 Nephi 3:27–31.)

2. On their return with Ishmael's family, Nephi's two oldest brothers bound him with cords and were going to leave him to be devoured by wild beasts. After Nephi prayed, the bands were miraculously loosed, and the pleadings of some of Ishmael's family defused the situation. (See 1 Nephi 7:6–21.)

3. After Ishmael died, another rebellion ensued, and Laman suggested that they kill both Lehi and Nephi. The voice of the Lord chastened them, dispelling their anger. (See 1 Nephi 16:34–39.)

4. After arriving in Bountiful, Nephi's brothers refused to help him build a ship and were about to throw him into the sea. Nephi became filled with the power of God and rebuked them. He later touched them, giving each a shock, so they finally agreed to help. (See 1 Nephi 17:17–55.)

5. During their sea voyage, Laman, Lemuel, and the sons of Ishmael again rebelled and tied up Nephi. After four days of abuse, a violent storm caused them to fear for their lives, so they loosed Nephi who prayed and calmed the storm. (See 1 Nephi 18:8–22.)

Laman, Lemuel, Sam, and Nephi all grew up in the same household, yet the oldest two brothers failed to develop the spiritual maturity of their younger siblings. They all heard the prophecies, visions, and admonitions of their father, yet they responded differently to these. Nephi's record helps us understand why. After Nephi observed his father prophesy in Jerusalem and teach his family at home, Nephi described the responses of all four brothers:

> And thus Laman and Lemuel, being the eldest, did murmur against their father. And they did murmur because they knew not the dealings of that God who had created them. Neither did they believe . . . the words of the prophets. And they were like unto the Jews who were at Jerusalem, who sought to take away the life of my father. . . . And it came to pass that I, Nephi, . . . did believe all the words which had been spoken by my father; wherefore, I did not rebel against him like unto my brothers. And I spake unto Sam, making known unto him the things which the Lord had manifested unto me by his Holy Spirit. And it came to pass that he believed in my words. (1 Nephi 2:12–13, 16–17)

We get additional insights into the lack of faith of Laman and Lemuel by observing their response to Lehi's vision of the tree of life. The older brothers complained that they did not understand. Nephi then asked if they had inquired of the Lord, and their response was, "We have not; for the Lord maketh no such thing known unto us" (1 Nephi 15:9). To this, Nephi retorted, "How is it that ye do not keep the commandments of the Lord? How is it that ye will perish, because of the hardness of your hearts? Do ye not remember the things which the Lord hath said?—If ye will not harden your hearts, and ask me in faith, believing that ye shall receive, with diligence in keeping my commandments, surely these things shall be made known unto you" (1 Nephi 15:10–11).

Nephi taught that the way to receive answers is to be diligent in keeping the commandments in spite of our questions and to not harden our hearts but to ask God in faith for understanding. Apparently, it is the attitude with which we face our questions that will determine how God will respond to us. However, Laman and Lemuel never passed that hurdle. They refused to follow the principles of obedience and sacrifice.

Nephi later described the faithless and disobedient nature of his older brothers when they refused to help him build the ship. He declared to them,

> Ye are swift to do iniquity but slow to remember the Lord your God. Ye have seen an angel, and he spake unto you; yea, ye have heard his voice from time to time; and he hath spoken unto you in a still small voice, but ye were past feeling, that ye could not feel his words; where-fore, he has spoken unto you like unto the voice of thunder, which did cause the earth to shake as if it were to divide asunder. (1 Nephi 17:45)

Finally, during the rebellion at sea, the older brothers again became angry with Nephi, saying, "We will not that our younger brother shall be a ruler over us" (1 Nephi 18:10). They refused to follow the man whom God had appointed as their spiritual leader and prophet.

From all of these incidents, we see that Laman and Lemuel espoused the following negative attributes:

1. They let their anger overpower them (see the five occasions described earlier).

2. They did not know or understand the dealings of God (1 Nephi 2:12).

3. They did not believe the words of past prophets (1 Nephi 2:13).

4. They would not follow the living prophet, first rebelling against their prophet father and then against their prophet brother (1 Nephi 2:11–12; 18:10).

5. They did not pray for answers to their questions (1 Nephi 15:7–9).

6. They did not keep the commandments (1 Nephi 15:10).

7. They did not ask in faith, believing they would receive answers (1 Nephi 15:11).

8. They preferred iniquity over remembering God (1 Nephi 17:45).

9. They had hard hearts to the point of being "past feeling" the still small voice of the Holy Ghost (1 Nephi 17:45).

Perhaps "past feeling" is the most telling attribute. Being past feeling is related to having a hard heart and is the same phrase that Mormon used to describe the depraved level of moral decay that the Nephite people had sunk to in his day (see Moroni 9:20). Laman and Lemuel had pauses in their murmurings, but their hearts did not change. Their pauses were merely reluctant compliance after rebuke or divine intervention. However, compliance is not obedience. It is not a lasting attitude of faithful righteousness that accompanies a true covenant relationship with God. Laman and Lemuel refused to exercise faith, even though they witnessed miracles. The privations they suffered only served to harden their hearts against the Lord and His anointed. Obedience and sacrifice were principles they scorned.

Signs and Miracles

The book of 1 Nephi also teaches that signs and miracles will not motivate wicked people toward obedience and sacrifice. Laman and Lemuel experienced many miraculous signs: a visit from an angel, the sudden loosening of cords from Nephi, hearing the voice of God, and feeling a shock from Nephi's touch. They saw, heard, and felt the power of God, yet Laman and Lemuel refused to be faithful and obey. Their experiences confirm a truth taught later to Joseph Smith: "Faith cometh not by signs, but signs follow those that believe" (D&C 63:9).

Sometimes people say they want to experience a sign before they will believe and obey. For example, people might want a prophet to perform a spectacular miracle, such as healing a snakebite. Truly, God can empower His prophets to do such things. In fact, Nephi reminded his brothers that "fiery flying serpents" had come among the children of Israel and bitten many, and the only thing they had to do to be healed was to look upon the staff or rod of Moses, which we later learn was a symbol of Christ. Nephi added, "and because of the simpleness of the way, or the easiness of it, there were many who perished (1 Nephi 17:41).

Nephi's recitation shows that a sign initiated by God can strengthen faith, but only if we humble ourselves and commit to obey God. When Laman and Lemuel saw signs, they rationalized that what they had seen were only deceptions performed by Nephi "by his cunning arts" (1 Nephi 16:38). Their response shows us that we should not seek for signs as precedents to our obedience and sacrifice. However, after we show our faith by keeping our covenants, we should be open to recognizing God's hand in blessing us and showing us signs that He is pleased with us. Once again, Nephi set the proper example for us, and Laman and Lemuel demonstrated attitudes that we should avoid if we choose to follow God's covenant path.

VISION OF THE TREE OF LIFE: MAKING AND KEEPING COVENANTS

The vision of the tree of life, which Lehi and Nephi both witnessed, can be seen as a manifestation of the rewards that can come to those who make and keep sacred covenants, including obedience and sacrifice, as well as showing what will come to those who do not. After describing the dream to his family, Lehi emphasized obedience as he "bade them to keep the commandments of God" (1 Nephi 8:38). Nephi made a similar connection when he described the dream to his brothers, explaining, "Wherefore, the wicked are rejected from the righteous, and also from that tree of life" (1 Nephi 15:36). Both prophets saw a clear connection between the vision of the tree of life and the principle of obedience.

This connection can also be seen in the plea Nephi made to his brothers to hold fast to the iron rod, which he described as the word of God. He said, "Wherefore, I, Nephi, did exhort them to give heed unto the word of the Lord; yea, I did exhort them with all the energies of my soul, and with all the faculty which I possessed, that they would give heed to the word of God and remember to keep his commandments always in all things" (1 Nephi 15:25).

However, obedience and sacrifice are not the only requirements for those who will partake of the fruit of the tree. This shared vision of Lehi and Nephi, with its path toward the tree of life, is best considered in the context of the entire covenant path, where obedience and sacrifice are only initial steps. The vision teaches us the importance of all our covenants as we proceed along the path toward eternal life. In this vision, the iron rod is said to represent the word of God. We commonly think of this as the scriptures, but the word of God is more than just the teachings and commandments found in the scriptures. God's word is His bond, His promises, His covenants. Elder Lance B. Wickman wrote,

In a broad sense, "the word of God" means the teachings and commandments. At a more specific level, it is the sacred covenants between God and man. Covenants bespeak commitment to living the commandments—God's law. It is living the law—not simply knowing it—that ultimately leads to happiness in this life and exaltation in eternity. . . . Accordingly, *the imagery of holding fast to the rod of iron means to make and keep sacred covenants.*[31]

Nephi and his father saw different groups of people advance toward the tree of life. Nephi wrote that his father "saw other multitudes pressing forward; and they came and *caught hold of the end of the rod of iron*; and they did press their way forward, *continually holding fast to the rod of iron*, until they came forth and fell down and partook of the fruit of the tree (1 Nephi 8:30; emphasis added). In the context of covenants, the phrase "caught hold of the end of the rod of iron" could symbolize the making of sacred covenants, and the phrase, "continually holding fast to the rod of iron" could symbolize the keeping of those covenants.

The vision of the tree of life reminds us that we need to make and keep all of our covenants, including the laws of obedience and sacrifice. Doing so will take us back to the presence of God where we can partake of the fruit of the tree of life. This fruit is "most sweet . . . and [will fill our] soul with exceedingly great joy" (1 Nephi 8:11–2). "Wherefore, it is the most desirable above all things. . . . Yea, and the most joyous to the soul" (1 Nephi 11:22–23).

THE RIGHTEOUS ARE FAVORED AND NEED NOT FEAR

When Laman and Lemuel saw that Nephi was going to try to build a ship, they complained, not wanting to help. It seems they were content to live in the relative comfort and ease they found in the land they called Bountiful. Nephi said, "they began to murmur against me, saying: Our brother is a fool, for he thinketh that he can build a ship; yea, and he also thinketh that he can cross these great waters" (1 Nephi 17:17).

The brothers continued to murmur, recounting the many afflictions that they and their wives had suffered through their multi-year journey in the wilderness. They bemoaned the loss of their possessions in Jerusalem and claimed, "And we know that the people who were in the land of Jerusalem were a righteous people; for they kept the statutes and judgments of the Lord, and all his commandments, according to the law of Moses" (1 Nephi 17:22).

Nephi had heard enough. He knew that the people of Jerusalem were not righteous, so he presented to his brothers a passionate review of God's miraculous blessings upon the children of Israel when Moses led them out of Egypt. He climaxed his lecture with these words:

> And now, do ye suppose that the children of this land, who were in the land of promise, who were driven out by our fathers, do ye suppose that they were righteous? Behold, I say unto you, Nay. Do ye suppose that our fathers would have been more choice than they if they had been righteous? I say unto you, Nay. Behold, the Lord esteemeth all flesh in one; he that is righteous is favored of God. (1 Nephi 17:33–35)

There we see Nephi's theme of obedience again: "He that is righteous is favored of God." A few verses later, Nephi added, "And he loveth those who will have him to be their God. Behold, he loved our fathers, and he covenanted with them, yea, even Abraham, Isaac, and Jacob; and he remembered the covenants which he had made; wherefore, he did bring them out of the land of Egypt" (1 Nephi 17:40). This teaches us that simply being a Latter-day Saint does not make us more choice than other people—we must be righteous in order for God to fulfill His covenants with us.

Nowhere in the book of 1 Nephi is the need for righteousness more dramatically emphasized than in the final chapter. It contains repeated warnings of the fire and destruction that will occur in the last days when "the fulness of the wrath of God shall be poured out upon all the children of men" (1 Nephi 22:16). Nephi's description is somber. It includes many apocalyptic words, such as blood, war, abomination, stubble, burned, destruction, fire, judgment, fear, tremble, and quake.

However, amidst his dire predictions, Nephi repeatedly sought to comfort the righteous who would read his warnings. Consider these verses:

- "For he [God] will not suffer that the wicked shall destroy the righteous" (1 Nephi 22:16).

- "Wherefore, he will preserve the righteous by his power, even if it so be that the fulness of his wrath must come. . . . Wherefore, the righteous need not fear; for thus saith the prophet, they shall be saved" (1 Nephi 22:17).

- "For behold, the righteous shall not perish; for the time surely must come that all they who fight against Zion shall be cut off" (1 Nephi 22:19).

- "And the righteous need not fear, for they are those who shall not be confounded" (1 Nephi 22:22).

- "And because of the righteousness of his people, Satan . . . hath no power over the hearts of the people, for they dwell in righteousness, and the Holy One of Israel reigneth" (1 Nephi 22:26).

- "But, behold, all nations, kindreds, tongues, and people shall dwell safely in the Holy One of Israel if it so be that they will repent" (1 Nephi 22:28).

Clearly Nephi wanted the righteous of the last days to know that, in spite of all of the destruction and turmoil around them, they need not fear. As he declared at the onset of this prophecy, "He that is righteous is favored of God" (1 Nephi 17:35). This should comfort us and help us remain true to all our covenants, including obedience and sacrifice, as the turmoil of the last days swirls around us.

How and Where Sacred Truths Are Taught

The book of 1 Nephi not only teaches us about the sacred covenant principles of obedience and sacrifice, but it also has lessons on where we can go to receive instruction on all sacred matters and how that instruction is usually received. After Nephi heard his father tell about his vision of the tree of life, he wrote, "I, Nephi, was desirous also that I might see, and hear, and know of these things, by the power of the Holy Ghost, which is the gift of God unto all those who diligently seek him" (1 Nephi 10:17). Nephi wanted to experience what his father had experienced, and he knew that such instruction, insights, and knowledge would come by revelation through the Holy Ghost. Nephi then further described the conditions under which he sought that revelation: "For it came to pass after [1] I had desired to know the things that my father had seen, and [2] believing that the Lord was able to make them known unto me, [3] as I sat pondering in mine heart" (1 Nephi 11:1).

Desire, faith and pondering—Nephi employed these three important precursors to receiving revelation. What then followed was a description of a special location where Nephi received the revelation he sought: "I was caught away in the Spirit of the Lord, yea, into an exceedingly high mountain, which I never had before seen, and upon which I never had before set my foot" (1 Nephi 11:1).

Mountaintop instruction became a recurring pattern for Nephi. He wrote that after arriving at Bountiful, "The voice of the Lord came unto me, saying: Arise, and get thee into the mountain. And it came to pass that I arose and went up into the mountain, and cried unto the Lord" (1 Nephi 17:7). Once Nephi was there, the Lord instructed him on how to build a ship. However, Nephi didn't learn everything he needed to know about ship building on that one occasion. As Nephi encountered new questions during the construction, he returned to the mountaintop and sought additional guidance. Nephi wrote that he built the ship "after the manner which the Lord had shown unto me; wherefore, it was not after the manner of men. And I, Nephi, did go into the mount oft, and I did pray oft unto the Lord; wherefore the Lord showed unto me great things" (1 Nephi 18:3).

In ancient times, God often used mountains as sacred locations for instructing his children and revealing important truths. Not only did He do so with Nephi but also with the brother of Jared (see Ether 3:1), with Moses (see Exodus 19:3, 20), and even with Jesus Christ (see Matthew 17:1–2). Today, temples serve this purpose. Indeed, Isaiah called temples, "the mountain of the Lord's house" (Isaiah 2:2; 2 Nephi 12:2).

Nephi's examples of where he went to receive sacred instruction and how he approached God are valuable lessons for us. We can take our desires and concerns to the temple. We can go with faith in Jesus Christ, believing that He is able to make His will known unto us, and then spend time in the temple sitting still, pondering and praying over our desires and concerns.

In my own life, as I have followed this pattern, I have often received answers in the form of quiet impressions and peaceful comfort. However, on rare occasions, "the Lord showed unto me great things." One very special experience came during a two-day priesthood temple trip in a day when temples were more distant and such excursions were typical. At the time, I desired direction for some personal challenges I was facing, so I relished the opportunity to ponder and pray while serving in back-to-back temple sessions, believing that God could give me some direction in that sacred place. During the second day of the trip, as I prayed in the celestial room, I suddenly felt a spiritual presence at my side and knew that it was my grandfather, Walter Jones, who had died when my father was fifteen. A sacred and personal experience ensued wherein my grandfather ministered to me with an overwhelming love and gave me a specific point of instruction to help with my challenges. All I could do was weep the remainder of that day in the temple as my grandfather continued to accompany me. The experience witnessed to me that angels do still minister on the earth (see Moroni 7:29), especially in temples. Great spiritual power resides in that sacred space. The veil is thinner there.

The instruction I received in the temple that day was not about building a ship. It had more to do with healing a soul and strengthening a family. Nevertheless, the guidance was specific and direct. Sometimes, however, the direction we receive is not revealed in a straightforward manner. The Lord's guidance is often less direct, such as what Nephi experienced in an earlier situation.

When Nephi sought understanding for the meaning of the tree of life, he was not given a direct answer. Instead, he was presented with another vision, this one of a virgin, "the mother of the son of God" (1 Nephi 11:18). The messenger guiding Nephi then asked if he knew the meaning of the tree, to which he replied, "Yea, it is the love of God, which sheddeth itself abroad in the hearts of the children of men; wherefore, it is the most desirable above all things" (1 Nephi 11:22). The messenger confirmed this, saying, "Yea, and the most joyous to the soul" (1 Nephi 11:23). The messenger had not given a direct answer to the question in Nephi's heart. Instead, he gave Nephi a vision of things that today we would find in the scriptures, and he encouraged Nephi to figure it out on his own. Then, when Nephi described his conclusion, the messenger confirmed that he was correct.

Often the Lord does not give direct answers to our questions, but he prompts us and gives us insights so we can make our own conclusions. For example, the Lord does not explain directly the meaning of all of the sacred instruction and symbols in the temple, but He provides the setting wherein the Spirit can guide us to come to our own conclusions in a way that will apply to our current life and situation. This method of instruction leads to learning that is individualized and lasting. It effects changes in our hearts and souls. In this way, the Lord teaches us through the Spirit according to our personal needs and circumstances in life.

Obedience and Sacrifice Point to Christ and Covenants

The principles of obedience and sacrifice relate directly to Jesus Christ. Jesus was obedient to the will of the Father in everything He did. He confirmed this himself, saying, "I seek not mine own will, but the will of the Father which hath sent me" (John 5:30). Also, there is no greater example of sacrifice than the Atonement of our Savior Jesus Christ. As Paul declared, "Christ also hath loved us, and hath given himself for us an offering and a sacrifice to God" (Ephesians 5:2). The book of 1 Nephi teaches these same principles of obedience and sacrifice, alongside a strong emphasis on Jesus Christ and covenants.

As noted earlier, the Book of Mormon records three occasions when Lehi led his family in the ordinance of animal sacrifice. In our day, we understand that these ordinances were intended to look forward to the sacrifice of Jesus Christ, and based on other teachings of Lehi and Nephi, it is clear that they understood the connection as well. In his second book, Nephi declared, "And, notwithstanding we believe in Christ, we keep the law of Moses, and look forward with steadfastness unto Christ, until the law shall be fulfilled. For, for this end was the law given" (2 Nephi 25:24–25). President M. Russell Ballard taught, "The law of sacrifice has always been a means for God's children to come unto the Lord Jesus Christ."[32]

This focus on Jesus Christ began in the first chapter of 1 Nephi. There, Nephi told of the inaugural vision that his father, Lehi, received wherein he saw, "One descending out of the midst of heaven, and he beheld that his luster was above that of the sun at noon-day" (1 Nephi 1:9). In this vision, Nephi wrote that Jesus Christ "stood before my father, and gave unto him a book, and bade him that he should read. And it came to pass that as he read, he was filled with the Spirit of the Lord" (1 Nephi 1:11–12). So from the earliest verses of the Small Plates of Nephi, we see that Lehi received a witness of the role of Jesus Christ.

Lehi then "went forth among the people, and began to prophesy . . . and he testified that the things which he saw and heard, and also the things which he read in the book, manifested plainly of the coming of a Messiah, and also the redemption of the world" (1 Nephi 1:18–19). Lehi's testimony of the Savior was firm. It was the foundation of his own commitment to be "obedient unto the word of the Lord" (1 Nephi 2:3).

In his vision of the tree of life, Nephi saw "A virgin, most beautiful and fair above all other virgins" (1 Nephi 11:15). He was then introduced to the concept of the condescension of God when he saw "the virgin again, bearing a child in her arms" and he heard the angel declare, "Behold the Lamb of God, yea, even the Son of the Eternal Father!" (1 Nephi 11:20–21). It was then that Nephi understood the meaning of the tree of life, which is the love of God. Nephi was next privileged to see a vision of the ministry of the Savior, including "multitudes of people who were sick, and who were afflicted with all manner of diseases, and with devils and unclean spirits; . . . And they were healed by the power of the Lamb of God" (1 Nephi 11:31). Finally, he stated that he saw that "the Son of the everlasting God was judged of the world; and I saw . . . that he was lifted up upon the cross and slain for the sins of the world" (1 Nephi 11:32–33). Nephi is a remarkable firsthand witness for Christ.

An additional focus on Christ in 1 Nephi is seen in how Lehi's family was led through the wilderness. The Lord had instructed them not use much fire for cooking or for light. He supported this requirement with a profound declaration that should be a guiding creed for us all. He told them, "And I will also be your light in the wilderness; and I will prepare the way before you, if it so be that ye shall keep my commandments; wherefore, inasmuch as ye shall keep my commandments ye shall be led towards the promised land; and ye shall know that it is by me that ye are led" (1 Nephi 17:13). Christ was Nephi's light, and Christ should be our light. If we will keep the commandments, being true to the laws of obedience and sacrifice, our path ahead will be illuminated.

The coming Messiah, Jesus Christ, was always on Nephi's mind. Near the end of his first book, Nephi prophesied of the Lord's future sacrifice, declaring, "And the world, because of their iniquity, shall judge him to be a thing of naught; wherefore they scourge him, and he suffereth it; and they smite him, and he suffereth it. Yea, they spit upon him, and he suffereth it, because of his loving kindness, and his long-suffering towards the children of men" (1 Nephi 19:9). Nephi then quoted prophecies of Christ from the brass plates and declared, "I Nephi, have written these things unto my people, that perhaps they would remember the Lord their Redeemer" (1 Nephi 19:18). Finally, he quoted two chapters from the book of Isaiah to his brothers, "that I might more fully persuade them to believe in the Lord their Redeemer" (1 Nephi 19:23).

While quoting Isaiah, Nephi recited these poignant words of the Lord: "Yea, they may forget, yet I will not forget thee, O house of Israel. Behold, I have graven thee upon the palms of my hands" (1 Nephi 21:15–16). This passage brings to mind a stanza of the inspired hymn by James Montgomery, "A Poor Wayfaring Man of Grief."

> Then in a moment to my view
> The stranger started from disguise.
> The tokens in His hands I knew;
> The Savior stood before mine eyes.[33]

Nephi knew the Lord. The Savior had stood before his eyes (see 1 Nephi 2:16; 2 Nephi 11:2–3). Nephi had seen the hands that would carry the tokens of His sacrifice—the palms that would be graven with scars from the cross where Jesus would obediently finish the work His Father had given Him. The scars in the Savior's hands are tokens or symbols of His sacrifice and love for us. Those tokens are also symbols of His part in the covenants He makes with us. Nephi's sacred record points to obedience and sacrifice—two of these covenants. We would all do well to follow the faithful examples of Lehi, Sariah, Sam, and Nephi by committing to live the principles of obedience and sacrifice in everything we do.

NEPHI'S CONCLUSION

Obedience and sacrifice are foundational covenants upon which all later commitments in the covenant path are established. Every point of instruction and direction we receive from the Lord is given with the understanding that we must obey it in order to receive the blessings associated with that instruction (see D&C 130:21). When we have first covenanted to obey God, we will not later murmur nor complain when we receive additional instructions from Him, whether they come by inspiration through the Holy Ghost or as pronouncements from His prophets. Additionally, when we are committed to make whatever sacrifice is necessary in order to obey God, our foundation for receiving further instructions and blessings from Him is fortified.

President Ezra Taft Benson has said, "When obedience ceases to be an irritant and becomes our quest, in that moment God will endow us with power."[34] Nephi was endowed with power because he always obeyed without reservation—obedience was his quest.

Indeed, obedience to God could be called Nephi's creed, for it influenced everything he did. This creed was first displayed in his early declaration, "I will go and do the things which the Lord hath commanded" (1 Nephi 3:7), and it was punctuated by the final words Nephi inscribed upon the Small Plates: "For thus hath the Lord commanded me, and I must obey. Amen" (2 Nephi 33:15). Nephi concluded his first book with this plea for continued obedience:

> Wherefore, my brethren, I would that ye should consider that the things which have been written upon the plates of brass are true; and they testify that *a man must be obedient to the commandments of God*. Wherefore, ye need not suppose that I and my father are the only ones that have testified, and also taught them. Wherefore, *if ye shall be obedient to the commandments*, and endure to the end, ye shall be saved at the last day. And thus it is. Amen. (1 Nephi 22:30–31; emphasis added)

This final passage of 1 Nephi underscores the theme of obedience in this book. It reminds us that both Nephi and his father, Lehi, taught obedience. In addition, the challenges their family endured show us that sacrifice is always required of those who choose to follow the covenant path toward an eternal promised land. From the day they left behind their comforts and treasures in Jerusalem until the day they disembarked from their tumultuous voyage in an unknown land, sacrifice was a daily part of their lives. Obedience and sacrifice are the covenant path themes of the book of 1 Nephi, and commitment to these principles is fundamental for each of us as we progress along this covenant path in our return to God's presence.

CHAPTER 3

2 NEPHI: THE GOSPEL

In his first book, Nephi told the story of his family's departure from Jerusalem and their travels to their new promised land. His personal experiences provided the backdrop for many lessons about obedience and sacrifice. In his second book, Nephi recounted very little narrative drama. Instead, his writings shifted mostly to doctrinal expositions presented in blessings, prophecies, sermons, and the expounding of scripture. These include a discussion of redemption and the Atonement of Jesus Christ, along with prophecies of apostasy and restoration from Lehi, Jacob, Isaiah, and Nephi himself. Nephi then ended this book with a beautiful treatise on the doctrine of Christ, expounding on what we know as the first principles and ordinances of the gospel.

As with the rest of the Small Plates, the book of 2 Nephi fulfills the purposes of the Book of Mormon by witnessing of Jesus Christ and the covenant blessings to Israel. In addition, 2 Nephi has its own subtheme that can be summarized very simply as *the gospel*. This, then, becomes the next step that the Small Plates of Nephi present in the path to return to God's presence—understanding and living the gospel of Jesus Christ.

SCRIPTURES DEFINING THE GOSPEL

In order to understand how 2 Nephi can be distilled to the theme of *the gospel*, we must first understand what is meant by the term. Many scriptures give insights on the meaning of the gospel, but a few are especially noteworthy, because they include succinct, dictionary-like declarations of "this is my gospel" or similar wording. Consider the following such passages. (Within these passages, some principles are highlighted in

bold or underlined text, and references to *the gospel* or similar terms are emphasized in *italics*. These will be explained later.)

D&C 33:11–12

Yea, **repent** and be **baptized**, every one of you, for a remission of your sins; yea, be **baptized even by water**, and then cometh the baptism of fire and of the **Holy Ghost**. Behold, verily, verily, I say unto you, *this is my gospel*; and remember that they shall have **faith in me** or they can in nowise be saved.

D&C 39:5–6

And verily, verily, I say unto you, he that receiveth my gospel **receiveth me**; and he that receiveth not my gospel receiveth not me. And *this is my gospel*—**repentance** and **baptism by water**, and then cometh the baptism of fire and the **Holy Ghost**, even the Comforter, which showeth all things, and teacheth the peaceable things of the kingdom.

D&C 84:26–27

And the lesser priesthood continued, which priesthood holdeth the key of the ministering of angels and the preparatory gospel; *which gospel is* the gospel of **repentance** and of **baptism**, and the remission of sins, and the law of carnal commandments, which the Lord in his wrath caused to continue with the house of Aaron among the children of Israel until John, whom God raised up, being filled with the **Holy Ghost** from his mother's womb.

D&C 76:40–42, 50–53, 70

And *this is the gospel*, the glad tidings, which the voice out of the heavens bore record unto us—that he came into the world, even Jesus, to be crucified for the world, and to bear the sins of the world, and to sanctify the world, and to cleanse it from all unrighteousness; that through him all might be saved whom the Father had put into his power and made by him; . . .

And again we bear record—for we saw and heard, and *this is the testimony of the gospel of Christ* concerning them who shall come forth in the resurrection of the just—they are they who received the testimony of Jesus, and **believed on his name** and were **baptized** after the manner of his burial, being buried in the water in his name, and this according to the commandment which he has given—that by keeping the commandments they might be washed and cleansed from all their sins, and receive the **Holy Spirit by the laying on of the hands** of him who is ordained and sealed unto this power; and who overcome by **faith**. . . . These are they whose bodies are celestial.

3 Nephi 27:13–16, 19–21

Behold I have given unto you my gospel, and *this is the gospel* which I have given unto you—that I came into the world to do the will of my Father, because my Father sent me. And my Father sent me that I might be lifted up upon the cross; and after that I had been lifted up upon the cross, that I might draw all men unto me, that as I have been lifted up by men even so should men be lifted up by the Father, to stand before me, to be judged of their works, whether they be good or whether they be evil—and for this cause have I been lifted up; therefore, according to the power of the Father I will draw all men unto me, that they may be judged according to their works. And it shall come to pass, that whoso **repenteth** and is **baptized** in my name shall be filled; and if he **endureth to the end**, behold, him will I hold guiltless before my Father at that day when I shall stand to judge the world. . . .

And no unclean thing can enter into his kingdom; therefore nothing entereth into his rest save it be those who have washed their garments in my blood, because of their **faith**, and the **repentance** of all their sins, and their **faithfulness unto the end**. Now this is the commandment: **Repent**, all ye ends of the earth, and come unto me and be **baptized** in my name, that ye may be sanctified by the reception of the **Holy Ghost**, that ye may stand spotless before me at the last day. Verily, verily, I say unto you, *this is my gospel*.

In addition, the following scriptures define "the doctrine of Christ," or "my doctrine." *The doctrine of Christ* and *the gospel of Jesus Christ* are equivalent terms—a fact that becomes clear when we recognize that they are defined in the scriptures by the same principles. Indeed, Sherem said to Jacob, "I have heard and also know that thou goest about much, preaching that which ye call *the gospel, or the doctrine of Christ*" (Jacob 7:6; emphasis added).[c]

Hebrew 6:1–2

> . . . *the principles of the doctrine of Christ* . . . of **repentance** from dead works, and of **faith** toward God, of the doctrine of **baptisms**, and of **laying on of hands**, and of resurrection of the dead, and of eternal judgment.

3 Nephi 11:32–35, 38–39

> Behold, verily, verily, I say unto you, I will declare unto you my doctrine. And *this is my doctrine*, and it is the doctrine which the Father hath given unto me; and . . . the Father commandeth all men, everywhere, to **repent** and **believe in me**. And whoso believeth in me, and is **baptized**, the same shall be saved; and they are they who shall inherit the kingdom of God. And whoso believeth not in me, and is not baptized, shall be damned. Verily, verily, I say unto you, that *this is my doctrine*, and I bear record of it from the Father; and whoso **believeth in me** believeth in the Father also; and unto him will the Father bear record of me, for he will visit him with fire and with the **Holy Ghost**. . . . And again I say unto you, ye must **repent**, and be **baptized** in my name, and become as a little child, or ye can in nowise inherit the kingdom of God. Verily, verily, I say unto you, that *this is my doctrine*.

Similar references to the doctrine of Christ are in 2 Nephi 31 and 32, which will be discussed later in this chapter as we examine what 2 Nephi adds to our understanding of the gospel.

One striking characteristic in all of the scriptures above is that they consistently refer to the first four principles of the gospel (**bolded** above); namely, faith in Jesus Christ, repentance, baptism, and the Holy Ghost. Not all passages include all four principles, and some refer to belief in

---

c Sherem was an anti-Christ, so not everything he said can be believed; however, his statement equating *the gospel* with *the doctrine of Christ* was not refuted by Jacob and is confirmed by comparing the principles used to describe these doctrines.

Christ or receiving Christ rather than faith in Christ, but the points we have come to know as the first principles of the gospel are consistently present in these scriptures that define *the gospel*. Additionally, one reference also includes what has sometimes been called the fifth principle of the gospel—enduring to the end.

A second characteristic is that many of the passages above refer to the Crucifixion and Resurrection of Jesus Christ and His atoning role in the Final Judgment and eternal reward (underlined above). The importance of these principles is further strengthened when we recognize that the two passages from 3 Nephi were spoken by Christ shortly after His Atonement and Resurrection.

The passage from Hebrews 6 is, perhaps, the most succinct definition, citing not only the first four principles of the gospel but also specifying resurrection and judgment. Echoing this passage, the Prophet Joseph Smith said, "The Doctrines of the Resurrection of the Dead and the Eternal Judgment are necessary to preach among the first principles of the Gospel of Jesus Christ."[35] An examination of all the scriptures above shows why this is so: By breaking the bands of death, Jesus provided for the resurrection of the dead, and by atoning for our sins, Jesus qualified Himself to administer eternal judgment for all mankind. These two doctrines point to the redemptive powers of Jesus Christ. Without them, the other principles of the gospel would have no effect.

In many passages of scripture, the redemptive power of Christ's Atonement is characterized by what will occur at the Final Judgment. We usually think of judgment in a negative light, but if we have followed the gospel path, the Final Judgment will be a glorious and joyful occasion, for Christ will intercede and declare that His Atonement has paid the price of our sins. We will rejoice during that Day of Judgment, knowing that Jesus Christ, our Friend and Redeemer, will be our ultimate judge and that He will pronounce us guiltless because of His Atonement (see D&C 45:3–5). Both Jacob and Moroni referred to the judgment bar as "the pleasing bar" of God for the repentant (see Jacob 6:13 and Moroni 10:34). As Elder Dieter F. Uchtdorf has said, "That Day of Judgment will be a day of mercy and love—a day when broken hearts are healed, when tears of grief are replaced with tears of gratitude, when all will be made right."[36]

When we examine all the scriptures that describe the gospel or the doctrine of Christ, it is clear why Joseph Smith said that the doctrines of resurrection and eternal judgment should be taught alongside the first principles of the gospel of Jesus Christ: These additional two principles point to the purpose for the other four or five—to bring us unto Christ so we can partake of the powers of His redemption. It is by following the steps we know as the first principles and ordinances of the gospel that we have the potential to be declared guiltless and saved in the kingdom of God when we stand before Him in our resurrected bodies at the Day of Judgment. Following the path defined by the first five principles and ordinances of the gospel qualifies us to be full beneficiaries of the other two.

I call resurrection and eternal judgment the redemption principles of the gospel (those carried out by Jesus Christ), to distinguish them from what have become known as the first principles of the gospel—faith in Jesus Christ, repentance, baptism, the gift of the Holy Ghost, and enduring to the end (principles which must be carried out by us). The redemption principles refer to the two main gifts from Jesus Christ: salvation from physical death and salvation from spiritual death, or, stated another way, salvation from death and sin. Salvation from physical death is a free gift given by Jesus Christ to all, but salvation from spiritual death and sin is given only to those who follow the first principles of the gospel. In the scriptures, the first of these two gifts is called the Resurrection, and the second is called either the Judgment or the Atonement. The gospel encompasses these two redemption principles along with the other principles.[d]

---

d All of these principles of the gospel are beautifully integrated in Mormon's farewell appeal to the latter-day remnant of Israel recorded in chapter 7 of his own book. His exhortation is centered on a plea to "lay hold upon the gospel of Christ" (Mormon 7:8). Mormon describes the role of both the Resurrection and the Judgment in fulfilling the purposes of the Redemption of Jesus Christ while also calling upon gathered Israel to follow the first principles of the gospel so that "it shall be well with you in the day of judgment" (Mormon 7:10). The short yet seminal chapter is recommended for further study on the meaning of the gospel.

What Is the Gospel?

The scriptures discussed above suggest the following two-part definition of *the gospel*:

a) The gospel is the good news that through the Atonement of Jesus Christ, all mankind may be redeemed from both death and sin, allowing us to stand before the Lord in resurrected bodies at the Day of Judgment and receive an eternal reward.

b) If we abide by the first principles and ordinances of the gospel, we will be declared guiltless and saved in the kingdom of God: Have faith in Jesus Christ, repent of all sin, be baptized by water for the remission of sins, be sanctified through the reception of the Holy Ghost, and endure to the end.

This definition is consistent with other descriptions of the gospel published by the Church.[e, f] If we condense this definition into its most essential parts and then convert it into statements of belief, we get the following equivalent declarations:

a) We believe that through the Atonement of Christ, all mankind may be saved, by obedience to the laws and ordinances of the Gospel.

b) We believe that the first principles and ordinances of the Gospel are: first, Faith in the Lord Jesus Christ; second, Repentance; third, Baptism by immersion for the remission of sins; fourth, Laying on of hands for the gift of the Holy Ghost.

---

e *Preach My Gospel* states, "According to the Book of Mormon the gospel of Jesus Christ includes (1) faith in the Lord Jesus Christ; (2) repentance through the Atonement of Christ; (3) baptism by immersion in Christ's name; (4) the gift of the Holy Ghost; and (5) enduring to the end (see 2 Nephi 31; 3 Nephi 11; and 3 Nephi 27). It also teaches us what we need to believe about Christ if we are to have faith in Him. . . . A purpose of the gospel of Jesus Christ is to cleanse people of their sins so they can receive His mercy at the day of judgment."[37]

f The Bible Dictionary states, "The word gospel means 'good news.' The good news is that Jesus Christ has made a perfect atonement for mankind that will redeem all mankind from the grave and reward each individual according to his or her works."[38]

These, of course, are the third and fourth articles of faith of the Church, which are part of our canonized scripture, and they confirm that the definition of the gospel given above is on track. Since my childhood days in Primary when I first memorized them, I have always seen these two articles of faith as connected—the end of the third seems to parallel the beginning of the fourth. No other articles of faith are so connected. The third says that salvation comes though Christ by obeying "the laws and ordinances of the Gospel," and the fourth delineates the essential laws or principles and ordinances we must follow to qualify for that salvation. Combined, these two articles of faith provide an additional, succinct definition of the gospel or the doctrine of Christ. What a testimony this provides to the internal consistency of the scriptures and doctrines revealed through the prophet Joseph Smith!

Now that we have come to a clear understanding of what is meant by *the gospel*, let us look at the book of 2 Nephi. The two parts of the gospel just described are exactly what we find therein. First, in the early chapters of 2 Nephi we find some of the most beautiful and doctrinally rich teachings on the Resurrection and Atonement of Jesus Christ in all of Holy Writ—particularly in chapters 2 and 9. Confirming the preeminence of these chapters, Elder Bruce R. McConkie wrote, "Our most explicit teaching on the Atonement of Christ are in 2 Nephi 2 and 9 and Alma 34."[39] So two of the three best chapters on the Atonement in all scripture are found in 2 Nephi. Other parts of the book, such as chapter 25, similarly testify powerfully of Christ and His Atonement. Second, at the end of the book, in chapters 31–33, we find an explanation of the first principles and ordinances of the gospel in Nephi's presentation of *the doctrine of Christ* that rivals all of the scriptures quoted above in scope, clarity, and literary beauty. Thus, both parts of the gospel are strongly emphasized in 2 Nephi, making *the gospel* a clear theme of the book.

With *the gospel* established as a covenant path theme of 2 Nephi, it becomes clear that understanding and committing to follow the gospel is one of the key steps in the path we must follow to return to God's presence. Indeed, I believe that one of the reasons the Lord gave us the book of 2 Nephi is to strengthen our understanding of the gospel, including helping us to understand what is meant by the phrase, "the law of the gospel" (see D&C 88:78; 104:18). The remainder of this chapter will explore this purpose.

THE CREATION, THE FALL, AND THE ATONEMENT

The words of blessing and instruction given by Lehi to his son, Jacob, in chapter 2 of 2 Nephi, show us that the Creation, the Fall, and the Atonement are integral parts of the gospel. As Elder Bruce R. McConkie has stated, "These three are the very pillars of eternity itself."[40] As pillars, they hold up everything else in the gospel. They are the three essential legs of the footstool of God called the gospel, and without any one leg, the stool would not stand.

The details of the stories of the Creation and the Fall are recited elsewhere in the scriptures, and Lehi had undoubtedly taught those details previously to his children from the brass plates. What Lehi focused on in his instructional blessing to Jacob was not the stories themselves, but the *purpose* of the Creation, the Fall, and the Atonement.

The purpose of these three pillars, and indeed, the purpose of the entire gospel plan of salvation was summarized by Lehi in these few words: "Men are, that they might have joy" (2 Nephi 2:25). Joy! What a glorious purpose! What a meaningful reason to exist! There is no one who does not want to have joy. President Russell M. Nelson has said, "When the focus of our lives is on God's plan of salvation . . . and Jesus Christ and His gospel, we can feel joy regardless of what is happening—or not happening—in our lives. Joy comes from and because of Him. He is the source of all joy. . . . For Latter-day Saints, Jesus Christ is joy!"[41] Clearly the purpose of the gospel of Jesus Christ, including the Creation, the Fall, and the entire plan of salvation, is to bring us joy.

Lehi taught the purpose for the gospel plan, but he didn't begin with that statement of purpose. He began by acknowledging to Jacob that this life is hard. He said, "And now, Jacob, I speak unto you: Thou art my firstborn in the days of my tribulation in the wilderness. And behold, in thy childhood thou hast suffered afflictions and much sorrow" (2 Nephi 2:1). It appears that the rest of Lehi's sermon-blessing was given to Jacob to explain how the challenges of life are designed to bring joy in spite of hardship. And to make that explanation, Lehi taught about the Creation, the Fall, and the Atonement.

Lehi began by speaking about Christ's Atonement, reminding Jacob that he had been blessed with a special spiritual experience with the Redeemer, wherein "thou has beheld in thy youth his glory," and reassuring Jacob that "the way is prepared from the fall of man, and salvation is free" (2 Nephi 2:4). Lehi expounded on this, declaring, "Wherefore, redemption cometh in and through the Holy Messiah; for he is full of grace and truth. Behold, he offereth himself a sacrifice for sin, to answer the ends of the law, unto all those who have a broken heart and a contrite spirit" (2 Nephi 2:6–7). Lehi further explained that there are two possibilities affixed as ends of the law: either punishment or happiness. He then added that "happiness . . . is affixed, to answer the ends of the atonement" (2 Nephi 2:10), or, to state this another way, the purpose of the Atonement is to bring about happiness. Lehi was trying to bring hope and joy into his son's difficult life.

Lehi then elaborated on the role of the Savior and His Atonement, including resurrection and judgment:

> There is no flesh that can dwell in the presence of God, save it be through the merits, and mercy, and grace of the Holy Messiah, who layeth down his life according to the flesh, and taketh it again by the power of the Spirit, that he may bring to pass the resurrection of the dead, being the first that should rise. Wherefore, he is the firstfruits unto God, inasmuch as he shall make intercession for all the children of men; and they that believe in him shall be saved. And because of the intercession for all, all men come unto God; wherefore, they stand in the presence of him, to be judged of him according to the truth and holiness which is in him. (2 Nephi 2:8–10)

Lehi's instruction makes it very clear that only through the Atonement can those with broken hearts and contrite spirits be cleansed from sin and achieve eternal happiness. His words further emphasize that this is made possible only through the merits, mercy, and grace of the Savior, who brings about the Resurrection and provides intercession for us all when we stand to be judged of him.

OPPOSITION IN ALL THINGS

Lehi did not focus solely on the happiness and joy that will be achieved after the Resurrection. He taught that this earth life, with its many opposing forces, was designed to bring joy and happiness by allowing us to experience their opposites: sorrow, misery, and tribulation. "For it must needs be, that there is an opposition in all things" (2 Nephi 2:11), he declared. This statement is especially poignant when we remember that Lehi began this sermon by consoling Jacob regarding his afflictions.

People with a purpose or challenge are generally happier than people with nothing to do. The design of our earth-life answers this need for everyone; however, difficulty arises when we experience a trial that is greater than we think we can handle. In such times as these, we need to look to God and seek inspiration on how to turn each obstacle or trial into a quest. Sometimes this will require the assistance of others, but the Holy Ghost can guide us to the help we need.

Consider the life of Steven Hawking. He had been a bright student of physics at Oxford University in the early 1960s and went on to do graduate study at Cambridge when he was first diagnosed with a rare form of the motor neuron disease known as ALS. He was only twenty-one. Walking became difficult, and his speech became slurred. Faced with these trials, he initially struggled with depression, but after receiving encouragement from his supervising professor, he decided to accept the disease as an additional challenge and move forward with his goals.[42] One biography states,

> In a sense, Hawking's disease helped turn him into the noted scientist he became. Before the diagnosis, Hawking hadn't always focused on his studies. "Before my condition was diagnosed, I had been very bored with life," he said. "There had not seemed to be anything worth doing." With the sudden realization that he might not even live long enough to earn his PhD, Hawking poured himself into his work and research.[43]

Steven Hawking went on to become one of the most brilliant and celebrated physicists of our time, in spite of the disease progressing until he became completely paralyzed and had to use a computerized synthesizer for speech. He passed away in 2018 at the age of seventy-six. His life story is aligned with the principles Lehi taught about opposition in all things. He turned his trials into quests and probably achieved more than he would have without the limitations of his disease.

Viktor Frankl, an Austrian psychiatrist who survived several Nazi concentration camps during World War II, likewise found purpose in suffering. He wrote that one of the key ways to find meaning in life is "by the attitude we take toward unavoidable suffering."[44] He added, "We must never forget that we may also find meaning in life even when confronted with a hopeless situation, when facing a fate that cannot be changed. For what then matters is to bear witness to the uniquely human potential at its best, which is to transform a personal tragedy into triumph, to turn one's predicament into a human achievement."[45]

These modern examples of triumph over adversity are consistent with Lehi's teachings. After introducing the principle of opposition, he set the stage for further explanation of this doctrine by rehearsing the creation of "all things," including "our first parents" and their experience in the Garden of Eden. He said, "It must needs be that there was an opposition; even the forbidden fruit in opposition to the tree of life; the one being sweet and the other bitter" (2 Nephi 2:15). Lehi explained how Satan, an enticer and source of opposition, tempted Adam and Eve to choose the forbidden fruit. Lehi then taught these profound truths:

> And now, behold, if Adam had not transgressed he would not have fallen, but he would have remained in the garden of Eden. . . . And they would have had no children; wherefore they would have remained in a state of innocence, having no joy, for they knew no misery; doing no good, for they knew no sin. But behold, all things have been done in the wisdom of him who knoweth all things. Adam fell that men might be; and men are, that they might have joy. (2 Nephi 2:22–25)

There is the grand explanation! In it lies the understanding of why Jacob, and indeed all mankind, must suffer afflictions and temptations and tribulation. It is one of the great lessons we are to glean from the story of the Creation and the Fall. It explains why God allows evil and suffering in the world.

With only the record in Genesis to guide them, most people of other faiths see the Fall as a bad thing. They think that we would all be living in a paradisiacal Eden today if Adam and Eve had not partaken of the forbidden fruit. The reality is that none of us would have even been born if it had not been for the Fall. Lehi stated this truth clearly in the first half of his beautiful, poetic couplet: *"Adam fell that men might be;* and men are, that they might have joy" (2 Nephi 2:25; emphasis added).[g]

After teaching about the Fall, Lehi returned full circle to the place he started: the Atonement. He emphasized that "the days of the children of men were prolonged . . . that they might repent while in the flesh" (2 Nephi 2:21). He then proclaimed that the Messiah is the source of redemption for those who do repent. These final words of his discourse declare his testimony of the Messiah and Redeemer:

> And the Messiah cometh in the fulness of time, that he may redeem the children of men from the fall. And because that they are redeemed from the fall they have become free forever, knowing good from evil; to act for themselves and not to be acted upon. . . . Wherefore, men are free according to the flesh; and all things are given them which are expedient unto man. And they are free to choose liberty and eternal life, through the great Mediator of all men, or to choose captivity and death, according to the captivity and power of the devil; for he seeketh that all men might be miserable like unto himself. And now, my sons, I would that ye should look to the great Mediator, and hearken unto his great commandments; and be faithful unto his words, and choose eternal life, according to the will of his Holy Spirit. (2 Nephi 2:26–28)

This testimony of Lehi attests that happiness and joy will only come when we, in the face of opposition, "choose liberty and eternal life,

---

g The following analogy might help those who think the Fall of Adam was a bad thing. Living in the Garden of Eden was a paradise experience: Adam and Eve got to walk and talk with God, there was no enmity between the animals, and food came plentifully with no effort. It was as if Adam and Eve were living on a mountaintop with everything available that they wanted and needed. However, they became aware that there was another mountaintop in the distance whose peak stood even higher—the mountaintop of exaltation. It still included life with God, but on that mountain everyone would share in all that God has, including having an exalted body like His and being organized in families. The problem was that there was a valley between the two mountains—a gulf that had to be crossed. The Fall was the descent of Adam and Eve from the mountain of the Garden of Eden, allowing everyone to be born, and this earth life is the quest to climb the higher mountain, with the help of the Atonement of Jesus Christ, toward eternal life with God in a state of exaltation.

through the great Mediator of all men" (2 Nephi 2:27). In other words, joy comes through choosing to engage the power of the Atonement of Jesus Christ in our lives by following the gospel path He has defined. In a later sermon of his own, Jacob reiterated this same principle, declaring, "Therefore, cheer up your hearts, and remember that ye are free to act for yourselves—to choose the way of everlasting death or the way of eternal life" (2 Nephi 10:23). This "way of eternal life" is the gospel path, also called the doctrine of Christ.

In chapter 2 of 2 Nephi, Lehi laid the foundation for understanding the gospel by teaching that only through God's divine plan, which included a creation, a fall, and an atonement, could we, the spirit children of God, acquire the freedom to choose for ourselves. This plan answers the innate longing we each have to be independent and choose for ourselves. It is an ingenious plan—one only God could have conceived—which allows us to be born into a mortal and fallen world where we can learn and grow from mistakes and yet be redeemed from those mistakes if we humble ourselves, repent, and "look to the great Mediator" (2 Nephi 2:28). It is an eternal plan that gives us physical bodies that will later be resurrected into perfect, eternal souls. It is a perfect plan whereby we have the potential to become like God. It is the plan of salvation. It is the plan of happiness and joy. This is the gospel of Jesus Christ.

RESURRECTION AND JUDGMENT COMPLETE THE ATONEMENT

The information taught in Lehi's sermon-blessing to Jacob formed a doctrinal foundation upon which Jacob built, later presenting his own remarkable sermon that testified of the Messiah and the covenants of Israel. Jacob's doctrinal discourse comprises chapters 6 through 10 of 2 Nephi and was presented over two days, probably at the temple, for he presented a later sermon at that holy place (see Jacob 2:2). The pinnacle of his sermon is chapter 9, which, like chapter 2, teaches much about the Atonement. However, while chapter 2 focuses on how the Atonement brings happiness and joy in the broad gospel plan, chapter 9 focuses on the role of the Atonement in our resurrection and judgment.

Jacob, perhaps more clearly than any other prophet, expounded on the two primary ways that Christ redeems us. Jacob spoke of an "escape from . . . death and hell, which I call the death of the body, and also the death of the spirit" (2 Nephi 9:10). He added,

And because of the way of deliverance of our God, the Holy One of Israel, this death, of which I have spoken, which is the temporal, shall deliver up its dead; which death is the grave. And this death of which I have spoken, which is the spiritual death, shall deliver up its dead; which spiritual death is hell; wherefore, death and hell must deliver up their dead, and hell must deliver up its captive spirits, and the grave must deliver up its captive bodies, and the bodies and the spirits of men will be restored one to the other; and it is by the power of the resurrection of the Holy One of Israel. (2 Nephi 9:11–12)

These two deaths, physical and spiritual, correspond to the two redemption principles of the gospel, resurrection and judgment. Jacob taught, "For as death hath passed upon all men, to fulfil the merciful plan of the great Creator, there must needs be a power of resurrection" (2 Nephi 9:6), later adding, "And it shall come to pass that when all men shall have passed from this first death unto life, insomuch as they have become immortal, they must appear before the judgment-seat of the Holy One of Israel; and then cometh the judgment, and then must they be judged according to the holy judgment of God" (2 Nephi 9:15).

Jacob's teachings show us that the principles of resurrection and judgment are integrated. He explained that without the Resurrection, the results of the First Judgment (sending us either to paradise or to hell, which here means spirit prison) would remain forever, and we would all become subject to the devil (see 2 Nephi 9:7–9). Without the Resurrection, even those who followed the gospel path would never have the blessing of standing before God at the Final Judgment day and being pronounced clean and saved in the kingdom of God. But with the Resurrection, "He delivereth his saints from that awful monster the devil, and death, and hell" (2 Nephi 9:19).

Focusing on the Atonement, Jacob explained the role of the redeemer in the gospel plan as follows:

And he cometh into the world that he may save all men if they will hearken unto his voice; for behold, he suffereth the pains of all men, yea, the pains of every living creature, both men, women, and children, who belong to the family of Adam. And he suffereth this that the *resurrection* might pass upon all men, that all might stand before him at the great and *judgment* day. And he commandeth all men that they must *repent*, and be *baptized* in his name, having perfect *faith* in the Holy One of Israel, or they cannot be saved in the kingdom of God. And if they will not *repent* and *believe* in his name, and be *baptized* in his name, and *endure to the end*, they must be damned; for the Lord God, the Holy One of Israel, has spoken it. (2 Nephi 9:21–24; emphasis added)

Although Jacob did not preface that statement with, "This is the gospel," this passage summarizes the gospel in words that are in complete harmony with the passages quoted at the beginning of this chapter, including the redemption principles of resurrection and judgment and all of the first principles of the gospel except the Holy Ghost. No wonder Sherem would later say to Jacob, "I have heard and also know that thou goest about much, preaching that which ye call the gospel, or the doctrine of Christ" (Jacob 7:6).

Jacob continued his sermon by emphasizing that there will be consequences for the wicked on the Day of Judgment. He proclaimed "wo" upon an array of sinners who die in their sins (see 2 Nephi 9:31–38), admonishing,

Turn away from your sins; shake off the chains of him that would bind you fast. . . . Prepare your souls for . . . the day of judgment, that ye may not shrink with awful fear; that ye may not remember your awful guilt in perfectness, and be constrained to exclaim: Holy, holy are thy judgments, O Lord God Almighty—but I know my guilt; I transgressed thy law, and my transgressions are mine; and the devil hath obtained me, that I am a prey to his awful misery. (2 Nephi 9:45–46)

Within the Church we don't often focus on the consequences for the wicked on the Day of Judgment because we are working with those who have already entered into the gospel path through baptism and who are striving to be more Christlike. Perhaps this is why we more frequently use the term *atonement* as opposed to *judgment* when we talk about the redemption principles of the gospel. The term *judgment* applies universally to everyone on earth, while the term *atonement* focuses on the power available to those who are striving to follow Christ. This becomes clear as we examine the next chapter of Jacob's sermon.

On the second day of his two-day discourse, Jacob prophesied of the coming of Christ to Jerusalem, the subsequent scattering of the Jews, and the latter-day gathering of Israel (see 2 Nephi 10). He then ended with this plea to "my beloved brethren" (Church members) to take advantage of the Resurrection and *the Atonement*:

Wherefore, my beloved brethren, reconcile yourselves to the will of God, and not to the will of the devil and the flesh; and remember, after ye are reconciled unto God, that it is only in and through the grace of God that ye are saved. Wherefore, may God raise you from death *by the power of the resurrection*, and also from everlasting death *by the power of the atonement*, that ye may be received into the eternal kingdom of God, that ye may praise him through grace divine. Amen. (2 Nephi 10:24–25; emphasis added)

Jacob's clear shift to the use of the term *atonement* in the same context where he had previously spoken of *judgment* shows how he would want all members of the Church to shift: from a motivation by fear of an impending judgment to a motivation by love of our Savior and the gift of grace found in His infinite Atonement. As Jacob said, "Remember, after ye are reconciled unto God, that it is only in and through the grace of God that ye are saved" (2 Nephi 10:24).

This portion of Jacob's sermon teaches that the two redemption principles of the gospel, resurrection and judgment, complete the effects of the Atonement in the eternal lives of those who follow the gospel path. Resurrection makes it possible for everyone to stand before God on the Day of Judgment, and then those who have been reconciled to Him by following the sanctifying laws and ordinances of the gospel will be declared saved through the grace and power of the Atonement of Jesus Christ.

Jacob's discourse on the redemption principles of the gospel also included this meaningful statement that echoes temple ritual, instruction, and clothing: "Wherefore, we shall have a perfect knowledge of all our guilt, and our uncleanness, and our nakedness; and the righteous shall have a perfect knowledge of their enjoyment, and their righteousness, being clothed with purity, yea, even with the robe of righteousness" (2 Nephi 9:14). Jacob's sermon is clearly covenant path instruction.

THE DOCTRINE OF THE ATONEMENT

Following is a list of the main points of doctrine and instruction we learn from 2 Nephi 9. These points not only enhance our understanding of the Atonement but also of the entire gospel plan of salvation, which is centered on the Atonement. They are worthy of our study and contemplation as we consider our covenant to live the law of the gospel.

Indeed, Jacob had his mind fixed on covenants as he began his sermon, stating that he had just read to the people two chapters from Isaiah, "that ye might know concerning the covenants of the Lord that he had covenanted with all the house of Israel" (2 Nephi 9:1).

1. Even though our flesh must die, in our bodies we shall see God because of the Lord who will come in the flesh and die for all men. (See 2 Nephi 9:4–5.)

2. As death will pass upon all, resurrection will also come to all, fulfilling the merciful plan of God. Resurrection could not come without the Fall and the transgression that initiated it, cutting mankind off from the presence of God. (See 2 Nephi 9:6.)

3. The Atonement is infinite, and it is a demonstration of the wisdom, mercy, grace, and goodness of God. Without it, there would be nothing beyond the First Judgment (which consigns our spirits to a place in the spirit world), so that corruption could not put on incorruption (meaning our bodies would never rise), our spirits would all become subject to the devil forever, and we would become angels to the devil. (See 2 Nephi 9:7–10.)

4. Because of the Holy One of Israel, all graves shall deliver up their dead. The spirits of those who are in a state of spiritual death will be delivered from hell (i.e., spirit prison; see D&C 76:106) to be reunited with their bodies from the grave, and the spirits of those who are righteous will be delivered from paradise to be reunited with their bodies from the grave. "And the bodies and the spirits of men will be restored one to the other; and it is by the power of the resurrection of the Holy One of Israel . . . and all men become incorruptible, and immortal, and they are living souls" (2 Nephi 9:11–13).

5. Resurrection will bring with it a perfect knowledge of things. We will know things in the same way we know things in the flesh, except that our knowledge will be perfect. (See 2 Nephi 9:13.) (Note that perfect knowledge is not promised in the spirit world.)

6. After being resurrected, those who carry guilt for their sins will have a perfect knowledge of that guilt and uncleanness and will

feel naked before God with respect to their guilt, while the righteous will have been cleansed by the Atonement and will have a perfect knowledge of their enjoyment and righteousness, and these shall be clothed with purity. Thus, we shall appear before the judgment-seat of Christ and be judged, and our righteousness or filth will remain. (See 2 Nephi 9:14–16.)

7. For those whose final fate is to dwell with Satan, their torment will be *as* a lake of fire and brimstone. (See 2 Nephi 9:16.) (The imagery is a figurative representation of the mental and spiritual torment the wicked will suffer, not a physical reality.)

8. We can trust God's promises. All His words and laws will be fulfilled. (See 2 Nephi 9:17.)

9. Through Christ, we can throw off the shame of the crosses of the world we have endured, and we can have full joy in the kingdom of God. (See 2 Nephi 9:18.) (Note that Jacob's use of joy here and his use of the word enjoyment in verse 14 are consistent with Lehi's use of the word joy as the purpose of life in 2 Nephi 2:25.)

10. God's mercy is great because He delivers us from hell, and He is great because He knows all things. (See 2 Nephi 9:19–20.) (This gives us reason to trust in Him.)

11. Christ suffered the pains of every man, woman, and child. This allows Him to save all who hearken to his voice and to bring about the Resurrection for everyone so they can stand before Him on Judgment Day. (See 2 Nephi 9:21–22.)

12. God commands everyone to follow the path of faith in Christ, repentance, baptism, and enduring to the end. Those who do not follow this law will be damned. (See 2 Nephi 9:23–25.)

13. Those who have received no law will have no punishment or condemnation. The mercies of Christ will have claim on them. Because of the Atonement, they will be delivered by His power, for the Atonement satisfies the demands of justice for them. (See 2 Nephi 9:25–26.)

14. The devil is cunning, and those who follow him are vain, weak, and foolish. "When they are learned they think they are wise, and they hearken not unto the counsel of God, for they set it aside, supposing they know of themselves, wherefore, their wisdom is foolishness and it profiteth them not. And they shall perish. But to be learned is good if they hearken unto the counsels of God" (2 Nephi 9:28–29).

15. Awful is the state of those who know the law and commandments of God and transgress them and die in their sins, for they shall remain in their sins when they stand accountable before God. (See 2 Nephi 9:27–38.)

16. "Remember, to be carnally-minded is death, and to be spiritually minded is life eternal." The righteous love the truth, while those who are unclean revile against the truth. (See 2 Nephi 9:39–40.)

17. The Lord's path is narrow but lies in a straight course, and the keeper of the gate is Christ, "and he employeth no servant there." He cannot be deceived. He despises those "who are puffed up because of their learning, and their wisdom, and their riches," but He will open the gate to those who "come down in the depths of humility." (See 2 Nephi 9:41–43.)

After teaching these principles, Jacob admonished his people to turn away from their sins and prepare for the Day of Judgment. He then he invited all to come unto Christ with these words:

> Come, my brethren, every one that thirsteth, come ye to the waters; and he that hath no money, come buy and eat; yea, come buy wine and milk without money and without price. Wherefore, do not spend money for that which is of no worth, nor your labor for that which cannot satisfy. Hearken diligently unto me, and remember the words which I have spoken; and come unto the Holy One of Israel, and feast upon that which perisheth not, neither can be corrupted, and let your soul delight in fatness. (2 Nephi 9:50–51)

Jacob then reminded his people to pray. He declared, "And behold how great the covenants of the Lord, and how great his condescensions unto the children of men" (2 Nephi 9:53). Clearly, the principles Jacob taught are tied to covenants.

Jacob's sermon teaches us much about the gospel, with special emphasis on Christ's redeeming gifts of the Resurrection and the atoning Judgment. This gospel—this doctrine of Christ—is a glorious doctrine. No wonder Jacob exclaimed repeatedly, "O the wisdom of God, his mercy and grace!" (2 Nephi 9:8), "O how great the goodness of our God" (2 Nephi 9:10), "O how great the plan of our God!" (2 Nephi 9:13), "O the greatness and the justice of our God!" (2 Nephi 9:17), "O the greatness of the mercy of our God, the Holy One of Israel!" (2 Nephi 9:19), and "O how great the holiness of our God!" (2 Nephi 9:20). How great indeed!

THE GOSPEL AND THE PLAN OF SALVATION

After reviewing the principles taught in chapters 2 and 9 of 2 Nephi, we can see that the plan of salvation is an integral part of the gospel of Jesus Christ. These two chapters include references to all of the following principles or doctrines that are typically included in discussions of the plan of salvation:

- Premortal life and the Creation (2 Nephi 2:13–17)
- The Fall and purpose of this life, including opposition in all things (2 Nephi 2:18–25; 9:45–46, 50–52)
- The Atonement of Jesus Christ (2 Nephi 2:3–10, 26–29; 9:7–10, 19–26)
- Death and a preliminary judgment to paradise or hell (spirit prison) (2 Nephi 9:10–13, 41)
- Resurrection (2 Nephi 9:6, 12–14)
- Final Judgment and rewards (2 Nephi 2:10; 9:15–18, 22–24)

It is interesting to note that Doctrine and Covenants 76, a revelation that we so often associate with the plan of salvation, declares at the onset, "And the record which we bear is the fulness of the gospel of Jesus Christ" (D&C 76:14), thus making a connection between the gospel and the plan of salvation. Section 76 not only contains descriptions of our possible final rewards, including the celestial, terrestrial, and telestial kingdoms, but it also contains one of the most beautiful and powerful witnesses of the resurrected Christ in all of scripture (see D&C 76:22–24). This latter-day revelation also contains a clear definition of the gospel, as quoted earlier (see D&C 76:40–44, 50–53, 70). A study of Doctrine and Covenants 76 will provide further insights into *the gospel* and its connection to the plan of salvation, including the Atonement of Jesus Christ.

Elder M. Russell Ballard has stated, "The plan of salvation is centered on the Savior's Atonement."[46] The gospel is also centered on the Atonement. The two overlap with a common center. In fact, they are essentially the same, as Elder Bruce R. McConkie made clear:

> What is the fulness of the everlasting gospel? It is the plan of salvation—the Father's eternal plan to save his children. It is the begetting of spirit children, the teachings and testings of our premortal existence, the creation of worlds without number, and (for us) our inheritance here on planet earth. It is the Fall of Adam, with its temporal and spiritual death, and the ransoming power of the Son of God, who abolished death and brought life and immortality to light through his laws. It is all of the laws, rites, and ordinances; all of the truths, powers, and performances; all of the keys, priesthoods, and privileges which bring to pass the immortality and eternal life of man. It is the Atonement of Christ, the Redemption of man, the opening of the graves, the wonder and glory of eternal life. It is faith, repentance, and baptism; it is the gifts of the Spirit, the revelations of heaven, and the unspeakable gift of the Holy Ghost. It is eternal marriage and eternal lives and eternal exaltation. It is to be one with the Father and the Son and to reign with them forever on their throne. It is the tests and trials of this mortal probation; it is sorrow and pain and death; it is overcoming the world and pursuing a godly course in spite of earth and hell; it is keeping the commandments and serving our fellowmen. And, finally, it is to sit down with Abraham, Isaac, and Jacob, and all the holy prophets, in the kingdom of God to go no more out.[47]

Sometimes we hear the term *the gospel* stated so frequently that we take it for granted; however, it encompasses all that is sacred in the plan of salvation. It includes the Creation, the Fall, and the Atonement, all in one word. It heralds salvation and ascension to our final glory, including resurrection of our corporal bodies and redemption from sin. It bespeaks the hope that comes with the eternal promise given to Adam that redemption would come after the Fall. It proclaims the purpose of our eternal lives:

"Men are, that they might have joy" (2 Nephi 2:25). These truths are all part of the fulness of the gospel of Jesus Christ.

OH LORD, WILT THOU REDEEM MY SOUL?

Chapter 4 of 2 Nephi also focuses on the Atonement of Jesus Christ, but in a different way. Chapters 2 and 9 focus on the redeeming power of the Atonement, but here, Nephi offers a prayer essentially asking God to bless him with the enabling power of the Atonement. This plea is part of what has been called the Psalm of Nephi, and it shows us that even a prophet of God needs help with his trials. Indeed, it confirms that we all need strength from the Atonement of Jesus Christ.

Nephi, an otherwise highly confident, dogmatically obedient prophet of God, began by humbly acknowledging his own weaknesses and dependence on the Lord. He declared, "I write the things of my soul" (2 Nephi 4:15), crying out,

> O wretched man that I am! Yea, my heart sorroweth because of my flesh; my soul grieveth because of mine iniquities. I am encompassed about, because of the temptations and the sins which do so easily beset me. And when I desire to rejoice, my heart groaneth because of my sins; nevertheless, I know in whom I have trusted. My God hath been my support; . . . He hath filled me with his love. . . . (2 Nephi 4:17–21)

Nephi's self-condemnation does not seem to be as concerned with specific sins as it is with his imperfect, sinful nature, which comes with mortality. In this, Nephi is similar to Paul, who also cried out, "O wretched man that I am!" (Romans 7:24) while also decrying his own sinful nature. They both bemoaned their weaknesses.

What was it that sparked Nephi's passionate plea at this time? The answer lies in the verses just preceding his emotional outpouring (see 2 Nephi 4:12–14). Nephi's father had just died. The two of them had been partners in the spiritual leadership of their family, but now Nephi carried this burden alone. Something then happened that provoked Nephi to admonish his family, yet his brothers and the sons of Ishmael responded again with anger. Had he been so passionate in his admonition that he had alienated them? He knew that he was not perfect and lamented his shortcomings. He regretted the anger that these rebellious ones so often stirred up in him. His father could no longer console him, so he poured out his heart in writing. After acknowledging his weaknesses, he rejoiced with praise to God and then cried out,

> Awake, my soul! No longer droop in sin. Rejoice, O my heart, and give place no more for the enemy of my soul. Do not anger again because of mine enemies. Do not slacken my strength because of mine afflictions. Rejoice, O my heart, and cry unto the Lord, and say: O Lord, I will praise thee forever; yea, my soul will rejoice in thee, my God, and the rock of my salvation. (2 Nephi 4:28–30)

Nephi then reached the climax of his psalm with the following heartfelt request to receive both the redeeming and enabling powers of the Atonement in his life:

> O Lord, wilt thou redeem my soul? Wilt thou deliver me out of the hands of mine enemies? Wilt thou make me that I may shake at the appearance of sin? May the gates of hell be shut continually before me, because that my heart is broken and my spirit is contrite! O Lord, wilt thou not shut the gates of thy righteousness before me, that I may walk in the path of the low valley, that I may be strict in the plain road! O Lord, wilt thou encircle me around in the robe of thy righteousness! (2 Nephi 4:31–33)

Is there anywhere in scripture a more passionate plea for the power of the Atonement of Jesus Christ? This should be an example to all of us who want that power more present in our lives. It shows us how to approach the Lord when we feel weak and need the enabling power of His Atonement—His grace—even though we are members of His Church and, like Nephi, have already entered into covenants with God.

Nephi's pleas, "O Lord, wilt thou redeem my soul?" and "O Lord, wilt thou encircle me around in the robe of thy righteousness!" remind us of a declaration Nephi made three chapters earlier: "But behold, the Lord hath redeemed my soul from hell; I have beheld his glory, and I am encircled about eternally in the arms of his love" (2 Nephi 1:15). It appears that Nephi had earlier felt confident in the Redemption and the love of the Lord; yet, while writing his psalm, Nephi felt weak and needed a renewed confirmation of the same. This shows us how tenuous our faith can be at times. Our need for the powers of the Atonement will never end.

Also, these passages, with reference to "the robe of thy righteousness" and "encircled about eternally in the arms of his love," remind us of the symbols and powers of the Atonement offered in the temple.

Nephi's psalm is a great example of the need for the enabling power of the Atonement of Jesus Christ. Studying it helps us understand the redemption principles of the gospel in a personal way.

Isaiah and Nephi: We Talk of Christ, We Rejoice in Christ

The Isaiah chapters of 2 Nephi similarly testify of Jesus Christ. One of the main reasons Nephi loved the writings of Isaiah so much was that they contain prophesies of Christ. The book of Isaiah was the closest thing that Nephi had to the Gospels. Surely, when he transcribed the following passages into his book, his soul swelled with joy for the coming of the Messiah, the Christ:

> Therefore, the Lord himself shall give you a sign—Behold, a virgin shall conceive, and shall bear a son, and shall call his name Immanuel. Butter and honey shall he eat, that he may know to refuse the evil and to choose the good. (2 Nephi 17:14)
>
> For unto us a child is born, unto us a son is given; and the government shall be upon his shoulder; and his name shall be called, Wonderful, Counselor, The Mighty God, The Everlasting Father, The Prince of Peace. (2 Nephi 19:6)

After quoting extensively from Isaiah, Nephi told about the destruction of Jerusalem that had occurred after his family had fled the city, and then he gave the following prophecy of Christ, which summarizes the mission of the Savior with more clarity and detail than any of the prophecies he had cited from Isaiah:

> And when the day cometh that the Only Begotten of the Father, yea, even the Father of heaven and of earth, shall manifest himself unto them in the flesh, behold, they will reject him, because of their iniquities, and the hardness of their hearts, and the stiffness of their necks. Behold, they will crucify him; and after he is laid in a sepulchre for the space of three days he shall rise from the dead, with healing in

his wings; and all those who shall believe on his name shall be saved in the kingdom of God. . . .

For according to the words of the prophets, the Messiah cometh in six hundred years from the time that my father left Jerusalem; and according to the words of the prophets, and also the word of the angel of God, his name shall be Jesus Christ, the Son of God. . . . and as the Lord God liveth, there is none other name given under heaven save it be this Jesus Christ, of which I have spoken, whereby man can be saved. (2 Nephi 25:12–13, 19–20)

How appropriate that in this book of 2 Nephi, with its theme of the gospel, Nephi declared that the name of the Messiah would be Jesus Christ. This is the earliest prophecy we have of this name—it was based on revelation from an angel of God almost six hundred years before Christ's coming.

Nephi then put into perspective the law of Moses with these words, explaining the purpose for which the law was given:

And, notwithstanding we believe in Christ, we keep the law of Moses, and look forward with steadfastness unto Christ, until the law shall be fulfilled. For, for this end was the law given; wherefore the law hath become dead unto us, and we are made alive in Christ because of our faith; yet we keep the law because of the commandments. . . .

Wherefore, we speak concerning the law that our children may know the deadness of the law; and they, by knowing the deadness of the law, may look forward unto that life which is in Christ, and know for what end the law was given. And after the law is fulfilled in Christ, that they need not harden their hearts against him when the law ought to be done away. (2 Nephi 25:24–25, 27)

Nephi knew that the law of Moses was not an end unto itself. He understood that the whole purpose of the law of Moses was to point toward Christ. Likewise, the whole purpose of the law of the gospel is to point us toward Christ. The law of Moses, however, was temporary, whereas the law of the gospel is eternal. Nevertheless, Jesus Christ is the center of both. Nephi testified of this Center with the following beautiful and bold declarations:

For we labor diligently to write, to persuade our children, and also our brethren, to believe in Christ, and to be reconciled to God; for we know that it is by grace that we are saved, after all we can do. . . .

And we talk of Christ, we rejoice in Christ, we preach of Christ, we prophesy of Christ, and we write according to our prophecies, that our children may know to what source they may look for a remission of their sins. . . .

And now behold, I say unto you that the right way is to believe in Christ, and deny him not; and Christ is the Holy One of Israel; wherefore ye must bow down before him, and worship him with all your might, mind, and strength, and your whole soul; and if ye do this ye shall in nowise be cast out. (2 Nephi 25:23, 26, 29)

These testimonies of Christ given by Nephi and Isaiah add to Jacob's writings, which have already been discussed. As Elder Jeffrey R. Holland has said, "Nephi, Jacob, and Isaiah bore a very special witness—they testified of the divinity of Jesus Christ, the Son of God, he who would be the central, commanding, presiding figure throughout the Book of Mormon."[48] All three of these witnesses had each personally seen the Savior (see 2 Nephi 11:2–3). This triad of testimonies demonstrates the law of witnesses, which says that 'in the mouth of two or three witnesses shall every word be established' " (2 Cor. 13:1).

In addition to the passages already quoted about Jesus Christ and His Atonement, there are many more scattered throughout 2 Nephi. The most prominent of these are included in Appendix B at the end of this chapter.

A PATTERN OF APOSTASY AND RESTORATION

The Isaiah chapters in 2 Nephi repeatedly describe cycles of sin and righteousness for the Israelites. The presence of these descriptions bears witness that patterns of apostasy and restoration are part of the gospel. They show that whenever man's wickedness brings an apostasy or a falling away from the light of the gospel, God promises to overcome that with a restoration of the truth. He has covenanted with His prophets that gatherings and restorations will always occur.

While presenting his great sermon on the Atonement in chapters 6–10 of 2 Nephi, Jacob read two chapters from Isaiah. He explained this inclusion by saying,

And now, my beloved brethren, I have read these things that ye might know concerning the covenants of the Lord that he has covenanted with all the house of Israel—that he has spoken unto the Jews, by the mouth of his holy prophets, even from the beginning down, from generation to generation, *until the time comes that they shall be restored to the true church and fold of God*; when they shall be gathered home to the lands of their inheritance, and shall be established in all their lands of promise. (2 Nephi 9:1–2; emphasis added)

Jacob was saying that he read from Isaiah so that his people would know about the Lord's covenants, including a promise that the house of Israel would be restored to the truth. Jacob knew that Isaiah testifies of restorations. A few chapters later, Nephi quoted a lengthy excerpt from Isaiah, comprising chapters 12–24. It begins,

And it shall come to pass in the last days, when the mountain of the Lord's house shall be established in the top of the mountains, and shall be exalted above the hills, and all nations shall flow unto it. And many people shall go and say, Come ye, and let us go up to the mountain of the Lord, to the house of the God of Jacob; and he will teach us of his ways, and we will walk in his paths. (2 Nephi 12:2–3)

It is easy to recognize that this is a prophecy of the latter-day restoration of the gospel that has been fulfilled, because people from around the world have gathered to learn about God in temples built initially in the mountain regions of Utah. Periods of apostasy and restoration are repeatedly described throughout the Isaiah chapters of 2 Nephi. Sometimes Isaiah wrote about ancient periods of apostasy and restoration, sometimes he wrote about modern ones, and sometimes his writings apply to both. Regardless, the pattern is consistent, and the promise is clear: God will always remember His covenants and restore all that was lost.

In a 1973 *Ensign* article, Elder Bruce R. McConkie presented "Ten Keys to Understanding Isaiah." He wrote,

Isaiah's . . . most detailed and extensive prophecies portray the latter-day triumph and glory of Jacob's seed. He is above all else the prophet of the Restoration. . . . [Isaiah's] emphasis is on the day of restoration and on the past, present, and future gathering of Israel. . . . But if we are to truly comprehend the writings of Isaiah, we cannot overstate or overstress the plain, blunt reality that he is in fact the prophet of the Restoration.[49]

In the same article, Elder McConkie provided a brief summary of all sixty-six chapters of the book of Isaiah, including the following descriptions of the fifteen Isaiah chapters quoted in 2 Nephi. Considering that Christ's first (messianic) coming and His second (millennial) coming are both restorations, every Isaiah chapter quoted in 2 Nephi includes discussions of apostasy and/or restoration, as shown in the next table.

Bruce R. McConkie's Summary of Events from Isaiah Chapters in 2 Nephi[49]

2 Ne. 7–8	Isa. 50–51	Scattering, gathering, Restoration, Second Coming. Isaiah 50:5–6 is messianic
2 Ne. 12	Isa. 2	Gathering of Israel to the temple in our day; latter-day state of Israel; millennial conditions and Second Coming of Christ
2 Ne. 13	Isa. 3	Status of Israel in her scattered and apostate condition before the Second Coming
2 Ne. 14	Isa. 4	Millennial
2 Ne. 15	Isa. 5	Apostasy and scattering of Israel; her dire state; restoration and gathering
2 Ne. 16	Isa. 6	Isaiah's vision and call. Isaiah 6:9–10 are messianic
2 Ne. 17	Isa. 7	Local history except Isaiah 7:10–16, which are messianic
2 Ne. 18	Isa. 8	Local wars and history; counsel on identifying true religion. Isaiah 8:13–17 are messianic.
2 Ne. 19–20	Isa. 9–10	Local history: destruction of wicked Israel by Assyrians to typify destruction of all wicked nations at Second Coming; Isaiah 9:1–7 is messianic.

2 Ne. 21	Isa. 11	Restoration; gathering of Israel; millennial era. Isaiah 11:1–5 are messianic and apply also to the Second Coming.
2 Ne. 22	Isa. 12	Millennial.
2 Ne. 23	Isa. 13	Overthrow of Babylon typifying Second Coming.
2 Ne. 24	Isa. 14	Millennial gathering of Israel; fall of Lucifer in War in Heaven; destruction preceding Second Coming.

Several books have been written to help us understand the writings of Isaiah. Such studies are helpful, but they are not necessary in order to see that the Isaiah chapters in 2 Nephi bear witness of Christ and show patterns of apostasy and restoration. We do not need to become Isaiah scholars to see this—all we need is the Spirit of the Lord to accompany us in our reading.

The themes of apostasy and restoration are not limited to the Isaiah chapters of 2 Nephi. Many notable passages about restoration and apostasy from 2 Nephi are included in Appendix B at the end of this chapter. The following chapters include prominent prophecies of apostasy and restoration, with special emphasis on the latter-day Restoration:

2 Nephi 3   Prophecy of Joseph Smith and the coming forth of the Book of Mormon

2 Nephi 26   Prophecy of Christ among the Nephites followed by Nephite apostasy and priestcrafts

2 Nephi 27   Prophecy of apostasy in last days and the coming forth of the Book of Mormon

2 Nephi 28   Prophecy of apostasy after the Bible is written

2 Nephi 29   Prophecy of the coming forth of the Bible and the Book of Mormon

2 Nephi 30   Prophecy of the gospel going to Jews and Gentiles followed by destruction of the wicked and peace for the righteous

These themes, repeatedly displayed in 2 Nephi, give us hope in the promise that a restoration will always follow an apostasy and a gathering will always follow a scattering. This pattern seems to stem from the doctrine of opposition in all things. The gospel includes many opposites: death and resurrection, sin and redemption, apostasy and restoration, scattering and gathering. Thus, the emphasis on apostasy and restoration in 2 Nephi fits doctrinally alongside sin and redemption. They are all part of the gospel of Jesus Christ.

The doctrine of opposition in all things was earlier discussed as a way to reconcile the presence of evil in the world: Evil must exist so that we can value the good. However, it is also helpful to think of this in reverse: Good exists to overcome evil. It is apparent that evil takes over whenever goodness is rejected, and this must be overcome by the power of God. Thus, the doctrine of opposition in all things also says that wherever and whenever evil has taken control, the power of the Atonement of Jesus Christ will overcome this.[h] Through Christ, goodness will always overcome evil, and a restoration will always overpower the darkness of an apostasy. This is a part of the gospel covenant.

The Final Restoration: Preparing for Christ

The book of 2 Nephi not only shows us a pattern of apostasy and restoration, it gives special emphasis to the two greatest periods of restoration of all time. The first of these is the restoration that occurred with the birth and mission of Jesus Christ and His atoning role in the Redemption of mankind. The second is the great and final Restoration that ushers in the Lord's Second Coming. This latter-day Restoration is an important part of the gospel.

The final Restoration began with Joseph Smith's prayer to know which church was true, but as Elder Dieter F. Uchtdorf has said, "The Restoration is an ongoing process; we are living in it right now."[50] This restoration will continue until the Lord completes it at the time of His Second Coming. Because we live in the middle of this latter-day era of

---

h I see a parallel with the second law of thermodynamics that states that entropy, which is disorder or chaos, will always increase in a system unless external energy is applied. Similarly, the Atonement of Jesus Christ is the source of energy that overcomes the chaos of Satan.

restoration, we usually see the early restoration events of the 1800s as one period and the millennial reign of Christ as a separate period. However, from his perspective three thousand years ago, Isaiah probably saw the events of the Restoration and the millennial reign of Christ as one period—the era of the Restoration of Zion. This perspective is justifiable, for there will be no global apostasy between these two latter-day events.

An example of this single-era view can be seen in the prophecy of the establishment of latter-day temples in the top of the mountains, cited earlier, which then merges with this prophecy of the millennial peace: "And they shall beat their swords into plow-shares, and their spears into pruning-hooks—nation shall not lift up sword against nation, neither shall they learn war any more" (2 Nephi 12:4).

This reminds us that a principal purpose of the latter-day Restoration is to prepare for Christ's return. When we realize this, the stories of the Restoration become Christ-centered rather than Joseph Smith-centered. This, however, does not diminish the role of the Prophet Joseph Smith in the Restoration of the gospel in these latter days. Indeed, 2 Nephi includes this promise that the Lord gave to Joseph of Egypt:

> A choice seer will I raise up out of the fruit of thy loins; and he shall be esteemed highly among the fruit of thy loins. And unto him will I give commandment that he shall do a work for the fruit of thy loins, his brethren, which shall be of great worth unto them, even to the bringing of them to the knowledge of the covenants which I have made with thy fathers. . . . And I will make him great in mine eyes; for he shall do my work. And he shall be great like unto Moses. (2 Nephi 3:7–9)

The book of 2 Nephi includes many prophecies of the latter-day Restoration given by Isaiah, Nephi, and Jacob, but they culminate in chapter 30 with a prophecy of Christ's millennial reign—a time when "the earth shall be full of the knowledge of the Lord as the waters cover the sea" (2 Nephi 30:15). Joseph Smith said,

> The building up of Zion is a cause that has interested the people of God in every age; it is a theme upon which prophets, priests and kings have dwelt with peculiar delight; they have looked forward with joyful anticipation to the day in which we live; and fired with heavenly and joyful anticipations they have sung and written and prophesied of this our day;

. . . [This is] a work that God and angels have contemplated with delight for generations past; that fired the souls of the ancient patriarchs and prophets; *a work that is destined to bring about the destruction of the powers of darkness, the renovation of the earth, the glory of God, and the salvation of the human family.*"[51]

The purpose of the latter-day Restoration and the building up of Zion is to prepare for the coming of the Lord in His glory and to bring souls unto Him. The Restoration truly is a Christ-centered event. The entire book of 2 Nephi focuses on Jesus Christ and His gospel.

THE DOCTRINE OF CHRIST: NEPHI'S CLOSING SERMON ON THE GOSPEL

In the final three chapters of his second book, Nephi presented a dissertation on the doctrine of Christ that beautifully describes how all disciples of Jesus Christ can incorporate the principles of the gospel in their lives in a way that will prepare them to be declared guiltless and saved in the kingdom of God on the Day of Judgment. Nephi began by saying that he believed he had written enough, "save a few words which I must speak concerning the doctrine of Christ" (2 Nephi 31:2). Twice more he referred to these teachings as "the doctrine of Christ" (see 2 Nephi 31:21, 32:6), and he ended his discussion by declaring that what he had written "are the words of Christ, and he hath given them unto me" (2 Nephi 33:10). Clearly, the doctrine of Christ is a doctrine declared *by* Christ, but it is also a doctrine *about* Christ. It is the doctrine by which we make the Atonement effective in our lives—by following the steps we call the first principles of the gospel.

Nephi began this sermon by writing about the first principles of the gospel. At the onset, he did not explicitly specify faith as one of those principles, but he did emphasize the importance of following the example of Jesus Christ, which is certainly an expression of faith. The first four principles of the gospel are thus each included in the following passage:

> And he said unto the children of men: Follow thou me. Wherefore, my beloved brethren, can we follow Jesus save we shall be willing to keep the commandments of the Father? And the Father said: Repent

ye, repent ye, and be baptized in the name of my Beloved Son. And also, the voice of the Son came unto me, saying: He that is baptized in my name, to him will the Father give the Holy Ghost, like unto me; wherefore, follow me, and do the things which ye have seen me do. (2 Nephi 31:10–12)

Here, Nephi began and ended with exhortations to follow Christ, explaining that we do so by following the first principles of the gospel. With this foundation, we will now examine what chapters 31 to 33 of 2 Nephi teach us about each of these four principles, plus a fifth that Nephi added later, which is enduring to the end.

FAITH IN JESUS CHRIST

As stated, Nephi began his three-chapter final sermon by addressing the need to follow the example of Jesus Christ, which requires faith in Him. Nephi later emphasized this need for on-going faith in Jesus Christ as we progress along the gospel path. He declared, "Ye have not come thus far save it were by the word of Christ with unshaken faith in him, relying wholly upon the merits of him who is mighty to save" (2 Nephi 31:19). However, Nephi's most powerful words on faith came at the end of his discourse, where he declared his personal faith in Jesus Christ and the charity it gave him:

> I glory in my Jesus, for he hath redeemed my soul from hell. I have charity for my people, and great faith in Christ that I shall meet many souls spotless at his judgment-seat. I have charity for the Jew. . . . I also have charity for the Gentiles. But behold, for none of these can I hope except they shall be reconciled unto Christ, and enter into the narrow gate, and walk in the strait path which leads to life, and continue in the path until the end of the day of probation. (2 Nephi 33:6–9)

What a glorious expression of faith in Christ! Because of that faith, Nephi said that he had hope for those who are reconciled unto Christ. To be reconciled unto Christ is to incorporate the power of His Atonement into our life, for the words *reconcile* and *atone* are synonyms. Those who have followed the steps outlined by the first principles of the gospel are those who are reconciled unto Christ.

Nephi continued his declaration of faith by testifying that he had been teaching the words of Christ: "And now, . . . hearken unto these words and believe in Christ; and if ye believe not in these words believe in Christ. And if ye shall believe in Christ ye will believe in these words, for they are the words of Christ, and he hath given them unto me; and they teach all men that they should do good" (2 Nephi 33:10).

Regardless of whether or not we believe anything else he wrote, Nephi wanted us to believe in Christ. It is important to recognize that the belief side of faith is not merely an exercise of a positive mental attitude. Faith is not an effort of optimistic thinking with confidence that a desired blessing will be granted. Those elements are good, but faith in a desired outcome is not what matters most—it is faith in Jesus Christ that is preeminent. Nephi emphasized belief and faith *in Christ*. When we exercise faith, we do not need to push out shadows of doubt regarding the possibility of a desired blessing. We need to push out shadows of doubt regarding our belief in Jesus Christ and His ability to change us regardless of the outcome.

Jesus healed many people during His mortal ministry, but before healing them, He invariably asked if they believed. I don't think He was merely asking if they believed that He could perform the miracle. Certainly, such a belief was a part of the required faith, but it was not the most important part. I believe that Jesus was really asking if they believed *in Him*. Did they believe that He was the Son of God and thus had the power to perform the desired miracle? Was their faith in Him strong enough that they would accept whatever outcome He thought was best for them? That is the type of faith that sometimes brings a physical miracle to heal the body, but always brings a spiritual miracle to heal the soul. That is faith in Jesus Christ.

Nephi's earlier admonition to follow the example of Jesus, along with his statement that the words of Christ "teach all men that they should do good" (2 Nephi 33:10) show us that faith is more than a belief or a declaration. True faith motivates us to take action in doing good. The combination of belief and righteous action bring forth the power of faith. Elder David A. Bednar taught this:

> True faith is focused in and on the Lord Jesus Christ and always
> leads to righteous action. The Prophet Joseph Smith taught that "faith

[is] the first principle in revealed religion, and the foundation of all righteousness" and that it is also "the principle of action in all intelligent beings" (*Lectures on Faith* [1985], 1). Action alone is not faith in the Savior, but acting in accordance with correct principles is a central component of faith. Thus, "faith without works is dead" (James 2:20).

The Prophet Joseph further explained that "faith is not only the principle of action, but of power also, in all intelligent beings, whether in heaven or on earth" (*Lectures on Faith*, 3). Thus, faith in Christ leads to righteous action, which increases our spiritual capacity and power.[52]

Faith in Jesus Christ is the first principle of the gospel, and demonstrating that faith through our actions is the first step we must take in our commitment to live His gospel.

REPENTANCE

Regarding repentance, Nephi declared, "And the Father said: Repent ye, repent ye, and be baptized in the name of my Beloved Son" (2 Nephi 31:11). Nephi then described what comprises a truly repentant attitude, saying, "Wherefore, my beloved brethren, . . . follow the Son, with full purpose of heart, acting no hypocrisy and no deception before God, but with real intent, repenting of your sins" (2 Nephi 31:13). This call for sincerity in repentance brings to mind a statement by Lehi that Nephi recorded earlier: "Behold, he [the Messiah] offereth himself a sacrifice for sin, to answer the ends of the law, unto all those who have a broken heart and a contrite spirit" (2 Nephi 2:7). This need to have "a broken heart and a contrite spirit" has been specified in several other scriptures as a prerequisite for baptism or for partaking of the sacrament (see 3 Nephi 9:20, Moroni 6:2, D&C 20:37, D&C 59:8–9). Humility and sincerity are the two overriding qualities that characterize a truly repentant person.

Nephi emphasized that repenting is an important part of following the Son. Repentance makes us worthy to approach Christ so we can partake of the powers of His Atonement. President Boyd K. Packer said, "No matter what we have done or where we have been or how something happened, if we truly repent, He [the Savior] has promised that He would atone. And when He atoned, that settled that. . . . The Atonement . . . can wash clean every stain no matter how difficult or how long or how many times repeated."[53]

Repentance makes us covenant people. In the chapter preceding Nephi's sermon on the doctrine of Christ, the ancient prophet wrote, "For behold, I say unto you that as many of the Gentiles as will repent are the covenant people of the Lord; and as many of the Jews as will not repent shall be cast off; for the Lord covenanteth with none save it be with them that repent and believe in his Son, who is the Holy One of Israel" (2 Nephi 30:2). Repentance prepares us to form a covenant with God through baptism, and to be cleansed by the reception of the Holy Ghost. Repentance is the second step of our commitment to live the gospel of Jesus Christ.

BAPTISM

Nephi's description of the doctrine of Christ began with a prophecy of the baptism of Jesus Christ by John the Baptist. Nephi then extended an invitation that is often repeated by missionaries: "And now, if the Lamb of God, he being holy, should have need to be baptized by water, to fulfil all righteousness, O then, how much more need have we, being unholy, to be baptized, yea, even by water!" (2 Nephi 31:5).

This was the first record that Joseph Smith encountered confirming that baptism was practiced by people who lived before Christ. Later he would learn that the covenant of baptism by immersion began with Adam (see Moses 6:64–65). The prominence of baptism at the onset of Nephi's revealed sermon on the doctrine of Christ confirms the eternal significance of this step.

Latter-day Saints are all familiar with the elements of the baptismal covenant as described by Moroni in the sacrament prayers and by Alma in Mosiah 18. The chart on the following page shows that Nephi taught the same principles in chapter 31 of 2 Nephi.

Elements of the Baptismal Covenant	Related Verses from 2 Nephi 31
. . . and witness unto thee . . . that they are willing to take upon them the name of thy Son (Moroni 4:3). . . . as ye are desirous to come into the fold of God, and to be called his people . . . (Mosiah 18:8)	Wherefore, my beloved brethren, I know that if ye shall follow the Son, . . . witnessing unto the Father that ye are willing to take upon you the name of Christ, by baptism . . . (2 Nephi 31:13)
. . . and witness unto thee . . . that they are willing to . . . keep his commandments which he hath given them . . . (Moroni 4:3) . . . as a witness before him that ye have entered into a covenant with him, that ye will serve him and keep his commandments . . . (Mosiah 18:8–9)	But notwithstanding he being holy, he . . . witnesseth unto the Father that he would be obedient unto him in keeping his commandments. (2 Nephi 31:7) After ye have repented of your sins, and witnessed unto the Father that ye are willing to keep my commandments, by the baptism of water. . . . (2 Nephi 31:14)
. . . and witness unto thee . . . that they are willing to . . . always remember him . . . (Moroni 4:3) . . . and to stand as witnesses of God at all times and in all things, and in all places that ye may be in . . . (Mosiah 18:9)	. . . he having set the example before them. And he said unto the children of men: Follow thou me. (2 Nephi 31:9–10) Wherefore, do the things which I have told you I have seen that your Lord and your Redeemer should do. (2 Nephi 31:17)
And now, as ye . . . are willing to bear one another's burdens, that they may be light; yea, and are willing to mourn with those that mourn; yea, and comfort those that stand in need of comfort . . . (Mosiah 18:10)	Wherefore, ye must press forward with a steadfastness in Christ, having a perfect brightness of hope, and a love of God and of all men. (2 Nephi 31:20)

The first two rows of this chart confirm important elements of our baptism covenant: We take upon us the name of Christ and we promise to keep the commandments. These are fundamental requirements that Christ has set for joining His Church. Also, in the third row, we can see, in a practical way, how we can always stand as a witness of God and always remember Christ: by following His example and being an example to others.

The final element of the baptismal covenant pertains to our relationship with other members of the Church. It says that we should bear one another's burdens and mourn with and comfort our fellow Saints when they need it. In other words, we should support and help one another as we grow together in our church community. This is an important part of the gospel and an important part of being a member of the Church. In addition to the verse shown from 2 Nephi 31, an earlier description from 2 Nephi also supports this concept. Nephi described the progress of his people after separating themselves from the Lamanites: "And the Lord was with us; and we did prosper exceedingly; for we did sow seed, and we did reap again in abundance. And we began to raise flocks, and herds, and animals of every kind. . . . And it came to pass that we lived after the manner of happiness" (2 Nephi 5:11, 27). A colonizing group cannot achieve that kind of happiness and success without unity and mutual support. They also built a temple (see 2 Nephi 5:16), which was a significant feat of cooperative effort and devotion. This is a testament to the power of a bond of fellowship and the mutual love and support that the covenant of baptism can bring.

Baptism is the third principle and first ordinance of the gospel. It is the center point or hinge on which the five principles of the gospel rotate. It is the gateway covenant—the doorway to many future blessings and covenants we will receive in our path to return to God. We should also remember that partaking of the sacrament is a renewal of that same covenant. They are two ordinances confirming one covenant. Whether through baptism or through the sacrament, we repeatedly promise to take upon us the name of Christ, to keep His commandments, to always remember Him by following His example, and to share in the burdens of our fellow Saints. In return, God promises to bless us with the gift of the Holy Ghost—the next step. Baptism is the third requirement in our commitment to live the gospel of Jesus Christ.

THE HOLY GHOST

The first three principles of the gospel prepare us for the fourth: receiving the gift of the Holy Ghost. As discussed earlier, the purpose of all of the first principles of the gospel is to bring us to Christ and prepare us to be declared guiltless on the Day of Judgment. In order to achieve this during our sojourn in this fallen world, we need a guide—an escort who can give us personalized direction for the unique trials and challenges we will encounter. The Holy Ghost is that customized guide. Nephi wrote, "For behold, again I say unto you that if ye will enter in by the way, and receive the Holy Ghost, *it will show unto you all things what ye should do*" (2 Nephi 32:5; emphasis added).

The great importance of following the guidance of the Holy Ghost was something Brigham Young learned as he prepared the Saints for unknown trials in their trek west. In February 1847, while residing in Winter Quarters, President Young had a dream wherein the Prophet Joseph Smith appeared to him and gave him this message:

> Tell the people to be humble and faithful and sure to keep the Spirit of the Lord and it will lead them right. Be careful and not turn away the small still voice; it will teach [you what] to do and where to go; it will yield the fruits of the kingdom. Tell the brethren to keep their hearts open to conviction so that when the Holy Ghost comes to them, their hearts will be ready to receive it. They can tell the Spirit of the Lord from all other spirits. It will whisper peace and joy to their souls, and it will take malice, hatred, envying, strife, and all evil from their hearts; and their whole desire will be to do good, bring forth righteousness, and build up the kingdom of God. Tell the brethren if they will follow the Spirit of the Lord they will go right.[54]

More recently, President Russell M. Nelson taught the same principle, declaring, "I promise you that if you will sincerely and persistently do the spiritual work needed to develop the crucial, spiritual skill of learning how to hear the whisperings of the Holy Ghost, you will have *all* the direction you will ever need in your life."[55]

Having the Holy Ghost guide us through life's challenges is a critical part of the gospel or the doctrine of Christ. Without it, no one would be able to know what Christ would have him or her do. However, Nephi taught that the direction of the Holy Ghost often comes in incremental impressions and that the Lord usually requires that we follow those impressions before more guidance will be given. Shortly before expounding on the doctrine of Christ, Nephi taught the following about how the Holy Ghost functions:

> Thus saith the Lord God: I will give unto the children of men line upon line, precept upon precept, here a little and there a little; and blessed are those who hearken unto my precepts, and lend an ear unto my counsel, for they shall learn wisdom; for unto him that receiveth I will give more; and from them that shall say, We have enough, from them shall be taken away even that which they have. Cursed is he that putteth his trust in man, or maketh flesh his arm, or shall hearken unto the precepts of men, save their precepts shall be given by the power of the Holy Ghost. (2 Nephi 28:30–31)

In his exposition on the doctrine of Christ, Nephi emphasized the importance of following the guidance of the Holy Ghost by drawing a three-way connection between speaking by the power of the Holy Ghost, speaking with the tongue of angels, and speaking the words of Christ. He said,

> Do ye not remember that I said unto you that after ye had received the Holy Ghost ye could speak with the tongue of angels? And now, how could ye speak with the tongue of angels save it were by the Holy Ghost? Angels speak by the power of the Holy Ghost; wherefore, they speak the words of Christ. Wherefore, I said unto you, feast upon the words of Christ; for behold, the words of Christ will tell you all things what ye should do. (2 Nephi 32:2–3)

It appears that Nephi wanted us to recognize what a great blessing it is to be guided by the Holy Ghost: It is as if we have angels or even Christ himself telling us what we should do. They are all equivalent.

When a person speaks by the power of the Holy Ghost, he speaks the words of Christ, meaning he says the things Jesus would have him say— things that uplift and build and strengthen others. So often when we communicate, we are so concerned about defending ourselves and building our own self-esteem that we don't worry about whether or not our words are helping the person we are talking to. The way we communicate with others can either strengthen our relationships with them and their relationships with Christ, or it can tear down those relationships. Nephi said that when we speak by the power of the Holy Ghost, we say what angels would say—we say the right things. He knew this from personal experience through interactions with his brothers (see 1 Nephi 17:48).

In addition to the things already discussed about the Holy Ghost, Nephi taught the following:

- The gift of the Holy Ghost is given after repentance and baptism. (See 2 Nephi 31:13, 17.)

- The Holy Ghost purifies us. Nephi taught, "For the gate by which ye should enter is repentance and baptism by water; and then cometh a remission of your sins by fire and by the Holy Ghost" (2 Nephi 31:17). We often speak of baptism as a cleansing ordinance, and perhaps this is not wrong since the promise of cleansing comes with baptism, but the Holy Ghost completes that purification by fire. Orson F. Whitney taught, "Water baptism begins the work of purification and enlightenment. Spirit baptism completes it."[56]

- The Holy Ghost "witnesses of the Father and of the Son" (2 Nephi 31:18).

- The Spirit teaches us to pray. When we do not understand gospel instruction or other spiritual matters, we should pray and ask God, and the Holy Ghost will guide us. (See 2 Nephi 32:4–5, 8–9.)

- When we speak by the power of the Holy Ghost, the Holy Ghost will carry the message *unto* the hearts of those listening. (See 2 Nephi 33:1.) It is incumbent upon the listener to invite that spirit in.

- Many people harden their hearts against the influence of the Holy Spirit. (See 2 Nephi 31:14; 33:2.)

We are blessed to have these teachings in 2 Nephi that instruct us on the role of the Holy Ghost as our guide along the gospel path back to God. As Nephi taught, the Holy Ghost "will show unto you all things what ye should do" (2 Nephi 32:5). Receiving and following the Holy Ghost is the fourth step in our commitment to live the gospel of Jesus Christ.

Endure to the End

Before ending his sermon on the doctrine of Christ, Nephi declared, "And I heard a voice from the Father, saying: Yea, the words of my Beloved are true and faithful. He that endureth to the end, the same shall be saved. And now, my beloved brethren, I know by this that unless a man shall endure to the end, in following the example of the Son of the living God, he cannot be saved" (2 Nephi 31:15–16).

The fact that God the Father would be the one to declare this principle to Nephi underscores the importance of enduring to the end if we are to be saved in the kingdom of God. Nephi expounded on this principle as follows:

> And now, my beloved brethren, after ye have gotten into this strait and narrow path, I would ask if all is done? Behold, I say unto you, Nay; for ye have not come thus far save it were by the word of Christ with unshaken faith in him, relying wholly upon the merits of him who is mighty to save. Wherefore, ye must press forward with a steadfastness in Christ, having a perfect brightness of hope, and a love of God and of all men. Wherefore, if ye shall press forward, feasting upon the word of Christ, and endure to the end, behold, thus saith the Father: Ye shall have eternal life. (2 Nephi 31:19–20)

The word *endure* can carry with it a feeling of drudgery—of hanging on to the bitter end, without joy or happiness. However, Nephi shifted this concept into its intended positive perspective by also using the equivalent term *press forward*. This teaches us that our attitude toward the principle of enduring to the end should be positive, proactive, and purposeful.

Nephi's counsel teaches how we are to press forward to the end. It is the same way we started: by focusing on Christ. He taught that we only got onto the path through a three-fold focus on Christ (see 2 Nephi 31:19):

1. By the word of Christ.

2. With unshaken faith in Christ.

3. By relying wholly upon the merits of Christ.

Nephi then declared that we are to endure to the end by following three additional steps that similarly focus on Christ (see 2 Nephi 31:20):

4. Press forward with a steadfastness in Christ.

5. Have a perfect brightness of hope.

6. Have a love of God and of all men.

It is remarkable how closely these latter three steps parallel the principles of faith, hope, and charity that were taught by Paul and Moroni hundreds of years later (see 1 Corinthians 13 and Moroni 7). The same three steps also parallel the first three principles of the gospel: (1) When we "press forward with a steadfastness in Christ" we are demonstrating faith in Him, (2) "A perfect brightness of hope" enters our hearts when we repent, and (3) we exhibit "a love of God and of all men" when we fulfill our baptismal covenants to keep the commandments and to bear one another's burdens. Thus, Nephi's plea to press forward with steadfastness, hope, and love mirrors his plea to follow the doctrine of Christ through faith, repentance, and baptism. Nephi taught that incorporating these principles into our daily lives will help us endure to the end.

At the end of 2 Nephi 31:20, Nephi added that we should feast upon the word of Christ. Today, the scriptures and teachings of modern prophets and apostles are our primary sources for the words of Christ. Earlier Nephi wrote, "My soul delighteth in the scriptures, and my heart pondereth them, and writeth them for the learning and the profit of my children" (2 Nephi 4:15). He also wrote, "I did liken all scriptures unto us, that it might be for our profit and learning" (2 Nephi 19:23). Feasting on the words of Christ in the scriptures and messages from His modern oracles will help us endure to the end.

In chapter 32, Nephi continued his counsel on how to endure to the end, saying, "I suppose that ye ponder somewhat in your hearts concerning that which ye should do *after* ye have entered in by the way" (2 Nephi 32:1; emphasis added). Nephi then emphasized three more points: He repeated his admonition to "feast upon the words of Christ" (2 Nephi 32:3), he taught that the Holy Ghost "will show unto you all things what ye should do" (2 Nephi 32:5), and he instructed that "ye must pray always" (2 Nephi 32:9). With these instructions, chapter 32 adds three additional ways to endure to the end:

7. Feast upon the words of Christ (which are today found in the scriptures and words of modern prophets and apostles).

8. Follow the Holy Ghost.

9. Pray always.

These three points form another trio we often hear. We attend church to partake of the sacrament and receive a renewal of the Holy Ghost. Add prayer and feasting on the words of Christ by studying the scriptures and the teachings of the prophets and apostles and you get the oft repeated "Primary answers." They are not only the answers we learn in Primary, but they are also the most important or primary steps we should take to endure to the end: Study the scriptures and words of modern prophets and apostles, pray always, and attend church to partake of the sacrament.

This process taught by Nephi is also taught in the New Testament. Peter called upon people to "Repent, and be baptized every one of you in the name of Jesus Christ for the remission of sins, and ye shall receive the gift of the Holy Ghost" (Acts 2:38). After citing this plea from Peter to follow the first principles of the gospel, the record states that the new converts "continued steadfastly in the apostles' doctrine and fellowship, and in breaking of bread, and in prayers" (Acts 2:42). So following the doctrinal teachings of the apostles, partaking of the sacrament, and praying are specified as the way they "continued steadfastly" or endured to the end. The parallel with Nephi's instruction is striking.

Nephi focused on the words of Christ, prayer, and following the Holy Ghost, because these three sources of guidance will tell or show us "what ye should do" (2 Nephi 31:3, 5). Nephi was essentially saying that he could not specify what we will need to do in every situation as we endure to the end, but we can receive customized guidance from the Lord for every situation, and this guidance will come from the words of Christ found through study, prayer, and direct inspiration from the Holy Ghost.

Nephi elaborated on how prayer will help us endure to the end:

> For if ye would hearken unto the Spirit which teacheth a man to pray, ye would know that ye must pray; for the evil spirit teacheth not a man to pray, but teacheth him that he must not pray. But behold, I say unto you that ye must pray always, and not faint; that ye must not perform any thing unto the Lord save in the first place ye shall pray unto the Father in the name of Christ, that he will consecrate thy performance unto thee, that thy performance may be for the welfare of thy soul. (2 Nephi 32:8–9)

Praying every day, multiple times a day, in the name of Christ, will help us always remember Him and remain faithful. Without it, we will drift from the covenant path. With it, God will bless our efforts. Prayer is a gift to help us press forward with steadfastness in Christ.

Nephi's instructions teach another important principle about spiritual guidance. He taught that the words of Christ will *tell* us what to do (see 2 Nephi 32:3), later adding that we should do the things which Christ would *say* (see 2 Nephi 32:6). He also said that the Holy Ghost will *show* us what to do (see 2 Nephi 32:5), and he finished by saying that we should pray before we *perform* anything unto the Lord (see 2 Nephi 32:9). *Tell* or *say*, *show*, and *perform*. These principles remind me of the **EDGE** method of teaching that I learned in Scouting: You first **E**xplain a skill, then **D**emonstrate it, then **G**uide a Scout in doing it with your coaching, and finally, you **E**nable him to do it on his own. That inspired approach is consistent with what I will call the **TSP** method for spiritual direction described by Nephi: the words of Christ (including the scriptures) **T**ell you what to do, the Holy Ghost will **S**how and guide you in what to do, and you should use prayer as you **P**erform your actions.

The **EDGE** and **TSP** methods both involve hearing, seeing, and doing, but the final objective is individual performance or action. Nephi spoke four times in chapter 32 of our need for action: "Tell you all things what *ye should do*" (verse 3). "Show unto you all things what *ye should do*" (verse 5). "The things he shall say unto you shall *ye observe to do*" (verse 6), and "ye must not *perform any thing* unto the Lord save in the first place ye shall pray" (verse 9). In fact, all of the first principles of the gospel are principles of action. The more we take righteous action, the more spiritual direction we will receive to help us endure to the end.

THE SACRAMENT HELPS US ENDURE TO THE END

In our day, the sacrament helps us remember to exercise steadfast faith in Jesus Christ, to gain hope in Christ though repentance, and to show a love of God and of all men by renewing our baptismal covenants to keep the commandments and bear one another's burdens. We are then promised continued direction from the Holy Ghost, which will help us endure to the end. Nephi's people did not have the ordinance of the sacrament—they had to rely on sacrificial offerings to remember this process. But since Christ's Resurrection, His Saints have been blessed to have the sacrament as the central focus of our weekly worship services. The sacrament is a ritual that focuses on the Atonement of Jesus Christ and facilitates our continuous improvement so that we are able to endure to the end. It is the process whereby we are given the opportunity weekly to cycle through each step of the gospel of Jesus Christ in hopes of improving a little each time we do.

The cycle is always the same. We exercise our faith by pondering on Jesus Christ, His teachings, and His Atonement. We humbly review our own lives and repent as needed. And we renew our baptismal covenants to follow Him. We are then promised a fresh infusion of the Holy Ghost to guide us through the week ahead. This is the continuous improvement process by which we are supposed to incorporate the power of the Atonement into our lives each week, pressing forward so that we will endure to the end with faith, hope, and charity.[i]

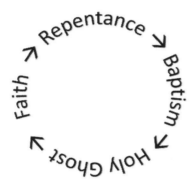

The Gospel Path or Cycle.
This is the Lord's four-step continuous improvement process.

---

i Quality Improvement experts of business and industry have developed various improvement processes. Some even emphasize four main steps, such as the Plan-Do-Check-Act Deming Cycle for quality improvement and the Measure-Analyze-Improve-Control process from Six Sigma techniques. However, these are man-made methodologies designed for improving processes and products. The Lord has established an improvement process designed to exalt His children eternally. It is called the gospel of Jesus Christ or the doctrine of Christ, and it centers on the Atonement of the Savior with the four principle steps being Faith-Repentance-Baptism-Holy Ghost.

Elder Dale G. Renlund confirmed this process of enduring to the end. He said, "Our theology does teach us . . . that we may be perfected by *repeatedly and iteratively* 'relying wholly upon' the doctrine of Christ: exercising faith in Him, repenting, partaking of the sacrament to renew the covenants and blessings of baptism, and receiving the Holy Ghost as a constant companion to a greater degree. As we do so, we become more like Christ and are able to endure to the end, with all that that entails."[57]

Even though we pass through each step of this gospel cycle almost weekly, we are not meant to repeat it on a flat plane, as if we were spinning in a circle. Rather, it should be a spiral, ascending upward as we improve with each repetition. It should be like a spiral staircase that takes us to heaven. This makes me think of Jacob's ladder or of the circular staircases built in many temples. Whenever I see one of those staircases, I think of the doctrine of Christ and the gospel cycle of faith, repentance, baptism (or its renewal), and the Holy Ghost—all of which we experience anew each week as we partake of the sacrament. Of course, these gospel steps should be accompanied by the other spiritual actions that Nephi taught: scripture study and prayer.

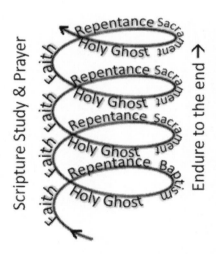

Repeating the gospel cycle is like a spiral staircase ascending to God.

When we follow this gospel cycle whole-heartedly each week as if it were a law to be followed, we gradually become more sanctified, more holy, and more Christlike. Key to our improvement is following the guidance of the Holy Ghost. Repeating this cycle so frequently helps us endure to the end, pressing forward with steadfastness in Christ, continually spiraling upward toward heaven. This is the gospel. This is the doctrine of Christ. It is God's process for changing our natures so that we become like Him, eventually standing before His judgment seat and being declared worthy to live eternally in God's presence. Indeed, Nephi made this objective clear with these words in the final verses of his discourse on the doctrine of Christ: "And you and I shall stand face to face before his bar; and ye shall know that I have been commanded of him to write these things, notwithstanding my weakness. And I pray the Father in the name of Christ that many of us, if not all, may be saved in his kingdom at that great and last day" (2 Nephi 33:11–12).

If we will study the words of Christ found in the scriptures and in the teachings of the prophets and apostles, pray always, and use the sacrament each week to help us follow the gospel improvement process, we will endure to the end. These steps help us pursue the process of sanctification with the continued guidance of the Holy Ghost.

AVOIDING BEHAVIORS THAT OFFEND THE SPIRIT

The sacrament prayers include this closing request: "That they may always have his Spirit to be with them" (Moroni 4:3). Having the Spirit with us at all times is very important to help us endure to the end, so we need to make sure that our behaviors do not cause the Holy Ghost to withdraw from us as we go through our voyage of life. Nephi's family had an episode during their voyage to the promised land that taught this lesson.

Nephi began his second book with a reminder of the rebellion at sea that had occurred by some members of the party: "And now it came to pass that . . . our father, Lehi . . . spake unto them concerning their rebellions upon the waters, and the mercies of God in sparing their lives, that they were not swallowed up in the sea" (2 Nephi 1:1–2). Nephi earlier described how that rebellion began:

> And after we had been driven forth before the wind for the space of many days, behold, my brethren and the sons of Ishmael and also their wives began to make themselves merry, insomuch that they began to dance, and to sing, and to speak with much rudeness, yea, even that

they did forget by what power they had been brought thither; yea, they were lifted up unto exceeding rudeness. (1 Nephi 18:9)

Dancing and singing are not necessarily bad, but Nephi's repeated use of the term *rudeness* gives us a clue that the behavior he observed had crossed a line. The Lord has stated in our day, "Therefore, cease from all your light speeches, from all laughter, from all your lustful desires, from all your pride and light-mindedness, and from all your wicked doings" (D&C 88:121).

It seems curious that laughter would be included in this admonition from the Lord. Everyone loves a good joke—many have been told in general conference that resulted in jovial laughter. However, the context with which the Lord condemns laughter in this verse is important. It is in the context of "light speeches," "lustful desires," "pride and light-mindedness," and "wicked doings." The type of laughter that occurs alongside these behaviors is usually in response to jokes and stories that are base and inappropriate.

There is a difference in being light-minded, which the Lord condemns, and being light-hearted, which usually connotes a joyful and merry attitude, for the Lord also stated, "If thou art merry, praise the Lord with singing, with music, with dancing, and with a prayer of praise and thanksgiving" (D&C 136:28). Merriment is good, but we need to be careful to not allow our pleasure to cross over into light-mindedness and rudeness. Nephi's brothers and the sons of Ishmael had clearly gone too far. Their mistake was not merely that they "began to make themselves merry," it was the way they carried this to excess so that it deteriorated to "exceeding rudeness." We can only speculate about the nature of that rudeness. Nephi was not specific, but it was bad enough that he feared that their standing with the Lord was in jeopardy.

Nephi had seen in the past what had occurred when there was murmuring and the Liahona stopped working. He did not want to lose that guidance at this critical time upon the sea. He wrote, "And I, Nephi, began to fear exceedingly lest the Lord should be angry with us, and smite us because of our iniquity, that we should be swallowed up in the depths of the sea" (1 Nephi 18:10). Unfortunately, that is exactly what did happen—the Liahona did stop working and they were almost capsized and drowned in the ocean.

Nephi's apprehension gives us a clue as to how we can judge whether our behavior has gone too far. Do we lose the guidance of the Holy

Ghost—our Liahona? In order to endure to the end, we need to have the Holy Ghost with us at all times. This is one reason why this story is being discussed here in association with 2 Nephi and the gospel rather than with 1 Nephi and obedience. The principle being taught in this story is not an issue of obedience to a specific commandment; rather, it illustrates the need to make sure that our behavior does not offend the spirit. Following the direction of the Holy Ghost is critical to enduring to the end, so we need to make sure that our actions always welcome its presence.

I remember one time as a BYU student when I attended the Provo Utah Temple with some friends. We sat together on a pew in the temple chapel as we waited for a session to begin. It was a busy Saturday morning, so the wait was longer than usual. We were happy to be together and began chatting among ourselves, eventually huddling over in our pew to tell stories and chuckle in semi-hushed tones. While nothing inappropriate was said, our attitude was not in keeping with the spirit of the temple, and we were disturbing others around us. A temple worker approached us and reminded us to be reverent. I remember being embarrassed and feeling that perhaps we had offended the Spirit. Sometimes an action that is okay in one setting can be wrong in another.

Unfortunately, those on Nephi's ship who were caught up in their raucous and rude behavior did not respond well to Nephi's correction when he "began to speak to them with much soberness" (1 Nephi 18:11). They got angry with Nephi, tied him up, and treated him harshly. Their rude behavior deteriorated into rebellion against one of the Lord's anointed leaders. With this, they had crossed an even more serious line into a state of full condemnation before God.

To rebel and speak evil against the Lord's anointed is a very serious offense in the eyes of God. Those who reject the guidance of the Lord's anointed will also lose the guidance of the Holy Ghost. Nephi wrote that when his father admonished the rebellious ones for their behavior, "they did breathe out much threatenings against anyone that should speak for me" (1 Nephi 18:17). Sometimes we see similar anger in our day among those who want to change or tear down the Church. The Lord will not tolerate such behavior for long. In the case of rebellion against Nephi, the Lord caused a great storm to arise and envelop the ship. It was driven back by the tempest for four days before the threat became so severe that the rebellious ones, fearing for their own lives, finally repented and loosened Nephi's bands.

The response of Nephi when he was released is also instructional. Even though his wrists and ankles "had swollen exceedingly . . . and great was the soreness thereof" (1 Nephi 18:15), Nephi did not dwell on the abuse nor admonish his captors further after his release. His actions seem to have been measured and calm. He wrote,

> And it came to pass after they had loosed me, behold, I took the compass, and it did work whither I desired it. And it came to pass that I prayed unto the Lord; and after I had prayed the winds did cease, and the storm did cease, and there was a great calm. And it came to pass that I, Nephi, did guide the ship, that we sailed again towards the promised land. (1 Nephi 18:21–22)

Nephi's quiet resumption of his leadership responsibilities, without vindictive rancor or retribution, confirms his role as one of the Lord's anointed. It is reminiscent of a prophecy about Jesus that Nephi afterward recorded: "They scourge him and he suffereth it; and they smite him, and he suffereth it. Yea, they spit upon him, and he suffereth it, because of his loving kindness and his long-suffering towards the children of men" (1 Nephi 19:9).

I once had a painful experience that taught me not to correct the Lord's representatives. While I was serving as a patron in the temple, a worker who was representing the Lord made a slight error in what he said to me. I was supposed to repeat it back, so when I did, I emphasized one syllable as a way of correcting and teaching him. Immediately after doing so, my mind went blank. I suddenly could not remember what it was that I had been saying or yet needed to say. It was quite remarkable. I immediately realized my mistake: I had been trying to correct a representative of the Lord. You don't do that! I paused and collected my thoughts, and then I started over, this time a more humble son of God.

The experience taught me an important lesson in a dramatic way: Don't correct the Lord's representatives. God knows His leaders and He sustains them, even with their flaws. Of course, this does not mean that I will not speak up and give counsel if that is my role or if I were ever to see a leader engage in something sinful or offensive. But I have learned to view Church leaders with charity, assuming they are acting with their best intentions as they seek to fulfill their callings before the Lord. I don't want to become like Laman and Lemuel, who refused to follow the Lord's anointed.

The incident of rebellion at sea by some of Nephi's family teaches us that we need to avoid behaviors that are rude, irreverent, or critical of the Lord's anointed. Nephi also wrote, "The Lord God hath commanded that men . . . should not take the name of the Lord their God in vain; that they should not envy; that they should not have malice; that they should not contend one with another" (2 Nephi 26:32).[j] Anything that might offend the Spirit could derail us from the covenant path. Our behaviors need to invite the guidance of the Holy Ghost at all times so that we can endure to the end.

The Law of the Gospel: Pathway to Salvation

We have been reviewing *the gospel* as one of the requirements along the covenant path that leads us back to God. It should not be surprising then to find that the Lord refers to the gospel as a covenant:

> I have prepared thee for a greater work. Thou shalt preach the fullness of *my gospel*, which I have sent forth in these last days, *the covenant* which I have sent forth to recover my people, which are of the house of Israel. (D&C 39:11; emphasis added)

> Verily I say unto you, blessed are you for receiving *mine everlasting covenant, even the fulness of my gospel*, sent forth unto the children of men, that they might have life and be made partakers of the glories which are to be revealed in the last days, as it was written by the prophets and apostles in days of old. (D&C 66:2; emphasis added)

The gospel is a covenant whose purpose is to recover the scattered house of Israel. It is a covenant sent forth to everyone on the earth so they

---

j Other scriptures related to this principle are: "Remember the great and last promise which I have made unto you; cast away your idle thoughts and your excess of laughter far from you" (D&C 88:69). "And see that there is no iniquity in the church, neither hardness with each other, neither lying, backbiting, nor evil speaking" (D&C 20:54). "But fornication, and all uncleanness, or covetousness, let it not be once named among you, as becometh saints; neither filthiness, nor foolish talking, nor jesting, which are not convenient: but rather giving of thanks" (Eph. 5:3–4). "Denying ungodliness and worldly lusts, we should live soberly, righteously, and godly, in this present world" (Titus 2:12).

can partake of the glories of the last days. This covenant is called the law of the gospel.

In the early days of this dispensation, the Lord told His Saints, "Teach ye diligently and my grace shall attend you, that you may be instructed more perfectly in theory, in principle, in doctrine, *in the law of the gospel*, in all things that pertain unto the kingdom of God, that are expedient for you to understand" (D&C 88:78; emphasis added). If we are to be instructed in the law of the gospel, we need to understand what it means.

Speaking from heaven before His appearance in Ancient America, Jesus declared that the law of Moses was fulfilled, and He outlined a different law that must be followed in order to be saved:

> Behold, I am Jesus Christ the Son of God. . . . And as many as have received me, to them have I given to become the sons of God; and even so will I to as many as shall believe on my name, for behold, by me redemption cometh, and in me is the law of Moses fulfilled. . . . And ye shall offer up unto me no more the shedding of blood; yea, your sacrifices and your burnt offerings shall be done away, for I will accept none of your sacrifices and your burnt offerings. And ye shall offer for a sacrifice unto me a broken heart and a contrite spirit. And whoso cometh unto me with a broken heart and a contrite spirit, him will I baptize with fire and with the Holy Ghost . . . Behold, I have come unto the world to bring redemption unto the world, to save the world from sin. Therefore, whoso repenteth and cometh unto me as a little child, him will I receive, for of such is the kingdom of God. Behold, for such I have laid down my life, and have taken it up again; therefore repent, and come unto me ye ends of the earth, and be saved. (3 Nephi 9:15–22)

This is the law of the gospel. It is a higher law than the law of Moses. During His ensuing visits to these righteous Nephites and Lamanites, Christ reiterated the principles of this higher law several more times. Two of these were cited in the beginning of the present chapter as definitions of what Christ called "my doctrine" (see 3 Nephi 11:32–39) or "my gospel" (see 3 Nephi 27:13–21). All of these teachings by Jesus Christ focus on redemption through Him and specify that we must follow the first principles and ordinances of the gospel in order to be saved. This is exactly what has been taught throughout 2 Nephi. Appendix A at the end of this chapter contains a brief review of Christ's teachings in Ancient America, demonstrating how they parallel the principles of the gospel taught in 2 Nephi.

In his sermon on the Atonement in chapter 9 of 2 Nephi, Jacob declared that Christ "suffereth the pains of all men . . . that the resurrection might pass upon all men, that all might stand before him at the great and judgment day" (2 Nephi 9:21–22). He then described specific steps we must follow to be saved:

> And he commandeth all men that they must repent, and be baptized in his name, having perfect faith in the Holy One of Israel, or they cannot be saved in the kingdom of God. And if they will not repent and believe in his name, and be baptized in his name, and endure to the end, they must be damned; for the Lord God, the Holy One of Israel, has spoken it. *Wherefore, he has given a law.* . . . (2 Nephi 9:23–25; emphasis added)

In these verses, Jacob taught the need to follow the first principles of the gospel in order to be saved, and immediately thereafter he declared, "Wherefore, he has given a law." [k] This is the law of the gospel. It is a law that says that those who sincerely follow the path of faith in Jesus Christ, repentance, baptism, receiving the Holy Ghost, and enduring to the end will inherit eternal life in the celestial kingdom.

Other scriptures support this same conclusion on the meaning of the law of the gospel. Doctrine and Covenants 88:18–21 makes it clear that those who inherit the celestial kingdom are "sanctified through the law which I have given unto you, even the law of Christ." Just as *the doctrine of Christ* and *the gospel* are synonyms, so also *the law of Christ* and *the law of the gospel* are synonyms. The requirements of this law that we must

---

k   In modern editions of the Book of Mormon, the phrase, "Wherefore, he has given a law" is the start of a new verse, and it is followed by a series of sequential logic statements attesting to the connection between law, punishment, condemnation, and mercy—linking these all to the Atonement of "the Holy One of Israel." (See 2 Nephi 9:25.) So the reference to law in this verse is most commonly connected with these subsequent statements and, thus, to all the laws of God. However, Jacob's use of the conjunction "wherefore" suggests that the phrase, "he has given a law" also applies to the verses that proceed it. Remember that when the Book of Mormon was originally translated, it had no verses or punctuation. Those were added later.

follow in order to be sanctified in the celestial kingdom are described in the Doctrine and Covenants, section 76, verses 40–42, 50–53, and 70, which were quoted at the start of this chapter. They say that salvation in the celestial kingdom comes through Jesus Christ by following the first principles and ordinances of the gospel. Taken together, these two passages in the Doctrine and Covenants provide an additional confirmation of the meaning of *the law of the gospel.*

With these insights from the scriptures, we can conclude that the definition of *the law of the gospel* is essentially the same as *the gospel* that was defined at the beginning of this chapter.[1] President Ezra Taft Benson likewise found the meaning of *the law of gospel* in the words that Jesus Christ used to describe *the gospel.* He said,

> The law of the gospel embraces all laws, principles, and ordinances necessary for our exaltation. We agree to exercise faith in Jesus Christ and sincere repentance borne out of a broken heart and a contrite spirit. As we comply with the ordinances of baptism and confirmation, and continue in faith and prayer, the power of the Savior's atoning sacrifice covers our sins and we are cleansed from all unrighteousness.
>
> Now this is the commandment: "Repent, all ye ends of the earth, and come unto me and be baptized in my name, that ye may be sanctified by the reception of the Holy Ghost, that ye may stand spotless before me at the last day. Verily, verily, I say unto you, this is my gospel" (3 Nephi 27:20–21).
>
> The law of the gospel is more than understanding the plan of salvation. It consists of partaking of the ordinances and the sealing powers culminating in a man being sealed up unto eternal life. "Being born again," said the Prophet Joseph Smith, "comes by the spirit of God through ordinances" (*Teachings of the Prophet Joseph Smith*, 162).[58]

President Benson's statement emphasizes that the law of the gospel includes the need to follow the first principles and ordinances of the gospel. Furthermore, his description interprets the law to include not only

---

1 It should not surprise us that *the gospel* and *the law of the gospel* mean essentially the same thing. The same is true with other laws in the covenant path, such as *obedience* and *the law of obedience*, which mean the same thing. Likewise do *sacrifice* and *the law of sacrifice*, *chastity* and *the law of chastity*, and *consecration* and *the law of consecration.*

these ordinances of salvation but also the temple ordinances of exaltation—a clear objective of the full covenant path.

THE LAW OF THE GOSPEL: A COMMUNITY COMMITMENT

At the end of his sermon on the doctrine of Christ, Nephi wrote, "But I, Nephi, have written what I have written, and I esteem it as of great worth, and especially unto my people. For I pray continually for them by day, and mine eyes water my pillow by night, because of them. . . . And I know that the Lord God will consecrate my prayers *for the gain of my people*" (2 Nephi 33:3–4; emphasis added). Everything Nephi said, wrote, and did was motivated by a concern for the spiritual and physical welfare of his people. He taught them the principles of the gospel not only as a pathway to eternal salvation, but also as a way to live together in a gospel community.

When we "are desirous to come into the fold of God, and to be called his people" (Mosiah 18:8), we engage in a community. We attend church where our faith in Jesus Christ can grow alongside others. We have to repent, confessing our sins to those people we have wronged and sometimes to Church leaders (see D&C 59:12). We are baptized and confirmed before other members of the Church (see D&C 20:37, 68), and we are instructed to "meet together oft" to renew our covenants through the sacrament (see Moroni 6:5–6). We receive callings and ministering assignments that require us to interact and serve one another. We "teach one another the doctrine of the kingdom" (D&C 88:77). The principles of the gospel are not intended to be carried out in isolation.

In April 1834, as the Church welcomed new immigrants into the Kirtland area, many members were poor, and many Church leaders were in debt. During this time of great temporal need, the Lord revealed the following:

> And it is my purpose to provide for my saints, for all things are mine. But it must needs be done in mine own way; and behold this is the way that I, the Lord, have decreed to provide for my saints, that the poor shall be exalted, in that the rich are made low. For the earth is full, and there is enough and to spare; yea, I prepared all things, and have given unto the children of men to be agents unto themselves. Therefore,

if any man shall take of the abundance which I have made, and impart not his portion, *according to the law of my gospel,* unto the poor and the needy, he shall, with the wicked, lift up his eyes in hell, being in torment. (D&C 104:15–18; emphasis added)

This passage describes how the Lord provides for His Saints, not for the world in general. The Lord makes it clear that sharing with fellow Saints who are in need is "according to the law of my gospel," explaining that every member should "take of the abundance which I have made, and impart . . . his portion . . . unto the poor and the needy."

Being willing to help one another in the Church is part of the covenant of baptism, which Alma described as being "willing to bear one another's burdens, that they may be light; yea, and . . . willing to mourn with those that mourn; yea, and comfort those that stand in need of comfort" (Mosiah 18:8–9).[m] This baptismal commitment is a central part of the gospel, so when we help our fellow Latter-day Saints who are in need we are acting "according to the law of my gospel."

This dimension of the law of the gospel is confirmed by similar instructions the Lord gave to the Kirtland Saints sixteen months earlier: "See that ye love one another; cease to be covetous; learn to impart one to another *as the gospel requires*" (D&C 88:123; emphasis added).

Paul taught the same principle in his letter to the Galatians, admonishing the Saints, "Bear ye one another's burdens, and so fulfil *the law of Christ*" (Galatians 6:2; emphasis added). The law or doctrine of Christ and the law of the gospel are equivalent terms, so Paul's counsel affirms that bearing one another's burdens fulfills the law of the gospel. Alma and Paul both understood this law.

This aspect of the law of the gospel appears to be the foundation of the Church's focus on ministering. Elder Ronald A. Rasband recounted the baptismal promises in Mosiah 18 to bear burdens, mourn with others,

---

m Similar to Alma, Paul gave this gospel instruction to the Romans on how to treat fellow Saints: "Be kindly affectioned one to another with brotherly love; in honour preferring one another; not slothful in business; fervent in spirit; serving the Lord; rejoicing in hope; patient in tribulation; continuing instant in prayer; *distributing to the necessity of saints*; given to hospitality. Bless them which persecute you: bless, and curse not. Rejoice with them that do rejoice, and *weep with them that weep*" (Romans 12:10–15, emphasis added; see entire chapter).

and comfort one another, explaining, "Our ministering one to another in the Church reflects our commitment to honor those very promises."[59] Ministering is an important way to live the law of the gospel.

President Spencer W. Kimball said, "God does notice us, and he watches over us. But it is usually through another person that he meets our needs. Therefore, it is vital that we serve each other in the kingdom. The people of the Church need each other's strength, support, and leadership in a community of believers as an enclave of disciples."[60] President Kimball's statement is a perfect description of the law of the gospel. It is a law for "a community of believers." Indeed, the law of the gospel is a law of community that says we should serve our fellow Saints, including sharing our means with them if needed. Paying fast offerings is one of the ways we do this.

Many people have heard the story of Joseph Millett, an early Mormon pioneer who settled in Southern Utah. His large family had already suffered through the death of his oldest daughter along with continued sickness and hunger when the following occurred, which he recorded in his journal:

> In 1871, one of my children came in [and] said that Brother Newton Hall's folks was out of bread, had none that day. I put our flour in [a] sack to send up to Brother Hall. Just then Brother Hall came. Says I, "Brother Hall, are you out of flour?"
>
> "Brother Millett, we have none."
>
> "Well, Brother Hall, there is some in that sack. I have divided [it out] and was going to send it to you. Your children told mine that you was out."
>
> Brother Hall began to cry. He said he had tried others, but could not get any. He went to the cedars and prayed to the Lord, and the Lord told him to go to Joseph Millett.
>
> [I replied,] "Well Brother Hall, you needn't bring this back if the Lord sent you for it. You don't owe me for it."
>
> You can't tell me how good it made me feel to know that the Lord knew that there was such a person as Joseph Millett.[61]

Brother Millet shared freely because he understood the law of the gospel. He did not describe his actions by that term, but he understood it in his heart and lived it, and as Brother Millet learned, the Lord always knows who of His children are committed to live the law of the gospel.

The law of the gospel is a law of community that emphasizes a covenant way of life as a social order.[n] It means we live by faith in Jesus Christ and come together as a body to teach one another and renew our covenants. It requires that we humbly admit the mistakes we make with one another and try to be better, always striving to follow the guidance of the Holy Ghost. In addition, it includes a covenant commitment to support one another as fellow Saints: "To bear one another's burdens, that they may be light; . . . to mourn with those that mourn; yea, and comfort those that stand in need of comfort" (Mosiah 18:8–9). As the Lord declared, "This is the way that I, the Lord, have decreed to provide for my saints . . . according to the law of my gospel" (D&C 104:16–18).

The book of 4 Nephi describes what can happen when an entire nation lives the law of the gospel. This record begins by stating, "Behold the disciples of Jesus had formed a church of Christ in all the lands round about. And as many as did come unto them, and did truly *repent* of their sins, were *baptized* in the name of Jesus; and they did also receive the *Holy Ghost*. And . . . the people were all *converted unto the Lord*, upon all the face of the land" (4 Nephi 1:1–2; emphasis added). Adherence to the first principles and ordinances of the gospel is clearly delineated. The Nephite record then describes the impact that living these principles had upon the people:

> And there were no contentions and disputations among them, and every man did deal justly one with another. And they had all things common among them; therefore there were not rich and poor, bond and free, but they were all made free, and partakers of the heavenly gift. . . . And the Lord did prosper them exceedingly in the land. . . . And they . . . were blessed according to the multitude of the promises which the Lord had made unto them. And they . . . did walk after the commandments which they had received from their Lord and their God, continuing in fasting and prayer, and in meeting together oft both to pray and to hear the word of the Lord. . . .

---

n This is not to say that the law of the gospel is equivalent to the United Order (which is sometimes also called the law of consecration). The United Order is but one social system under which some Saints have tried to live the law of the gospel; however, this law can be followed regardless of the social system in which people live. Indeed, Latter-day Saints can follow the law of the gospel within every government and social order they reside in throughout the world.

And it came to pass that there was no contention in the land, because of the love of God which did dwell in the hearts of the people. And there were no envyings, nor strifes, nor tumults, nor whoredoms, nor lyings, nor murders, nor any manner of lasciviousness; and surely there could not be a happier people among all the people who had been created by the hand of God. . . . But they were in one, the children of Christ, and heirs to the kingdom of God. And how blessed were they! For the Lord did bless them in all their doings. (4 Nephi 1:2–3, 7, 11–12, 15–16, 18)

Like Nephi's people who "lived after the manner of happiness" (2 Nephi 5:27), these later descendants of Lehi "could not be a happier people" (4 Nephi 1:16). This is the power of living the law of the gospel. It is the law by which Jesus and His disciples establish Zion in Ancient America. It includes supporting one another while living all of the principles of the gospel of Jesus Christ as a covenant way of life.

Greater Views upon My Gospel

After Joseph Smith lost the first 116 pages of his translation of the Book of Mormon, the Lord told him that he should not retranslate that portion, but that he should instead translate the separate account that Nephi had written on a smaller set of plates. The Lord declared, "Behold, there are many things engraven upon the [small] plates of Nephi which do throw *greater views upon my gospel*" (D&C 10:45; emphasis added). Nowhere in the Small Plates are greater views upon the gospel taught more completely than in the book of 2 Nephi.

The gospel, which is also called the doctrine of Christ, is the covenant path theme of 2 Nephi. The book teaches about the plan of salvation and purpose of life, including the Creation and the Fall. It confirms that the gospel is centered on the Atonement of Jesus Christ, including His Resurrection and the Judgment where He will declare that those who have followed the law of the gospel are redeemed from sin. This law assures salvation in the celestial kingdom for those who follow the path of faith in Jesus Christ, repentance, baptism, and receiving the Holy Ghost. But following the law of the gospel is not meant to be a one-time occurrence. By repeatedly renewing these principles, along with praying always and feasting upon the words of Christ, we can endure to the end.

Following the guidance of the Holy Ghost is essential to enduring to the end. The book of 2 Nephi began with a reminder of the rebellion that occurred during the voyage of Nephi's family across the seas. That story teaches how important it is to retain the guidance of the Spirit and not allow our actions to deteriorate into rude behavior, rebellion against the Lord's anointed, or any other unholy and inappropriate conduct.

The law of the gospel is a law of hope and optimism. God's part in this covenant is a promise that because of Jesus Christ, for every death there will be a resurrection, for every sin there is a path to redemption, for every apostasy God has promised a restoration, and for every scattering of covenant people there will be a gathering. Like the law of gravity, which says that whatever goes up must come down, the law of the gospel says that because of Christ's Atonement, whatever goes down must come up! For those who follow the doctrine of Christ, all bad will be overcome by good, all wrongs will be righted, and all darkness will be overpowered by light.

Near the end of his second book, Nephi made this concluding declaration about the gospel or doctrine of Christ: "And now, behold, my beloved brethren, this is the way; and there is none other way nor name given under heaven whereby man can be saved in the kingdom of God. And now, behold, this is the doctrine of Christ, and the only and true doctrine of the Father, and of the Son, and of the Holy Ghost, which is one God, without end. Amen" (2 Nephi 31:21). Understanding and following this doctrine is an important step in the covenant path that leads us back to God.

APPENDIX A
A NEW LAW TAUGHT BY JESUS CHRIST

After His Resurrection in Jerusalem and Ascension into heaven, Jesus Christ appeared to the ancient inhabitants of America and taught that the law of Moses was fulfilled and that the people should follow a new law that He described as "my doctrine" (see 3 Nephi 11:32–39) and later as "my gospel" (see 3 Nephi 27:13–21). This doctrine or law teaches that because of Christ's Resurrection and Atonement, when He judges the world, He will declare salvation for those who follow the first principles and ordinances of the gospel.

Christ began his Sermon at the Temple with a preamble that reiterated the importance of following those principles and ordinances. He said, "Blessed are ye if ye shall believe in me and be baptized, after that ye have seen me and know that I am. . . . Yea, blessed are they who shall . . . come down into the depths of humility and be baptized, for they shall be visited with fire and with the Holy Ghost, and shall receive a remission of their sins" (3 Nephi 12:1–2). The presentation of this doctrine at the onset of Christ's sermon shows that these gospel principles are the foundation for the higher law so beautifully taught in the Beatitudes and other teachings that followed. They also affirm that this special sermon is instruction directed to those who have entered into a covenant relationship with God through baptism.

New insights can come if we study these teachings of Christ through the lens of instruction on how members of the Church are to support one another as part of their baptismal covenants. For example, when we read, "And again, blessed are all they that mourn, for they shall be comforted" (3 Nephi 12:4), we think of the words of Alma at the waters of Mormon (see Mosiah 18:10) and realize that we are to be the agents who provide the needed comfort. And when we read that we should not be angry and should reconcile with others before we come before the Lord (see 3 Nephi 12:22–25), we realize that we should strive to resolve our differences with members of our ward or family before we partake of the sacrament. Many more insights can be gained by studying these teachings of Christ through this lens.

In this sermon, Christ taught, "Therefore those things which were of old time, which were under the law, in me are all fulfilled. Old things are done away, and all things have become new" (3 Nephi 12:46–47). As a part of this new law, Christ's Sermon at the Temple, recorded in 3 Nephi, and His Sermon on the Mount, recorded in Matthew, have been described as a "higher law" by President James E. Faust[62] and others.[63, 64] These signature sermons of Jesus Christ teach how to live the law of the gospel in a higher way.

The things that Jesus taught and did during His visit to Lehi's descendants parallel remarkably the principles of the gospel taught in 2 Nephi and discussed earlier in this chapter. These include the following:

- Christ witnessed of His own Resurrection and Atonement. (3 Nephi 9:15–22; 10:4–7; 11:11–16; 27:14–19)

- Christ taught the redemption principles of resurrection and judgment. (3 Nephi 26:3–5; 27:14, 15, 19, 24–27)

- Christ taught the first principles and ordinances of the gospel and their role as prerequisites for salvation. (3 Nephi 9:15–22; 11:32–39; 12:1–2; 27:13–21)

- Christ gave the authority to baptize to twelve disciples and instructed them to baptize the people.° (3 Nephi 11:18–28; 19:10–13)

- Christ twice administered the sacrament to the people. (3 Nephi 18:1–14; 20:3–9)

- Christ taught the importance of enduring to the end by focusing on Him. (3 Nephi 15:9; 27:16–17)

- Christ taught the need to study His words and other scriptures, to pray always, and to meet together often. (3 Nephi 10:14; 23:1–6; 18:15–22; 20:1)

---

o The Nephites already possessed priesthood authority and had been baptized before Christ came (see 3 Nephi 7:23–26). The fact that Christ personally renewed this authority and instructed the people to be baptized again not only emphasizes the importance of this ordinance but also shows that a new dispensation had begun with lines of authority refreshed and purified.

- Christ repeatedly stated that His joy was full, reminding us that "men are, that they might have joy." (2 Nephi 2:25; 3 Nephi 17:20; 27:30–31)

- Christ quoted prophecies of Isaiah. He taught that "the words of Isaiah should be fulfilled" and declared, "Great are the words of Isaiah." (3 Nephi 22; 20:11; 23:1–3)

- Christ taught about the scattering and gathering of Israel and promised that all of His covenants with Israel shall be fulfilled. (3 Nephi 16; 20:10–46; 21; 22)

- Christ prophesied of the latter-day gathering of Israel and the coming forth of the Book of Mormon. (3 Nephi 20:22–46; 21; 22)

The book of 3 Nephi ends with this invitation, which Mormon said Jesus Christ commanded him to write: "Turn, all ye Gentiles, from your wicked ways; and repent of your evil doings, . . . and come unto me, and be baptized in my name, that ye may receive a remission of your sins, and be filled with the Holy Ghost, that ye may be numbered with my people who are of the house of Israel" (3 Nephi 30:2). These teachings of Jesus Christ in 3 Nephi confirm that the principles taught in 2 Nephi reflect His doctrine. They teach a new and higher law—the law of the gospel.

APPENDIX B

HIGHLIGHT PASSAGES ON THE
ATONEMENT, APOSTASY, AND RESTORATION

Following are some the key passages about Christ and His Atonement, the Apostasy, and the Restoration found in 2 Nephi and not already quoted in this chapter. These come from Nephi's own writings as well as quotes from his brother Jacob and the prophet Isaiah—three witnesses of the Atonement, Apostasy, and Restoration.

CHRIST AND HIS ATONEMENT

Nevertheless, the Lord has shown unto me that they [the Jews] should return again. And he also has shown unto me that the Lord God, the Holy One of Israel, should manifest himself unto them in the flesh; and after he should manifest himself they should scourge him and crucify him, according to the words of the angel who spake it unto me. (2 Nephi 6:9)

And behold, according to the words of the prophet, the Messiah will set himself again the second time to recover them; wherefore, he will manifest himself unto them in power and great glory, unto the destruction of their enemies, when that day cometh when they shall believe in him; and none will he destroy that believe in him. (2 Nephi 6:14)

Therefore, cheer up your hearts, and remember that ye are free to act for yourselves—to choose the way of everlasting death or the way of eternal life. Wherefore, my beloved brethren, reconcile yourselves to the will of God, and not to the will of the devil and the flesh; and remember, after ye are reconciled unto God, that it is only in and through the grace of God that ye are saved. Wherefore, may God raise you from death by the power of the resurrection, and also from everlasting death by the power of the Atonement, that ye may be received into the eternal kingdom of God, that ye may praise him through grace divine. Amen. (2 Nephi 10:23–25)

And now I, Nephi, write more of the words of Isaiah, for my soul delighteth in his words. For I will liken his words unto my people, and I will send them forth unto all my children, for he verily saw my Redeemer, even as I have seen him. And my brother, Jacob, also has seen him as I have seen him; wherefore, I will send their words forth unto my children to prove unto them that my words are true. Wherefore, by the words of three, God hath said, I will establish my word. Nevertheless, God sendeth more witnesses, and he proveth all his words. Behold, my soul delighteth in proving unto my people the truth of the coming of Christ; for, for this end hath the law of Moses been given; and all things which have been given of God from the beginning of the world, unto man, are the typifying of him. And also my soul delighteth in the covenants of the Lord which he hath made to our fathers; yea, my soul delighteth in his grace, and in his justice, and power, and mercy in the great and eternal plan of deliverance from death. And my soul delighteth in proving unto my people that save Christ should come all men must perish. (2 Nephi 11:2–6)

And there shall come forth a rod out of the stem of Jesse, and a branch shall grow out of his roots. And the Spirit of the Lord shall rest upon him, the spirit of wisdom and understanding, the spirit of counsel and might, the spirit of knowledge and of the fear of the Lord. (2 Nephi 21:1–2)

APOSTASY

O house of Jacob, come ye and let us walk in the light of the Lord; yea, come, for ye have all gone astray, every one to his wicked ways. (2 Nephi 12:5)

For behold, the Lord, the Lord of Hosts, doth take away from Jerusalem, and from Judah, the stay and the staff, the whole staff of bread, and the whole stay of water— . . . And the people shall be oppressed, every one by another, and every one by his neighbor; the child shall behave himself proudly against the ancient, and the base against the honorable. . . . For Jerusalem is ruined, and Judah is fallen, because their tongues and their doings have been against the Lord, to provoke the eyes of his glory. (2 Nephi 13:1, 5, 8)

And now go to; I will tell you what I will do to my vineyard—I will take away the hedge thereof, and it shall be eaten up; and I will break down the wall thereof, and it shall be trodden down; and I will lay it waste; it shall not be pruned nor digged; but there shall come up briers and thorns; I will also command the clouds that they rain no rain upon it. (2 Nephi 15:5–6)

Wo unto them that call evil good, and good evil, that put darkness for light, and light for darkness, that put bitter for sweet, and sweet for bitter! Wo unto the wise in their own eyes and prudent in their own sight! Wo unto the mighty to drink wine, and men of strength to mingle strong drink; who justify the wicked for reward, and take away the righteousness of the righteous from him! (2 Nephi 15:20–23)

And he said: Go and tell this people—Hear ye indeed, but they understood not; and see ye indeed, but they perceived not. Make the heart of this people fat, and make their ears heavy, and shut their eyes—lest they see with their eyes, and hear with their ears, and understand with their heart, and be converted and be healed. Then said I: Lord, how long? And he said: Until the cities be wasted without inhabitant, and the houses without man, and the land be utterly desolate; and the Lord have removed men far away, for there shall be a great forsaking in the midst of the land. (2 Nephi 16:9–12)

And if they speak not according to this word, it is because there is no light in them. (2 Nephi 18:20)

Wo unto them that decree unrighteous decrees, and that write grievousness which they have prescribed; to turn away the needy from judgment, and to take away the right from the poor of my people, that widows may be their prey, and that they may rob the fatherless! (2 Nephi 20:1–2)

For the Spirit of the Lord will not always strive with man. And when the Spirit ceaseth to strive with man then cometh speedy destruction, and this grieveth my soul. (2 Nephi 26:11)

He commandeth that there shall be no priestcrafts; for, behold, priestcrafts are that men preach and set themselves up for a light unto the world, that they may get gain and praise of the world; but they seek not the welfare of Zion. (2 Nephi 26:29)

Yea, and there shall be many which shall say: Eat, drink, and be merry, for tomorrow we die; and it shall be well with us. And there shall also be many which shall say: Eat, drink, and be merry; nevertheless, fear God—he will justify in committing a little sin; yea, lie a little, take the advantage of one because of his words, dig a pit for thy neighbor; there is no harm in this; and do all these things, for tomorrow we die; and if it so be that we are guilty, God will beat us with a few stripes, and at last we shall be saved in the kingdom of God. Yea, and there shall be many which shall teach after this manner, false and vain and foolish doctrines, and shall be puffed up in their hearts, and shall seek deep to hide their counsels from the Lord; and their works shall be in the dark. (2 Nephi 28:7–9)

For behold, at that day shall he [the devil] rage in the hearts of the children of men, and stir them up to anger against that which is good. And others will he pacify, and lull them away into carnal security, that they will say: All is well in Zion; yea, Zion prospereth, all is well—and thus the devil cheateth their souls, and leadeth them away carefully down to hell. And behold, others he flattereth away, and telleth them there is no hell; and he saith unto them: I am no devil, for there is none—and thus he whispereth in their ears, until he grasps them with his awful chains, from whence there is no deliverance. (2 Nephi 28:20–22)

And because my words shall hiss forth—many of the Gentiles shall say: A Bible! A Bible! We have got a Bible, and there cannot be any more Bible. (2 Nephi 29:3)

RESTORATION

For Joseph truly testified, saying: A seer shall the Lord my God raise up, who shall be a choice seer unto the fruit of my loins. Yea, Joseph truly said: Thus saith the Lord unto me: A choice seer will I raise up out of the fruit of thy loins; and he shall be esteemed highly among the fruit of thy loins. And unto him will I give commandment that he shall do a work for the fruit of thy loins, his brethren, which shall be of great worth unto them, even to the bringing of them to the knowledge of the covenants which I have made with thy fathers. And I will give unto him a commandment that he shall do none other work, save the work which I shall command him. And I will make him great in mine eyes; for he shall do my work. And he shall be great like unto Moses, whom I have said I would raise up unto you, to deliver my people, O house of Israel. . . . And thus prophesied Joseph, saying: Behold, that seer will the Lord bless; and they that seek to destroy him shall be confounded. . . . And his name shall be called after me; and it shall be after the name of his father. And he shall be like unto me; for the thing, which the Lord shall bring forth by his hand, by the power of the Lord shall bring my people unto salvation. (2 Nephi 3:6–9, 14, 15)

[Spoken to Joseph of old:] Wherefore, the fruit of thy loins shall write; and the fruit of the loins of Judah shall write; and that which shall be written by the fruit of thy loins, and also that which shall be written by the fruit of the loins of Judah, shall grow together, unto the confounding of false doctrines and laying down of contentions, and establishing peace among the fruit of thy loins, and bringing them to the knowledge of their fathers in the latter days, and also to the knowledge of my covenants, saith the Lord. (2 Nephi 3:12)

In that day shall the branch of the Lord be beautiful and glorious; the fruit of the earth excellent and comely to them that are escaped of Israel. . . . And the Lord will create upon every dwelling-place of mount Zion, and upon her assemblies, a cloud and smoke by day and the shining of a flaming fire by night; for upon all the glory of Zion shall be a defence. (2 Nephi 14:2, 5)

And he will lift up an ensign to the nations from far, and will hiss unto them from the end of the earth; and behold, they shall come with speed swiftly; none shall be weary nor stumble among them. (2 Nephi 15:26)

The people that walked in darkness have seen a great light; they that dwell in the land of the shadow of death, upon them hath the light shined. (2 Nephi 19:2)

And it shall come to pass in that day that his burden shall be taken away from off thy shoulder, and his yoke from off thy neck, and the yoke shall be destroyed because of the anointing. (2 Nephi 20:27)

And he shall set up an ensign for the nations, and shall assemble the outcasts of Israel, and gather together the dispersed of Judah from the four corners of the earth. (2 Nephi 21:12)

For the Lord will have mercy on Jacob, and will yet choose Israel, and set them in their own land; and the strangers shall be joined with them, and they shall cleave to the house of Jacob. And the people shall take them and bring them to their place; yea, from far unto the ends of the earth; and they shall return to their lands of promise. And the house of Israel shall possess them, and the land of the Lord shall be for servants and handmaids; and they shall take them captives unto whom they were captives; and they shall rule over their oppressors. (2 Nephi 24:1–2)

And the Lord will set his hand again the second time to restore his people from their lost and fallen state. Wherefore, he will proceed to do a marvelous work and a wonder among the children of men. (2 Nephi 25:17)

And it shall come to pass that the Lord God shall bring forth unto you the words of a book, and they shall be the words of them which have slumbered. And behold the book shall be sealed; and in the book shall be a revelation from God, from the beginning of the world to the ending thereof. . . . Wherefore, at that day when the book shall be delivered unto the man of whom I have spoken, the book shall be hid from the eyes of the world, that the eyes of none shall behold it save it be that three witnesses shall behold it, by the power of God, besides him to whom the book shall be delivered; and they shall testify to the truth of the book and the things therein. And there is none other which shall view it, save it be a few according to the will of God, to bear testimony of his word unto the children of men; for the Lord God hath said that the words of the faithful should speak as if it were from the dead. (2 Nephi 27:6–7, 12–13)

But behold, there shall be many—at that day when I shall proceed to do a marvelous work among them, that I may remember my covenants which I have made unto the children of men, that I may set my hand again the second time to recover my people, which are of the house of Israel. (2 Nephi 29:1)

Wherefore, because that ye have a Bible ye need not suppose that it contains all my words; neither need ye suppose that I have not caused more to be written. For I command all men, both in the east and in the west, and in the north, and in the south, and in the islands of the sea, that they shall write the words which I speak unto them; for out of the books which shall be written I will judge the world, every man according to their works, according to that which is written. (2 Nephi 29:10–11)

Wherefore, the things of all nations shall be made known; yea, all things shall be made known unto the children of men. There is nothing which is secret save it shall be revealed; there is no work of darkness save it shall be made manifest in the light; and there is nothing which is sealed upon the earth save it shall be loosed. Wherefore, all things which have been revealed unto the children of men shall at that day be revealed; and Satan shall have power over the hearts of the children of men no more, for a long time. And now, my beloved brethren, I make an end of my sayings. (2 Nephi 30:16–18)

CHAPTER 4

JACOB: CHASTITY

Like the previous two books, the book of Jacob testifies powerfully of Jesus Christ, which is one of the primary purposes of the Book of Mormon in general and of the Small Plates of Nephi in particular. In addition, two other topics stand out. One is the scattering and gathering of Israel, as so beautifully told in the allegory of the tame and wild olive trees in chapter 5. This clearly fits in with the other primary purpose of the Book of Mormon—to show that God fulfills his covenant promises to the house of Israel. The other prominent topic is chastity. No other book of scripture covers this topic so extensively in a single sermon, suggesting that chastity is the covenant path theme of the book of Jacob. This chapter will proceed to review the teachings in the book of Jacob through the lens of the law of chastity.

PRECIOUS, SACRED, AND GREAT

Jacob began his book by explaining that his brother, Nephi, had instructed him to write on the Small Plates "a few of the things which I considered to be most precious" (Jacob 1:2). He was to touch only lightly on secular history and instead emphasize "preaching which was sacred, or revelation which was great, or prophesying" (Jacob 1:4).

A focus on Christ also motivated Jacob. Nephi had instructed him that he was to write "for Christ's sake, and for the sake of our people" (Jacob 1:4). Jacob explained that they knew of Christ because of their faith, and their "many revelations, and the spirit of much prophecy" (Jacob 1:6). Thus, he wrote, "We labored diligently among our people, that we might persuade them to come unto Christ, and partake of the goodness of God" (Jacob 1:7). It was in this spirit that Jacob included his sermon on chastity in his book. Jacob saw chastity as a topic that is precious, sacred, and great, and he knew that living a chaste life would help his people come unto Christ. When we commit to any of the steps in the covenant path we are coming unto Christ.

The sanctity of the law of chastity is made clear in the book of Jacob. Three times Jacob stated that he taught this principle at the temple (see Jacob 1:17, 2:2, 2:11). In fact, he said that the Lord specifically instructed him to teach this principle at that location, saying, "Get thou up into the temple on the morrow, and declare the word which I shall give thee unto this people" (Jacob 2:11). It sounds as if God wanted to emphasize that chastity is a temple covenant.

We might wonder why the principle of chastity would be included as a separate commitment along the covenant path, because it could certainly be considered as part of the earlier covenant of obedience. Yet it does stand out as a separate covenant topic. Perhaps this is because God wants to emphasize how much He values virtue and chastity. He knows that disobedience to this particular commandment has a high potential to deteriorate the fabric of families, separate us from God, and keep us from receiving exaltation.

When God placed us here on earth, He gave us powerful sexual urges so that we would naturally obey His command to "be fruitful and multiply and replenish the earth" (Genesis 1:28) and thus provide bodies for all of His spirit children who needed to come to earth. However, He also knew that these strong urges would lead to abuse of the powers of procreation, so from the beginning He set boundaries for their use, decreeing that they should only be used within the bounds of a special covenant relationship called marriage. To underscore the importance of these boundaries, He specified the law of chastity as an antecedent, preparatory covenant that we must agree to before entering into the covenant of marriage. Obeying the law of chastity protects the sanctity of marriage and family. Chastity is a principle that is precious, sacred, and great.

TEACH WITH ALL DILIGENCE

Jacob wrote, "And we did magnify our office unto the Lord, taking upon us the responsibility, answering the sins of the people upon our own heads if we did not teach them the word of God with all diligence" (Jacob 1:19). Jacob elaborated further on that diligence that motivated him:

Now, my beloved brethren, I, Jacob, according to the responsibility which I am under to God, to magnify mine office with soberness, that I might rid my garments of your sins, I come up into the temple this day that I might declare unto you the word of God. And ye yourselves know that I have hitherto been diligent in the office of my calling; but I this day am weighed down with much more desire and anxiety for the welfare of your souls than I have hitherto been. (Jacob 2:2–3)

Why did Jacob emphasize this motivation for doing his duty? Perhaps it was because he was about to discuss a topic that he dreaded and wished he did not have to address—especially in such a public setting. Chastity is, by its nature, a personal and sensitive subject, and it makes most people uncomfortable to discuss it. Jacob expounded in length on his discomfort in having to address this topic:

Yea, it grieveth my soul and causeth me to shrink with shame before the presence of my Maker, that I must testify unto you concerning the wickedness of your hearts. And also it grieveth me that I must use so much boldness of speech concerning you, before your wives and your children, many of whose feelings are exceedingly tender and chaste and delicate before God . . . Wherefore, it burdeneth my soul that I should be constrained, because of the strict commandment which I have received from God, to admonish you according to your crimes. (Jacob 2:6–9)

Clearly, Jacob did not want to talk about this subject. However, he returned again to the necessity of doing his duty with these words, "But, notwithstanding the greatness of the task, I must do according to the strict commands of God, and tell you concerning your wickedness and abominations, in the presence of the pure in heart, and the broken heart, and under the glance of the piercing eye of the Almighty God" (Jacob 2:10).

Many parents today also struggle with discomfort when talking about sexuality and chastity. However, as stated in the *Family Home Evening Resource Manual*, "God expects parents in the Church to teach their children about procreation and chastity and to prepare them for dating and marriage."[65] In addition, the Church publication, *A Parent's Guide*, states,

The Lord has placed on you as a parent the primary responsibility to teach your children. Though this is a great responsibility, it is also a divine privilege to have Heavenly Father's children entrusted to your care. One of the most important concepts that the Lord expects you to teach your children is the righteous meaning and use of intimate physical relations between a man and a woman.[66]

The example of Jacob can help us overcome our inhibitions so we can teach chastity with confidence and courage.

PRIDE AND RICHES

Before delving further into the topic of chastity, Jacob addressed pride and riches—two issues that, like chastity, strongly affect marriages. Pride and a focus on riches can both tear away at the fabric of a marriage, leading to a breakup of the family, so it seems fitting that Jacob would address these vices before tackling chastity.

Pride is a mental attitude rooted in a comparison to others. C. S. Lewis famously wrote, "Pride gets no pleasure out of having something, only out of having more of it than the next man . . . It is the comparison that makes you proud: the pleasure of being above the rest. Once the element of competition is gone, pride is gone."[67] Jacob taught this same principle, declaring,

> You have obtained many riches; and because some of you have obtained more abundantly than that of your brethren ye are lifted up in the pride of your hearts, and wear stiff necks and high heads because of the costliness of your apparel, and persecute your brethren because ye suppose that ye are better than they. . . . Think of your brethren like unto yourselves, and be familiar with all and free with your substance, that they may be rich like unto you. . . . And the one being is as precious in his [God's] sight as the other. (Jacob 2:13, 17, 21)

Pride can cause great damage to a marriage. Pride always seeks to defend itself, saying, "I am right and you are wrong," or, "My ways are better than your ways." I remember an occasion early in my own marriage when I wanted to defend myself, but I knew in my heart that I was the one in error, so I owned up to my mistake and admitted that I was wrong. I don't remember the specifics of the incident, but I do remember feeling the Holy Ghost come over me after I admitted my error. It came with a feeling of love from Heavenly Father that more than compensated for the shame I felt in relinquishing my pride. This decision early in my marriage made it easier for me to be humble about other mistakes that followed throughout the years. It contributed to much more happiness in my life than defending my pride would have ever done.

Pride often can also cause us to focus on gaining more material possessions than others have. An excessive focus on wealth can tear marriages apart. Jacob put riches in their proper perspective, saying, "But before ye seek for riches, seek ye for the kingdom of God. And after ye have obtained a hope in Christ ye shall obtain riches, if ye seek them; and ye will seek them for the intent to do good—to clothe the naked, and to feed the hungry, and to liberate the captive, and administer relief to the sick and the afflicted" (Jacob 2:18–19).

Many people are relieved when they read this, because it shows that God's people are not expected to live in poverty. It acknowledges that the pursuit of wealth is not inherently wrong. In fact, it is okay to seek riches if we put God first and use our wealth to bless others—it is a question of priorities. Speaking of meeting their temporal needs, Jesus taught His disciples, "Seek ye first the kingdom of God, and his righteousness; and all these things shall be added unto you" (Matthew 6:33). This is why Jacob sanctioned the pursuit of wealth only "after ye have obtained a hope in Christ" (Jacob 2:19). Our desires should be centered first on Jesus Christ and His kingdom. When they are, we will not be motivated by pride.

THEY SEEK TO EXCUSE THEMSELVES

Jacob shifted from pride to the topic of chastity, calling it "a grosser crime" (Jacob 2:22). He reprimanded his people, saying that the Lord told him that "they seek to excuse themselves in committing whoredoms, because of the things which were written concerning David, and Solomon his son" (Jacob 2:23). The Lord acknowledged that polygamy had been practiced in the past, but He condemned those two Israelite kings, both of whom had taken wives in ways not sanctioned by God (see 2 Samuel 11:27, 1 Kings 11:1–2).

God instructed the Nephites, "Wherefore, I the Lord God will not suffer that this people shall do like unto them of old. . . . For there shall not any man among you have save it be one wife; and concubines he shall have none" (Jacob 2:26–27). This is the same direction God has given us today. As stated in the Doctrine and Covenants, "Monogamy is God's standard for marriage unless He declares otherwise" (D&C Official Declaration 1, heading). The law of chastity says that sexual intimacy may occur only within the bond of marriage between one husband and one wife.

Through Jacob, the Lord provided an insight into one reason why plural marriage had been sanctioned in the past, saying, "For if I will, saith the Lord of Hosts, raise up seed unto me, I will command my people; otherwise they shall hearken unto these things" (Jacob 2:30). God used polygamy to raise up a righteous seed in the days of the Old Testament patriarchs, and based upon this explanation given to Jacob, it is likely one of the reasons God also commanded its use in the early years of our dispensation. But the Lord also told Jacob that in the days when plural marriage was practiced in Jerusalem, it deteriorated into wickedness, bringing sorrow to many. The Lord said, "For behold, I, the Lord, have seen the sorrow, and heard the mourning of the daughters of my people in the land of Jerusalem, yea, and in all the lands of my people, because of the wickedness and abominations of their husbands" (Jacob 2:31).

The Lord told the Nephites that the standard of monogamous chastity and virtue was required of them because, "I have led this people forth out of the land of Jerusalem, by the power of mine arm, that I might raise up unto me a righteous branch from the fruit of the loins of Joseph" (Jacob 2:25). In other words, they were separated from the culture they had known in order to be a righteous branch of covenant people. We need to similarly separate ourselves from the culture of sexual indulgence around us. This will usually not entail relocating our homes, but it will require us to make our homes safe havens, free from the carnal focus of the world around us.

Jacob's primary point in discussing polygamy was to condemn those who justify their sins. Nearly all who commit sexual sin seek to justify their actions in one way or another. Some justify their sexual escapades because of the shortcomings of their spouse. Such excuses are pure selfishness. Others justify themselves "because everyone does it." It is true that many in the world do not hold to the high standard of sexual morality that the Lord has established through the law of chastity, but such standards are required of us as covenant people who believe in eternal families. Jacob taught that we should not justify our sins.

GOD DELIGHTS IN CHASTITY

The Lord declared, through Jacob, "For I, the Lord God, delight in the chastity of women. And whoredoms are an abomination before me; thus saith the Lord of Hosts" (Jacob 2:28). Of course, the chastity of women will not prevail without the chastity of men. In fact, Jacob came down very hard on men, saying,

> And I will not suffer, saith the Lord of Hosts, that the cries of the fair daughters of this people, which I have led out of the land of Jerusalem, shall come up unto me against the men of my people, saith the Lord of Hosts. For . . . they shall not commit whoredoms, like unto them of old, saith the Lord of Hosts. And now behold, my brethren, . . . ye have come unto great condemnation; for ye have done these things which ye ought not to have done. (Jacob 2:32–34)

The same standard is required of both men and women. As stated in "The Family: A Proclamation to the World": "God has commanded that the sacred powers of procreation are to be employed only between man and woman, lawfully wedded as husband and wife."[68] All who violate this law break their covenants and come under great condemnation.

In discussing Jacob's sermon, President Dallin H. Oaks said,

> In the second chapter of the book that bears his name, Jacob condemns men for their "whoredoms" (Jacob 2:23, 28). . . . What were these grossly wicked "whoredoms"? No doubt some men were already guilty of evil acts. But the main focus of Jacob's great sermon was not with evil acts completed, but with evil acts contemplated.
>
> Jacob began his sermon by telling the men that "as yet, [they had] been obedient unto the word of the Lord" (Jacob 2:4). However, he then told them he knew their thoughts, that they were "beginning to labor in sin, which sin appeareth very abominable . . . unto God" (Jacob 2:5). "I must testify unto you concerning the wickedness of your hearts" (Jacob 2:6), he added. Jacob was speaking as Jesus spoke when He said, "Whosoever looketh on a woman to lust after her hath committed adultery with her already in his heart" (Matt. 5:28; see also 3 Ne. 12:28; D&C 59:6; D&C 63:16).[69]

Elder Oaks then proceeded to preach against pornography. The law of chastity requires us to avoid such sins of the mind and heart. One *Ensign* article states,

> The letter of the law of chastity is to have sexual experiences only with one's spouse, the man or woman with whom legal marriage covenants have been made. But the spirit of this law encompasses far more. It requires that we keep sacred and appropriate all of our sexual desires—and all related behaviors. To have physical desires is not evil. But to dwell upon them is evil. This is lust—the mental pursuit of anything that would be spiritually damaging.[70]

Jacob knew this and expounded on sexual sins in more detail during his actual sermon than he recorded in his book. For us, he summarized, "And now I, Jacob, spake many more things unto the people of Nephi, warning them against fornication and lasciviousness, and every kind of sin, telling them the awful consequences of them" (Jacob 3:12).

Lasciviousness is an old word that refers to any lewd or lustful sexual behavior. The most common display of this in our day is pornography. President Gordon B. Hinckley denounced pornography, saying,

> Pornography, with its sleazy filth, sweeps over the earth like a horrible, engulfing tide. It is poison. Do not watch it or read it. It will destroy you if you do. It will take from you your self-respect. It will rob you of a sense of the beauties of life. It will tear you down and pull you into a slough of evil thoughts and possibly of evil actions. Stay away from it. Shun it as you would a foul disease, for it is just as deadly. Be virtuous in thought and in deed. God has planted in you, for a purpose, a divine urge which may be easily subverted to evil and destructive ends.[71]

That statement was made over twenty years ago. Since then, the scourge of pornography has grown more and more pervasive. With that growth, the Church's emphasis on this topic has shifted from warnings of addictions and devastation to assurances that exposure does not guarantee an addiction and that repentance and recovery are always possible. President Dallin H. Oaks gave this reassurance:

> All of us need the Atonement of Jesus Christ. Those struggling with pornography need our compassion and love as they follow needed

principles and steps of recovery. Please do not condemn them. They are not evil or without hope. They are sons and daughters of our Heavenly Father. Through proper and complete repentance, they may become clean, pure, and worthy of every covenant and temple blessing promised by God.[72]

What a beautiful, hopeful statement! Those touched by pornography have no need to panic. We have the Atonement and its promise of purification through repentance. The Atonement of Jesus Christ is the greatest safety net the world has ever known. It can bring people back to their covenants.

However, having a safety net does not mean we can let down our guard. We should not become apathetic toward pornography and accept its ever-growing presence as an expression of a normal part of life. There is nothing normal about pornography. It continues to destroy marriages and families. As one slogan declares, "Porn kills love."[73] Pornography demeans the value of the human soul, presenting it only as an object of base lust and carnal desire. Women are most often the ones who are so objectified, so it is no wonder that the Lord declared, "I . . . delight in the chastity of women" (Jacob 2:28).

Lehi used the brass plates and the stories they contained from the five books of Moses (Genesis through Deuteronomy in our Bible) to teach Jacob and his brothers (see 1 Nephi 5:11–15). One of the stories in these books is the tale of Joseph in Egypt and how he kept the law of chastity in spite of temptation from Potiphar's wife. I had an experience where that story helped me withstand temptation to indulge in pornography.

Near the end of my undergraduate studies, I worked one summer as an intern in Southern California. It was a fun time as I participated in the young single adult program at church and enjoyed the area's beaches, amusement parks, and other activities. Someone told me that I could get a good price on a suit in a clothing district of Los Angeles, so I went there one Saturday morning. I found a suit I liked at a great price and started walking back to my car when I suddenly found myself in front of an adult bookstore. I stopped. I looked through the windows and saw enticing pictures and displays inside. I stood there and thought, "Here I am, all alone in this big city where no one knows me. Now is my chance to sample some of the things the world has to offer. I could go inside and no one would know."

However, I knew that God would know. Suddenly, I thought of Joseph of Egypt and what he did when Potiphar's wife had tried to seduce him. I knew I needed to do the same, so I turned and ran! I ran down that sidewalk in Los Angeles with my new suit flapping in the breeze behind me as I transferred all of that temptation energy into flight. It was good I was running, because when I rounded the next corner, I passed by a similar store. I just kept on running and didn't stop until I reached my car a few blocks away.

I have always felt that my choice to keep my covenants on that day saved me from falling into a pit that would have been extremely difficult to climb out of. My decision to run from temptation also fortified me against new temptations that came later. I have always felt a love for Joseph of Egypt and am grateful for the stories of his life. Jacob's younger brother was named after him. Jacob likely knew the story of Joseph in Egypt and used it to teach his own children about the law of chastity.

My experience occurred almost two decades before the Internet proliferated a scourge of sleaze across the globe like never before. Today, people are faced with all kinds of technology-based "whoredoms" and "lasciviousness" such as Internet pornography, sexting, virtual sex, and many other deviant sexual behaviors. To keep our covenants, we must avoid these and any other improper relationships, real or virtual. Modern technologies make possible new ways of sinning, but the class of sin is very old and must still be shunned. We may have to run from it by quickly shutting off our electronic device and talking with someone who can help us process what we have seen. As Jacob declared, "Whoredoms are an abomination before me; thus saith the Lord of Hosts" (Jacob 2:28). We are blessed to have his teachings to remind us, as Latter-day Saints, that we are expected to live the law chastity.

These cautions, however, must be balanced with an understanding of the beauty and magnificence of a healthy sexual relationship that should exist between a husband and a wife. President Hinckley's warning about pornography included this statement: "God has planted in you, for a purpose, a divine urge."[74] This divine urge is good, not bad. Its two-fold purpose has been confirmed by modern prophets and is stated in *For the Strength of Youth*: "Physical intimacy between husband and wife is beautiful and sacred. It is ordained of God for the creation of children and for the expression of love between husband and wife."[75] Jacob's warnings were not given to condemn sexuality, but to guard against its misuse and thus elevate it to the divine and holy purposes God intended for it. Chastity is a holy covenant that has a positive side as well as a negative one.

VICTIMS: THOSE WITH HEARTS
PIERCED WITH DEEP WOUNDS

Jacob had a tender spot in his heart for those who are the victims of sexual sin: innocent spouses and children. He expressed words of compassion from the Lord for these victims and added consolation of his own, saying,

> For behold, I, the Lord, have seen the sorrow, and heard the mourning of the daughters of my people . . . in all the lands of my people, because of the wickedness and abominations of their husbands. . . .
>
> Ye have broken the hearts of your tender wives, and lost the confidence of your children, because of your bad examples before them; and the sobbings of their hearts ascend up to God against you. And because of the strictness of the word of God, which cometh down against you, many hearts died, pierced with deep wounds. (Jacob 2:31, 35)

Jacob's words are touching. If wayward parents could see the future shattered lives of their spouses and children before breaking their marital vows, they might restrain the fire of their adulterous passions. If they could see the future "sobbings of their [children's] hearts ascend up to God" or see the day when their children's "hearts died, pierced with deep wounds," then they might work harder to repair their existing marriage relationship rather than seek fulfillment elsewhere. Unfortunately, we live in a day when self-fulfillment is usually given priority over self-sacrifice and the well-being of the family. People are told that they should seek their own happiness regardless of the cost to others. Too often, this attitude increases the level of unhappiness for everyone involved.

Jacob was dealing with a situation where wives were the victims of the sexual sins of their husbands. That is frequently the case in our day as well, but not always. Sometimes the husband has remained loyal while the wife has broken the law of chastity. Regardless, children are always victims.

For all who suffer from broken covenants and betrayal, God has again provided the safety net of the Atonement of Jesus Christ. Jacob directed the victims of sin to look to that power for comfort and strength:

But behold, I, Jacob, would speak unto you that are pure in heart. Look unto God with firmness of mind, and pray unto him with exceeding faith, and he will console you in your afflictions, and he will plead your cause, and send down justice upon those who seek your destruction. O all ye that are pure in heart, lift up your heads and receive the pleasing word of God, and feast upon his love; for ye may, if your minds are firm, forever. (Jacob 3:1–2)

These are beautiful words of consolation and instruction for all victims of sin. God will console you. He will plead your cause. You are entitled to feast upon His love. These blessings are available to the victims of sin because of the Atonement of Jesus Christ.

Jacob's admonition, "Look unto God with firmness of mind," encourages those who suffer from the sins of others to have the confidence that comes from faith in God. Jacob added, "Pray unto him with exceeding faith," and "receive the pleasing word of God." That word usually comes through the scriptures or the words of living prophets. The formula for spiritual direction and support never changes: Have faith, pray, and study the scriptures and words of living oracles. Then, Jacob directed, "Feast upon his love; for ye may, if your minds are firm, forever" (Jacob 3:2).

Jacob's phrase "for ye may" emphasizes that victims who follow this formula are *entitled* to the blessings of feasting upon the love of God. We know that the power behind this love comes from the Atonement of Jesus Christ. Alma later described how Christ would gain this power, saying, "And he shall go forth, suffering pains and afflictions and temptations of every kind; . . . and he will take upon him their infirmities, that his bowels may be filled with mercy, according to the flesh, that he may know according to the flesh how to succor his people according to their infirmities" (Alma 7:11–12). Truly, Christ is the Great Healer, and Jacob made it clear that those who have suffered as innocent victims of sexual sin can feast upon His love forever.

YE MAY BRING YOUR CHILDREN UNTO DESTRUCTION

Jacob had harsh words for those who bring pain to their families through disobedience to the law of chastity. He said, "Wherefore, ye shall remember your children, how that ye have grieved their hearts because of the example that ye have set before them; and also, remember that ye may, because of your filthiness, bring your children unto destruction, and their sins be heaped upon your heads at the last day" (Jacob 3:10).

While some children of those who participate in sexual sin will shun the mistakes of their parents and seek consolation through Christ, others will end up repeating those same sins when they get older. It often takes three or four generations before traditions of sin are discarded. The Lord taught this when he told Moses, "The Lord God . . . will by no means clear the guilty; visiting the iniquity of the fathers upon the children, and upon the children's children, unto the third and to the fourth generation" (Exodus 34:6, 7; see also D&C 98). Likewise, Jacob warned those who disobey the law of chastity: "Ye may, because of your filthiness, bring your children unto destruction."

Children are excellent mimics. It is amazing how they will notice their parents' most subtle behaviors and repeat those behaviors themselves. They do not even have to be direct witnesses of their parents' sins in order to incorporate their attitudes into their own lives and repeat their sins. Elder Richard L. Evans taught,

> Sometimes some parents mistakenly feel that they can relax a little as to conduct and conformity or take perhaps a so-called liberal view of basic and fundamental things—thinking that a little laxness or indulgence won't matter—or they may fail to teach or to attend Church, or may voice critical views. Some parents . . . seem to feel that they can ease up a little on the fundamentals without affecting their family or their family's future. *But, if a parent goes a little off course, the children are likely to exceed the parent's example.*[76]

Some men indulge in pornography frequently and justify it saying that at least they are not committing adultery. Such a man does not realize the impact his behavior could have on his children unto the third and fourth generations. Even if he can maintain the self-discipline of not letting his habit move beyond viewing, it is still infidelity to his wife. He is breaking his covenants by committing adultery in his heart (see 3 Nephi 12:27–29). If he does not repent, it is very likely that some of his children will repeat their father's sins and maybe even go much farther than he has. This could occur not only because they could take on the carnal attitude of their father, but also because they could lose the protection of the presence of the Holy Ghost in their home. Perhaps the unrepented sins of such a father could also disqualify him in the next life from intervening as an unseen angel in behalf of his posterity "unto the third and fourth generation" when they are similarly tempted.

Elder Vaughn J. Featherstone quoted Oscar W. McConkie, the father of Elder Bruce R. McConkie, who "counseled that when we violate any commandment, however small, our youth may choose to violate a commandment later on in life perhaps 10 times or 100 times worse and justify it on the basis of the small commandment we broke."[77]

If we want to see our children remain faithful to their covenants, we need to hold firmly to standards of righteousness ourselves. God will hold us accountable if we do not. The proclamation on the family states, "We warn that individuals who violate covenants of chastity, who abuse spouse or offspring, or who fail to fulfill family responsibilities will one day stand accountable before God."[78] Nevertheless, such sins should not bring hopelessness. The Lord's warning to Moses about the effects of sin on future generations, quoted earlier, also includes these words of comfort: "The Lord God [is] merciful and gracious, longsuffering, and abundant in goodness and truth, keeping mercy for thousands, forgiving iniquity and transgression and sin" (Exodus 34:6–7).

Sexual sins can be repented of. Three times Jacob added a qualifier to his pronouncements of consequences for sexual sin, saying, "except ye repent" or "unless ye shall repent" (see Jacob 3:4–5, 8). Jacob made it clear that the long-term consequences of sexual sin are reversible, and experience teaches that the sooner we repent, the more we diminish the short-term consequences for ourselves and for our families. Heartfelt repentance from sexual sins purges their stain from our souls as thoroughly as repentance from any other type of sin. The repentance process for these serious sins may be difficult, but this does not mean that the forgiveness is any less complete. The final pronouncement from the Lord for all repented sin is the same: "Behold, he who has repented of his sins, the same is forgiven, and I, the Lord, remember them no more" (D&C 58:42).

PREVENTING A CURSE UPON THE LAND

The book of Jacob teaches that disobedience to the law of chastity not only has consequences for the individual and his or her family, but also for communities and nations. When immoral standards become accepted as the norm for a nation, the underpinnings of the family structure are in peril, and God withholds His blessings.

Jacob taught the Nephites that their disobedience to the law of chastity was an abomination before the Lord and that it would bring a curse upon the land, leading to the destruction of the entire Nephite nation:

> For I, the Lord God, delight in the chastity of women. And whoredoms are an abomination before me; thus saith the Lord of Hosts. Wherefore, this people shall keep my commandments, saith the Lord of Hosts, or *cursed be the land for their sakes.* . . .
>
> For they shall not lead away captive the daughters of my people because of their tenderness, *save I shall visit them with a sore curse, even unto destruction*; for they shall not commit whoredoms, like unto them of old, saith the Lord of Hosts. And now behold, my brethren, ye know that these commandments were given to our father, Lehi; wherefore, ye have known them before; and *ye have come unto great condemnation*; for ye have done these things which ye ought not to have done. Behold, *ye have done greater iniquities than the Lamanites*, our brethren. (Jacob 2:28–29, 33–35; emphasis added)

Jacob's statement that the sexual sins of the Nephites made their iniquities greater than those of the Lamanites probably surprised his people. They saw the Lamanites as dark, loathsome, and wicked, while they saw themselves as delightsome and righteous. However, Jacob taught that because the Lamanites held true to values that strengthen families, the Lord would bless them in the long run, while cursing the land for the Nephites if they would not repent. Here are Jacob's words:

> But, wo, wo, unto you that are not pure in heart, that are filthy this day before God; for *except ye repent the land is cursed for your sakes*; and the Lamanites, which are not filthy like unto you . . . shall scourge you even unto destruction. And the time speedily cometh, that except ye repent they shall possess the land of your inheritance. . . . Behold, *the Lamanites . . . are more righteous than you*; for they have not forgotten the commandment of the Lord, which was given unto our father—that they should have save it were one wife, and concubines they should have none, and there should not be whoredoms committed among them. And now, this commandment they observe to keep; wherefore . . . the Lord God will not destroy them, but will be merciful unto them; and one day they shall become a blessed people. Behold,

their husbands love their wives, and their wives love their husbands; and their husbands and their wives love their children; and their unbelief and their hatred towards you is because of the iniquity of their fathers. (Jacob 3:3–7; emphasis added)

This shows the high level of importance the Lord places on the basic principle of chastity, which strengthens the foundation of families. When that foundation is in place for a nation, the Lord can rebuild faith, but when basic moral values are lost, the family structure deteriorates and God's blessings on that society end. Jacob's prophecy regarding the future of the Nephite and Lamanite nations was fulfilled, as witnessed in the final letter that Mormon wrote to his son, Moroni:

> And notwithstanding this great abomination of the Lamanites, it doth not exceed that of our people [the Nephites] in Moriantum. For behold, many of the daughters of the Lamanites have they taken prisoners; and after depriving them of that which was most dear and precious above all things, which is chastity and virtue—and after they had done this thing, they did murder them in a most cruel manner, torturing their bodies even unto death; and after they have done this, they devour their flesh like unto wild beasts, because of the hardness of their hearts; and they do it for a token of bravery. (Mormon 9:9–10)

What horrible depths of depravity the Nephites had fallen to! In the end, the Lamanites, in spite of their own wickedness and lack of faith in God, still maintained a higher respect for the law of chastity than did the Nephites. This is one reason why God preserved the Lamanites while the Nephites were destroyed. This is a witness to the importance God places on families and virtue.

The downfall of the Nephite nation stands as a testimony of the truth of the following caution in the proclamation on the family: "We warn that the disintegration of the family will bring upon individuals, communities, and nations the calamities foretold by ancient and modern prophets."[79] Jacob's warning should motivate covenant-keeping Latter-day Saints to promote high moral values in each of the nations in which we live.

BEAR THE SHAME OF THE WORLD

The world, in general, does not agree with the emphasis that we, as a church, place on chastity. We are often seen as puritanical or old fashioned. Many people around us think that any sexual behavior is permissible between consenting parties, and they ridicule those who advocate the values of chastity and marriage. Perhaps Jacob knew that this would be so when he wrote, "Wherefore, we would to God that we could persuade all men not to rebel against God, to provoke him to anger, but that all men would believe in Christ, and view his death, and suffer his cross and *bear the shame of the world*" (Jacob 1:8; emphasis added).

Even though standing up for the law of chastity may bring ridicule and criticism, the Lord will bless us if we will not hesitate to "bear the shame of the world" by speaking up for this principle. More important, we should set a quiet example by always living it. Chastity is a foundational covenant that fosters an atmosphere of trust and confidence between husband and wife and with God. It also helps ensure an emotionally healthy family environment for raising children. Some people will notice these characteristics in covenant-keeping families and will desire the peace and happiness they see in them.

One area where the chasm between the world's view and God's view on chastity has widened is regarding same-sex marriage. The First Presidency and the Twelve Apostles have consistently taught that sexual relations are to be kept within the bounds of marriage between one man and one woman. However, they also acknowledge that those who struggle with same gender attraction did not choose to have the inclinations they live with.[80] All should be treated with respect and fairness, remembering Jacob's declaration, "And the one being is as precious in his sight as the other" (Jacob 2:21). The following passage from Jacob 4 may be helpful in dealing with this issue:

> Behold, great and marvelous are the works of the Lord. How unsearchable are the depths of the mysteries of him; and it is impossible that man should find out all his ways. And no man knoweth of his ways save it be revealed unto him. . . . Wherefore, brethren, seek not to counsel the Lord, but to take counsel from his hand. For behold, ye yourselves know that he counseleth in wisdom, and in justice, and in great mercy, over all his works. Wherefore, beloved brethren, be reconciled unto him through the atonement of Christ, his Only Begotten Son, and ye may obtain a resurrection, according to the power of the resurrection which is in Christ. . . . (Jacob 4:8–11)

There is much we don't understand, but as stated in the ninth article of faith, "We believe . . . that God . . . will yet reveal many great and important things pertaining to the Kingdom of God," and perhaps this is one area where He will reveal more. In the meantime, we should not seek to counsel the Lord, nor should we seek to counsel the prophets and apostles who are His spokesmen; rather, we should have faith that He counsels in wisdom, justice, and mercy. Above all, we should "be reconciled unto him through the atonement of Christ" and have hope that these issues will be resolved in the Resurrection if not before. Jacob later added that we should not be like the Jews of old who were guilty of "looking beyond the mark" (Jacob 4:14). We must keep focused on the Atonement of Jesus Christ and continue to follow all that He reveals through His living prophets, including their counsel to treat all people with love, respect, and compassion.

FAMILIES AND THE ALLEGORY OF ZENOS

Chapter 5 of the book of Jacob contains the allegory of the tame and wild olive trees, which Jacob presumably transcribed from a record by the prophet Zenos found on the Brass Plates. Jacob's inclusion of this allegory helps fulfill one of the main purposes of the Small Plates of Nephi—to testify that the promises of the Lord to the remnants of His covenant people, Israel, will be fulfilled. However, this allegory also teaches many principles that can apply to raising a family in the vineyard of the world, including some passages that can apply to marriage and to living the law of chastity.

The allegory says that a tree can bring forth both tame and wild fruits: "And [the Lord] said unto the servant: Look hither and behold the last [tree]. Behold, this have I planted in a good spot of ground; and I have nourished it this long time, and only a part of the tree hath brought forth tame fruit, and the other part of the tree hath brought forth wild fruit; behold, I have nourished this tree like unto the others" (Jacob 5:25).

Of course, this passage alludes to the Nephites and Lamanites, one nation being tame and the other wild. However, it can also apply to individuals. We each have both tame and wild tendencies within us. Paul wrote of the internal conflict he experienced between his spiritual and carnal tendencies, lamenting, "For what I would [desire to do], that do I not; but what I hate, that do I" (Roman 7:15). We all need to nourish the tame and purge the wild that dwells within us. The tame fruits of our sexual powers are our children and the strengthened love we have for our spouse. What we must avoid is going down paths that will lead to the wild fruit of our passions—extra-marital affairs, pornography addictions, broken covenants, broken homes, and pain-filled lives.

Pruning is another of the symbols in the allegory that has an application in our struggles with sin. Zenos wrote, "And it came to pass that the master of the vineyard went forth, and he saw that his olive tree began to decay; and he said: I will prune it, and dig about it, and nourish it, that perhaps it may shoot forth young and tender branches, and it perish not. And it came to pass that he pruned it, and digged about it, and nourished it according to his word" (Jacob 5:4–5).

Sin brings spiritual decay, and the Lord usually responds with pruning. This pruning shows up in our lives as difficult challenges or humbling experiences. Formal Church discipline can also be a type of pruning, and such pruning can motivate us to repent. However, not all pruning comes as a consequence of sin. The Lord uses pruning to promote new growth. Regardless of the cause, pruning is always an opportunity to humble ourselves and seek improvement in our lives.

Marriages can sometimes include pruning, transplanting, and grafting in the form of divorces, remarriages, and the blending of families. Sometimes moving to distant places, far from extended family, can also be difficult. Those who experience these life challenges can find in Jacob 5 some promises that their experiences can ultimately result in healthy growth and good fruit:

> And behold, saith the Lord of the vineyard, I take away many of these young and tender branches, and I will graft them whithersoever I will. . . . And it came to pass that the Lord of the vineyard went his way, and hid the natural branches of the tame olive tree in the nethermost parts of the vineyard, some in one and some in another, according to his will and pleasure.
>
> And it came to pass that the Lord of the vineyard said unto the servant: Come, let us go to the nethermost part of the vineyard, and behold if the natural branches of the tree have not brought forth much fruit also. . . . And it came to pass that they went forth whither the master had hid the natural branches of the tree, and he said unto the servant: Behold these; and he beheld the first that it had brought forth much fruit; and he beheld also that it was good. (Jacob 5:8, 14, 19–20)

The most prominent action described in the allegory is to nourish. Nourishing is mentioned twenty-two times in Jacob 5. In the following passage, the Lord of the vineyard describes how much He nourished the tree that had grown wild branches:

> And it came to pass that the servant of the Lord of the vineyard did according to the word of the Lord of the vineyard, and grafted in the branches of the wild olive tree. And the Lord of the vineyard caused that it should be digged about, and pruned, and nourished, saying unto his servant: It grieveth me that I should lose this tree; wherefore, that perhaps I might preserve the roots thereof that they perish not, that I might preserve them unto myself, I have done this thing. Wherefore, go thy way; watch the tree, and nourish it, according to my words. (Jacob 5:10–12)

Likewise, we should not give up on family members who have grown wild branches and are not keeping their covenants. We can follow the direction of the Lord of the vineyard who said, "It grieveth me that I should lose this tree," and then commanded his servant to "watch the tree, and nourish it." The day may come when such trees—and people—will begin to give good fruit.

The Lord of the vineyard also described how He nourished the trees that had tame or natural branches:

> And it came to pass that they went forth whither the master had hid the natural branches of the tree, and he said unto the servant: Behold these; and he beheld the first that it had brought forth much fruit; and he beheld also that it was good. And he said unto the servant: Take of the fruit thereof, and lay it up against the season, that I may preserve it unto mine own self; for behold, said he, this long time have I nourished it, and it hath brought forth much fruit. (Jacob 5:20)

Likewise, we need to nourish our existing marriages and families—our tame or natural branches. Successful marriages do not spring forth immediately after the ceremony is performed. Marriage covenants need to be nourished. As stated in the proclamation on the family, "Successful marriages and families are established and maintained on principles of faith, prayer, repentance, forgiveness, respect, love, compassion, work, and wholesome recreational activities."[81] These principles must be practiced over time in order to bring success. "This long time have I nourished it," said the Lord of the vineyard. We need to nourish our marriages and families with similar long-term commitment and patience.

Jacob's recitation of the allegory of the olive trees reminds us that we are a covenant people loved by the Lord of the vineyard and that everything He does is for our benefit. He fulfills His covenant promises, and we should too.

HARDEN NOT YOUR HEARTS

Following his recitation from the prophet Zenos, Jacob summarized principles from the allegory and called upon his people to repent. He described two outcomes in life: "And how blessed are they who have labored diligently in his vineyard; and how cursed are they who shall be cast out into their own place!" (Jacob 6:3). Jacob continued with a plea that is especially noteworthy when it is considered with respect to the law of chastity: "Wherefore, my beloved brethren, I beseech of you in words of soberness that ye would repent, and come with full purpose of heart, and cleave unto God as he cleaveth unto you. And while his arm of mercy is extended towards you in the light of the day, harden not your hearts" (Jacob 6:4–5).

We may have had a struggle with the law of chastity, but if we repent and harden not our hearts, His arm of mercy is extended toward us. Also, responding in-kind to the way God reaches out to us "in the light of the day" is helpful in repentance. Sexual sin thrives in secrecy. Many people have not been able to overcome its grasp until they became completely transparent about their struggles. An accountability partner is often helpful. Sometimes the assistance of a professional counselor or coach is needed in order to bring into "the light of the day" underlying emotional wounds that are often at the root of a pornography addiction. As a minimum, a person needs to confess openly to his or her bishop and spouse and be honest when relapses occur.

For those who have entered into sacred covenants with God and then fall into sin without repenting, Jacob's prognosis is dire:

> For behold, after ye have been nourished by the good word of God all the day long, will ye bring forth evil fruit, that ye must be hewn down and cast into the fire? Behold, will ye reject these words? Will ye reject the words of the prophets; and will ye reject all the words which have been spoken concerning Christ, after so many have spoken concerning him;

and deny the good word of Christ, and the power of God, and the gift of the Holy Ghost, and quench the Holy Spirit, and make a mock of the great plan of redemption, which hath been laid for you? (Jacob 6:7–8)

As covenant people, we have to be careful not to adopt the attitudes of the world regarding sexual behavior. There are many in the world who claim to be good Christians, yet they blatantly transgress the law of chastity. They claim that His grace and mercy will redeem them even though they disobey this law, when in fact their behavior shows that they are rejecting the words of the prophets as well as the good word of Christ. If we fall into the same trap, we will suppress the influence of the Holy Ghost—one of the greatest consequences of unrepented sin. Jacob's scathing rebuke continued,

> Know ye not that if ye will do these things, that the power of the redemption and the resurrection, which is in Christ, will bring you to stand with shame and awful guilt before the bar of God? And according to the power of justice, for justice cannot be denied, ye must go away into that lake of fire and brimstone, whose flames are unquenchable, and whose smoke ascendeth up forever and ever, which lake of fire and brimstone is endless torment. (Jacob 6:9–10)

Nevertheless, such sinners are not without hope, for Jacob added this invitation: "O then, my beloved brethren, repent ye, and enter in at the strait gate, and continue in the way which is narrow, until ye shall obtain eternal life. O be wise; what can I say more?" (Jacob 6:11–12). As stated earlier, sexual sins can be repented of. The consequences of such sins do not have to be eternal. We should repent and continue along the covenant path toward eternal life, which includes abstinence outside of marriage and fidelity within marriage. This is the path of wisdom, and Jacob admonished, "O be wise; what can I say more?"

Jacob ended this segment of his book with a departing salutation: "Finally, I bid you farewell, until I shall meet you before the pleasing bar of God, which bar striketh the wicked with awful dread and fear. Amen" (Jacob 6:13). The judgment bar of God will be a pleasing bar for those who repent and keep their covenants, but it will be a place of awful dread and fear for the wicked. If we will cling to the law of chastity as a standard of protection and power, we will be blessed with joy and eternal life when we stand with Jacob before the pleasing bar of God.

Spiritual Power from Christ

Jacob began his book with a testimony of Christ, declaring, "We knew of Christ and his kingdom, which should come. Wherefore we labored diligently among our people, that we might persuade them to come unto Christ, and partake of the goodness of God, that they might enter into his rest" (Jacob 1:6–7). At the end of his book, Jacob came full-circle, again testifying of Christ through the story of an encounter with a man named Sherem. Although their confrontation did not involve the law of chastity, it reminds us of the need to be anchored in Jesus Christ in order to gain spiritual power. Our covenants, including chastity, secure this anchor.

Sherem was a man who "began to preach among the people, and to declare unto them that there should be no Christ. And . . . this he did that he might overthrow the doctrine of Christ. . . . wherefore, he could use much flattery, and much power of speech, according to the power of the devil" (Jacob 7:2, 4). In spite of Sherem's efforts to shake Jacob from his faith, the prophet remained firm. He said, "The Lord God poured in his Spirit into my soul, insomuch that I did confound him in all his words" (Jacob 7:8).

Jacob refuted Sherem by referring to the witness of Christ in the scriptures and adding his own personal testimony of the Savior. He said, "They [the scriptures] truly testify of Christ. Behold, I say unto you that none of the prophets have written, nor prophesied, save they have spoken concerning this Christ. And this is not all— . . . it has been made manifest unto me by the power of the Holy Ghost; wherefore, I know if there should be no atonement made all mankind must be lost" (Jacob 7:11–12).

When Sherem asked for a sign, Jacob agreed, saying, "If God shall smite thee, let that be a sign unto thee that he has power, both in heaven and in earth; and also, that Christ shall come. And thy will, O Lord, be done, and not mine" (Jacob 7:14). God fulfilled Jacob's words, and Sherem was smitten. He died some days later, admitting "that he had been deceived by the power of the devil" and confessing, "I have lied unto God" (Jacob 7:18–19).

Jacob's testimony—that all the prophets have testified of Christ, and that without His Atonement all mankind would be lost—was a powerful witness. Jacob was able to testify with such power because, as he said, "The Lord God poured in his Spirit into my soul" (Jacob 7:8). Jacob's narrative shows that spiritual power comes to covenant-keeping people who testify of Jesus Christ. It can be used to break down the false arguments of wicked people like Sherem who seek to "overthrow the doctrine of Christ" and "lead away the hearts of the people" (Jacob 7:2–3).

The presence of this lesson in the book of Jacob, with its subtheme of chastity, can remind us to use our testimony of Christ as a bulwark against all kinds of spiritual attacks—including assaults by Satan tempting us to commit sexual sin. A close friend once told me of a time when he found himself in a situation where an opportunity to break the law of chastity lay directly before him. He felt so strongly tempted that even thoughts of his wife and family were not barriers to him—but then he thought of his love for the Savior. "I could not do that to Christ," he told me. This thought prevented him from yielding to sin.

Elder Jeffrey R. Holland said, "In exploiting the body of another—which means exploiting his or her soul—one desecrates the Atonement of Christ, which saved that soul and which makes possible the gift of eternal life."[82] My friend did not do that because he was anchored in his love for the Lord and in the power of His Atonement.

Nearly everyone faces sexual temptation. It comes with having physical bodies and hormones. As stated earlier, sexual desires are good and proper when used for their divine purposes. However, they also provide one of the universal tests of this mortal life. This may be one reason why God has singled out the law of chastity as one of the covenant steps on the path to exaltation. It is a test of our self-discipline and our love for the Savior.

There is a connection between sexual purity and being able to receive the power of the Atonement of Jesus Christ in our lives. The virtue that accompanies living the law of chastity is a prerequisite to that power, which comes through the priesthood and through the Holy Ghost. A passage in Doctrine and Covenants 121 makes this clear:

> Let thy bowels also be full of charity towards all men, and to the household of faith, and *let virtue garnish thy thoughts unceasingly; then* shall thy confidence wax strong in the presence of God; and the doctrine of the priesthood shall distil upon thy soul as the dews from heaven. The Holy Ghost shall be thy constant companion, and thy scepter an unchanging scepter of righteousness and truth; and thy dominion shall be an everlasting dominion, and without compulsory means it shall flow unto thee forever and ever. (D&C 121:45–46; emphasis added)

Virtue brings confidence before God. It endows us with the doctrine of the priesthood and ensures the companionship of the Holy Ghost. These blessings are available to all covenant people, male and female, and are well worth the price of the self-discipline required to keep the law of chastity.

Jacob understood the importance of keeping covenants and gave special emphasis to keeping the law of chastity, but his primary focus was on Jesus Christ. After inscribing his temple sermon about chastity onto the Small Plates of Nephi, he described the reason he kept this record:

> For, for this intent have we written these things, that they may know that we knew of Christ, and we had a hope of his glory many hundred years before his coming; and not only we ourselves had a hope of his glory, but also all the holy prophets which were before us. Behold, they believed in Christ and worshiped the Father in his name, and also we worship the Father in his name. And for this intent we keep the law of Moses, it pointing our souls to him; and for this cause it is sanctified unto us for righteousness . . . Wherefore, we search the prophets, and we have many revelations and the spirit of prophecy; and having all these witnesses we obtain a hope, and our faith becometh unshaken, insomuch that we truly can command in the name of Jesus and the very trees obey us, or the mountains, or the waves of the sea. (Jacob 4:4–6)

These words, coming on the heels of Jacob's powerful sermon on chastity, can remind us why we should want to remain pure and clean and virtuous: because of our love for the Savior. We can liken Jacob's words to us and to our adherence to the law of chastity by declaring, "*I know of Christ, and I have a hope of His glory. I believe in Christ and worship the Father in His name. I keep the law* of chastity because, like the law of Moses, *it points my soul to Christ. And for this cause, the law of chastity is sanctified unto me for righteousness.*"

Indeed, if we will keep this law and *search the prophets* regarding it, then, like Jacob, we will gain spiritual power. We will *have many revelations and the spirit of prophecy* so that we can *obtain hope* and have *our faith become unshaken,* and we will be able *to command miracles in the name of Jesus,* either through the priesthood or through our faith and prayers according to His will.

The law of chastity is a great blessing. As the covenant path theme of the book of Jacob, this topic is precious, sacred, and great. Jacob taught that keeping this law brings blessings to our nations, our families, and to us. It is prerequisite to receiving power from Christ and is an essential step on the covenant path back to God.

CHAPTER 5

ENOS:
PRAYER

The writings of Enos comprise only twenty-seven verses in the Small Plates of Nephi, but his experience with prayer is instructive to all who seek the blessings of God. There are several prayers in the scriptures that stand out as significant examples of how to communicate with God. Among these are the Lord's Prayer (see Matthew 6:9–13), His intercessory prayer prior to His Crucifixion (see John 17), His prayers during his visits to the Nephites (see 3 Nephi 17:11–25 and 19:19–35), and the prayer of Joseph Smith in Liberty Jail (see D&C 121). However, none of these is as relatable to the common person as the example given by humble Enos, the son of Jacob. His experience points to prayer as the covenant path theme of the book of Enos.

Enos began his narrative by telling of a time when he "went to hunt beasts in the forest" (Enos 1:3). His original objective had been to seek physical sustenance, but in the quiet solitude of the forest, he became contemplative and shifted instead to the pursuit of spiritual nourishment as "the words which [he] had often heard [his] father speak concerning eternal life, and the joy of the saints, sunk deep into [his] heart" (Enos 1:3).

Enos wrote, "And my soul hungered; and I kneeled down before my Maker, and I cried unto him in mighty prayer and supplication for mine own soul" (Enos 1:4). The spiritual anxiety of Enos was so great that he admitted, "All the day long did I cry unto him; yea, and when the night came I did still raise my voice high that it reached the heavens" (Enos 1:4). However, Enos's prayer did not focus solely on himself. It started there, but like the concentric circles that form when a pebble is tossed into a still pond, his prayer spread outward. It advanced from a concern for his own soul to supplication for his family and fellow Nephites. From there it went to the unbelieving Lamanites and finally to the future surviving descendants of Father Lehi. Enos's prayer had such a systematic structure and order to it that we might say that he gave us an example of an "order of prayer."

Prayers are an important part of temple worship. In a general conference talk, President N. Eldon Tanner once described a temple prayer circle.[83] The *Encyclopedia of Mormonism* says, "The prayer circle is a part of Latter-day Saint temple worship, usually associated with the endowment ceremony."[84]

The experience of Enos appears to be a type for such prayers. In holy temples, most of which are adorned with scenes of nature such as in Enos's forest, we set aside our pursuit of physical sustenance and material wealth and pray unto our Maker for our own souls and for others in need of blessings. Often we put the names of loved ones (or even our own name) on the temple prayer roll,[85] and when we reach the point in the temple ceremony where a prayer is said for these souls, we exercise our faith in their behalf, much like Enos did.

Rarely, if ever, will any of us pray all day and into the night for someone, but when we enter names on temple prayer rolls, supplications will continue in behalf of those persons for long periods of time. Indeed, it is in the temples of the Church that Enos's model of praying for someone all day and into the night occurs regularly. This chapter will review the record of Enos through the lens of temple prayers.

THY SINS ARE FORGIVEN THEE

After introducing himself, Enos began his book by writing, "And I will tell you of the wrestle which I had before God, before I received a remission of my sins" (Enos 1:2). He had gone hunting, but he began to think upon the words of his father, Jacob, whom we know was a spiritual man. Enos had undoubtedly heard many of his father's sermons, for he wrote, "And the words which I had often heard my father speak concerning eternal life, and the joy of the saints, sunk deep into my heart" (Enos 1:3).

This motivated Enos to begin a prayer that was probably unlike any he had before offered to God. It was a prayer that came from the depths of his soul with such desire and fervor that he was able to sustain this prayer for the entire day and into the night. Enos did not give us the details of his supplication other than to say that it was a wrestle, but his lengthy pleadings were rewarded. He recorded a remarkable exchange with God that ended his wrestle:

> And there came a voice unto me, saying: Enos, thy sins are forgiven thee, and thou shalt be blessed. And I, Enos, knew that God could not lie; wherefore, my guilt was swept away. And I said: Lord, how is it done? And he said unto me: Because of thy faith in Christ, whom thou hast never before heard nor seen. And many years pass away before he shall manifest himself in the flesh; wherefore, go to, thy faith hath made thee whole. (Enos 1:5–8)

What a blessing to know that his sins were forgiven. He was pronounced clean and pure before God. How did it happen? It was because Enos had such great faith in Christ, whom he had "never seen nor heard." The Lord emphasized, "Thy faith hath made thee whole." This example from Enos gives us hope that through our faithfulness, we too may become clean before God. Such a pronouncement would prepare us for further intimate communication with God through prayer, just as it did for Enos.

The importance of being cleansed is similarly emphasized in Doctrine and Covenants 88, a revelation given to the Prophet Joseph Smith that he aptly called an "olive leaf . . . plucked from the Tree of Paradise" (D&C 88 heading):

> And I give unto you . . . a commandment that you assemble yourselves together, and organize yourselves, and prepare yourselves, and sanctify yourselves; yea, purify your hearts, and cleanse your hands and your feet before me, that I may make you clean; that I may testify unto your Father, and your God, and my God, that you are clean from the blood of this wicked generation. . . . Also, I give unto you a commandment that ye shall continue in prayer and fasting from this time forth. (D&C 88:74–76)

The example of Enos models this same approach of being cleansed by God before engaging in a special and inspired prayer experience.

The Joy of the Saints

Describing the spark that ignited his faithful prayer, Enos said that "the words which I had often heard my father speak concerning eternal life, and the joy of the saints, sunk deep into my heart" (Enos 1:3). A sense of unity and love with fellow Saints is an essential element for truly powerful prayer. If we can surround ourselves with others who have similar faith "concerning eternal life" and invite them to unite their faith with ours, then that combined faith will strengthen our prayers.

We often see this model of unity and faith demonstrated in invitations among close family and friends to pray for a loved one. Usually it is for the sake of one who has an illness or some personal struggle. Often it is combined with fasting. Sometimes a group will gather together in one place and pray for a particular need, while other times a plea goes out to pray wherever we are. Regardless, we often sense that the combined unity of faith with other Saints will magnify the power of our prayers beyond what we can do on our own.

When we pray with this sort of unity, we are participating in what could be called an "order of prayer." In this application, the word *order* refers to a fellowship, much like a fraternal club may be called an order. There is strength when we unite our faith in the prayer with others. The Lord said, "If two of you shall agree on earth as touching any thing that they shall ask, it shall be done for them of my Father which is in heaven. For where two or three are gathered together in my name, there am I in the midst of them" (Matthew 18:19–20).

Brother Truman G. Madsen emphasized the importance of unity in prayer as follows:

> Why is it that when a ward comes together in fasting and prayer, it makes a greater difference somehow than if anyone had done so alone? In part because such united efforts of the Saints are a testimony unto the heavens—a witness that Christ and his purposes take precedence over our hostilities and personality problems. The revelation says, "Be agreed as touching all things whatsoever ye ask" (D&C 27:18). Or again, "If ye are not one ye are not mine" (D&C 38:27). . . . The effectual, fervent power of united prayer cannot be overestimated. Powerful prayer unites the "Saints—unity expands the power of prayer."[86]

This kind of unity in prayer was experienced at a time of need for my wife's family. Her father was a WWII veteran who was injured while fighting in France in 1944. His leg was amputated, and about a decade later, he developed diabetes. The effects of the two maladies had a slow, deteriorating effect on his body. In later years, he reached a point where he could not wear his prosthetic leg or leave home. His greatest desire was to attend church. Calls went out to family, friends, and ward members to pray that he would be well enough to attend church. A week after these united prayers of faith, he was again wearing his prosthetic and attending church. The joy of the Saints who loved him was great as his friends and family recognized the tender mercies of the Lord in his behalf.

Inspiration in What to Pray For

The 2009 Book of Mormon institute manual says this regarding the prayer of Enos:

> Enos did not wrestle with God. The record states that Enos wrestled before God in prayer. Such wrestling is the struggle to find and express one's real desires under the inspiration of the Holy Ghost. Praying in this manner requires that a person eliminate vain, trite, or insincere repetitions and to pour the deepest desires of his or her heart into words. Each phrase becomes an expression of yearning and desire to do God's will. Such prayers are assisted and guided by the Holy Spirit, "for we know not what we should pray for as we ought: but the Spirit itself maketh intercession for us with groanings which cannot be uttered" (Romans 8:26).[87]

In his prayer, Enos requested things that appear to have been inspired by the Holy Ghost. After praying for himself and receiving confirmation of his own worthiness before God, Enos said, *"I began to feel a desire* for the welfare of my brethren, the Nephites; wherefore, I did pour out my whole soul unto God for them" (Enos 1:9; emphasis added). Enos struggled in the spirit for his people, but it appears that his desires for their future were restrained by that spirit, for the Lord responded, "I will visit thy brethren according to their diligence in keeping my commandments . . . wherefore, I will visit thy brethren according as I have said; and their transgressions will I bring down with sorrow upon their own heads" (Enos 1:10).

Next, Enos prayed for the Lamanites, asking, "If it should so be, that my people, the Nephites, should fall into transgression, and by any means be destroyed, and the Lamanites should not be destroyed, that the Lord God would preserve a record of my people, the Nephites; even if it so be by the power of his holy arm, that it might be brought forth at some future day unto the Lamanites, that, perhaps, they might be brought unto salvation" (Enos 1:13).

The response of the Lord was in agreement with this inspired request by Enos, for he added, "And I did cry unto God that he would preserve the records; and he covenanted with me that he would bring them forth unto the Lamanites in his own due time" (Enos 1:16).

The fact that the requests of Enos were aligned with the will and fore-knowledge of God is borne out by the remaining record in the Book of Mormon. We who know the end of the record can see that the Spirit was telling Enos what to pray for.

What follows in Enos's record is further validation that his pleas were inspired by the Holy Ghost. Enos wrote, "And the Lord said unto me: Thy fathers have also required of me this thing; and it shall be done unto them according to their faith; for their faith was like unto thine" (Enos 1:18). Enos's ancestral fathers, Jacob, Nephi, and Lehi, had faith similar to that of Enos, and thus the Spirit had filled them with the same desires, inspiring similar requests from them.

Enos's example of prayer teaches us that the best prayers are inspired prayers. They are prayers where our will becomes united with the will of the Father. The Bible Dictionary gives this description of prayer:

> Prayer is the act by which the will of the Father and the will of the child are brought into correspondence with each other. The object of prayer is not to change the will of God but to secure for ourselves and for others blessings that God is already willing to grant but that are made conditional on our asking for them. . . . We pray in Christ's name when our mind is the mind of Christ, and our wishes the wishes of Christ—when His words abide in us (John 15:7). We then ask for things it is possible for God to grant.[88]

In the New Testament, the Lord's Prayer includes the phrase, "Thy will be done" (Matthew 6:10), and the Savior's prayer in Gethsemane included the phrase, "Nevertheless, not my will, but thine be done" (Luke 22:42). Although Enos did not include a similar phrase in his prayer, his pleadings were aligned with the will of the Father. Enos prayed with such faith that he was completely in tune with the spirit, and his will became matched to God's, so that the words he prayed came to him through the Holy Ghost. Thus, his will was already God's will when he spoke those words. His approach was not, "I want one thing, but if You don't, then Thy will be done." It was, "My will is Thy will." Of course, there are times when it is appropriate to plead for our righteous desires but then acknowledge that they might not be God's will. Even Christ did this. But there are other times when we will be given to know God's will so we can make requests that are aligned with His purposes.

This same principle is seen in the prayers offered by the Nephite disciples of Christ during his visit to them after His Resurrection: "And it came to pass that when Jesus had thus prayed unto the Father, he came unto his disciples, and behold, they did still continue, without ceasing, to pray unto him; and they did not multiply many words, for *it was given unto them what they should pray*, and they were filled with desire" (3 Nephi 19:24; emphasis added). The Lord explained the same in our day, saying, "And if ye are purified and cleansed from all sin, ye shall ask whatsoever you will in the name of Jesus and it shall be done. But know this, *it shall be given you what you shall ask*; and as ye are appointed to the head, the spirits shall be subject unto you" (D&C 50:29–30; emphasis added). Other scriptures also affirm this approach.[p] Notice that a prerequisite for this type of prayer is that we must be "purified and cleansed from all sin." This had indeed occurred for Enos, as discussed earlier.

This approach of praying for things as directed by the Holy Ghost might also be called an "order of prayer," but in a different sense than the order of fellowship described earlier. This order of prayer is one where the words and desires of the prayer follow a specific order of transmission: from the Spirit, to us, and then to God. All petitionary prayers that follow this order will not only be granted, but they will also be spiritually nourishing to our souls. They will fill us with the Holy Ghost and make our will at one with the Lord's. This approach could be called the "true order of prayer."

The "true order of prayer" is a phrase that President Russell M. Nelson has used. He said, "Jesus taught us how [to pray]. We pray to our Heavenly Father, in the name of Jesus Christ, by the power of the Holy Ghost. This is the 'true order of prayer,' in contrast to 'vain repetitions' or recitations given to 'be seen of men.'"[89] This emphasis that the "true

---

p Related scriptures are (1) "If ye abide in me, and my words abide in you, ye shall ask what ye will, and it shall be done unto you" (John 15:7). (2) "For we know not what we should pray for as we ought: but the Spirit itself maketh intercession for us with groanings which cannot be uttered" (Romans 8:26). (3) "He that asketh in the Spirit asketh according to the will of God; wherefore it is done even as he asketh" (D&C 46:30). (4) "All things shall be done unto thee according to thy word, for thou shalt not ask that which is contrary to my will" (Helaman 5:10).

order of prayer" includes praying "by the power of the Holy Ghost" and without "vain repetitions" is consistent with the prayer model of Enos that teaches us to pray until we are filled with desires and with words born of the Holy Ghost.

I have experienced the blessing of specific direction during prayer. My wife and I have always prayed together beside our bed before retiring. One night, during one of these prayers, I felt an impression that one of our teenage sons had a concern. After the prayer, I said to my wife, "I think something is bothering Brad. I'm going to go talk to him." I went into his room where he was preparing for bed. We talked, and he expressed some concerns he was facing. I asked if he wanted a father's blessing. He said he would, so I dressed and gave him one, counseling him in ways that I felt inspired to do at the time.

It wasn't until many months later that I learned that there was more to this story than I had known. During a campfire testimony meeting at a Latter-day Saint Boy Scout encampment, Brad recounted his experience. He said that earlier in the day, as he struggled with his concerns, he wondered if he should ask for a father's blessing, but he wasn't sure if his worries were serious enough to warrant such a request. So he prayed to God, saying, "If I should have a blessing, please guide my father to offer me one." I am so grateful that my wife and I had established the proper prayer habits that put me in the frame of mind to be guided by the Spirit for the sake of my faithful son. The Lord had guided me, not only in what to pray for, but also in what action I should take to bring about the desired blessing.

Praying for things as inspired by the Holy Ghost may be the highest order of prayer. Such prayers may not occur frequently, but when they do happen, the results are memorable and often miraculous. Inspired prayers are a gift for those who are traveling along the covenant path.

BECAUSE OF THY FAITH IN CHRIST

After Enos prayed under inspiration for various groups of people, the Lord said unto him, "Whatsoever thing ye shall ask in faith, believing that ye shall receive in the name of Christ, ye shall receive it" (Enos 1:15). Enos responded with this short, emphatic declaration: "And I had faith" (Enos 1:16). What was this faith that was so powerful that it motivated God to promise answers to Enos's prayers? What was the power behind this faith that had led God to forgive Enos of his sins? When Enos asked how it was done, God replied, "Because of thy faith in Christ, whom thou hast never before heard nor seen" (Enos 1:8).

Faith in Jesus Christ brings power, and God knew that Enos had great faith in Christ, because He saw that Enos made and kept covenants with Him. After Enos pled with the Lord that the Nephite records would be preserved, he said that the Lord "covenanted with me that he would bring them forth unto the Lamanites in his own due time. And I, Enos, knew it would be according to the covenant which he had made; wherefore, my soul did rest" (Enos 1:16–17). Combining faithful covenant keeping with prayer will magnify the power of those prayers and prepare us to more often experience the joy of having the Spirit guide us in what to pray for.

If we can learn to pray like Enos did, then we will be prepared to enter into the presence of the Lord. Indeed, we will be able to declare, like Enos did, "And I soon go to the place of my rest, which is with my Redeemer; for I know that in him I shall rest. And I rejoice in the day when my mortal shall put on immortality, and shall stand before him; then shall I see his face with pleasure, and he will say unto me: Come unto me, ye blessed, there is a place prepared for you in the mansions of my Father. Amen" (Enos 1:27). We will then be ushered into the presence of God.

THREE GENERATIONS OF INSPIRED PRAYERS

The book of Enos contains a model of prayer that teaches many lessons. One of these, discussed earlier, is that the Holy Ghost can guide us in what to pray for. When this occurs, as the Bible Dictionary says, "our mind is the mind of Christ, and our wishes the wishes of Christ."[90] Most instances of this are usually subtle and simple; however, occasionally an experience of inspired prayer is so dramatic that it can affect the course of a life or even a nation.

When Enos prayed for the future survival of the Lamanites and their restoration to the truth, the Lord told him that his fathers had prayed for the same thing (see Enos 1:13–18). Three generations had desired family blessings that were inspired by the Holy Ghost, including Lehi (see 2 Nephi 4:3–7), Jacob (see Jacob 3:5–6), and now Enos. The same has been true in my own family where three generations have been inspired to pray in specific ways for blessings on their posterity. Following are three stories from my family history, each demonstrating prayers that were inspired by the Holy Ghost.

MY GRANDMOTHER'S INSPIRED PRAYER

During World War II, my Uncle Bud was drafted into the army and sent to the Pacific where he eventually found himself at the height of the war in the Philippines. His recently widowed mother would occasionally receive letters from him, but she usually knew little about where he was or what battles he might be in. Her stress for her soldier son was great. His younger brother, my father, wrote years later, "I well remember a very distraught mother who spent many hours in her bedroom, on her knees, praying for Bud's safety." She was a faithful Latter-day Saint mother who, bereft of her eternal companion, had only her Father in Heaven to give her comfort and guidance as she worried about the possibility of also losing her eldest son.

One night, after praying for all of her children and especially for the safety and protection of Bud, she went to sleep. She had a dream where she saw Bud dodging bullets while he was carrying something. She awoke, feeling that her son's life was in danger and that she should pray for him right then. She got out of bed, knelt, and prayed, earnestly pleading for his life. She continued praying until she finally felt at peace.

When Bud returned home, he verified the scene in his mother's dream. He had been a cook in charge of preparing food for the soldiers and then getting that food to them on the front lines. Since the kitchens were farther back from the fighting, he would form carrying parties from local Filipino volunteers who would work for food. They often had to traverse jungle terrain where enemy snipers lay in-wait for them. More than once, he narrowly escaped being shot.

Uncle Bud was grateful for the inspired prayers of his mother, which he believed saved his life. Later in life, he said of her, "My mother was a tremendous, tremendous person. That is one woman that anyone could be proud of—I was. She was a dear, dear lady. If everyone could just follow her footsteps! I have never seen a woman that was so religious, so honest, and reliable."[91]

MY FATHER'S INSPIRED PRAYER

In the mid-1970s, my family lived in Meridian, Idaho, where my father ran a furniture refinishing business in a shop behind our house. When my sister, Anne, was in her senior year of high school, she attended classes in the mornings and worked at a bank in the afternoons as part of a work-training program. She drove a battered, old, gold Chevy that my father had acquired for the teenage drivers in our family to use.

One evening as Anne was driving home, cruising at the posted speed limit with very little traffic around, a big, black truck, which was traveling toward her in the adjacent lane, suddenly turned directly in front of her, crossing her lane in order to enter a business at Anne's right. On her left was an irrigation ditch between the on-coming lane and a parking lot for a junior high school. Anne wrote of the incident:

> I slammed on my brakes but was going too fast, and I knew I would hit him HARD if I did not do something. I turned my car to the left, hoping to swerve and miss him—not knowing if there was any other traffic behind him. I was successful in missing him, but I was still going too fast and just kept going off the road. I jumped the ditch and somehow ended up in the parking lot of the junior high school. My engine died, but I was fine, outside of being shaken. The man in the black truck came running right over to me. He kept apologizing, telling me he did not see me at all. He admitted he was at fault and told me he would be happy to pay for any damages to the car. We walked around it, and I could not find anything that had changed. I got back in the car and started the engine, and it started right up. Everything seemed fine. The man gave me a slip of paper with his name and phone number. Nothing seemed to be harmed, so I saw no need to call the police.
>
> When I pulled into the driveway at home, Dad came out of his workshop immediately. This was odd because he usually stayed inside the shop and worked while his children would go about their activities. I thought, "How does he know what just happened?" I got out of the car and started to cry. Dad asked if I was all right. I nodded my head and proceeded to tell him the story. When I finished, Dad took me in his arms and hugged me close. He told me how grateful he was that I was not harmed.[92]

My father then told Anne his side of the story. When he had awakened that morning, he had a strong feeling that one of his children was going to be hurt badly that day. He said he got on his knees and pleaded with Heavenly Father to protect his endangered child from harm or accident. He had no idea which of his eight children was to come in harm's way, but it did not matter. He had been warned by the Spirit of an impending danger, so he knew what to pray for. He told Anne that he did not get up from his knees until he felt peaceful. Our entire family was grateful for a father who was in tune with the Spirit enough to receive that warning and who then prayed in faith until he received peace that all would be well.

MY OWN INSPIRED PRAYER

My daughter, Camilla, has always loved soccer. She grew up playing on recreational soccer teams with friends in our community. As they got older, some of her friends played in the more challenging travel soccer league, but she did not because it required Sunday play. The varsity high school soccer coaches were involved with the travel league, and if a girl did not play in that league, she was not likely to be selected for the varsity soccer team.

Camilla trained very hard in high school, and she was elated when she found her name on the varsity team roster her junior year. However, she wondered if she would get any play time when she learned that the only reason she had made the team was because some of the other girls on the team, including the team captain, had pressed the coaches to add her.

For the first three games of the season, Camilla sat on the bench, and she was getting discouraged. My wife and I were concerned for her and tried to encourage her. We prayed for her. The next game was on a Saturday morning at a town three hours away. We sent her off on a bus with her team and wished her well, sorry that we could not be with her. My thoughts were with her all morning as I worked on several projects at home. I hoped that her coaches would finally put her in the game that day. I feared what would happen to her self-esteem if she went one more game without any playtime.

Around noon, I was in my living room, working on some wiring behind my stereo system. Suddenly there came into my mind these words: "Pray for Camilla right now!" I felt a sense of urgency. I quickly looked at my watch and realized that her game must be in play right then. I was already on my knees, so I immediately bowed my head and prayed, asking that the Lord would impress my daughter's coaches to put her into the game. I knew that this high school soccer game was an insignificant event in the world right then, but I also knew that the personal development and boost of self-confidence that might come to my daughter from a positive experience on the soccer field that day *did* matter to Heavenly Father.

So I prayed earnestly that He would somehow impress her coach to give her some play time. I felt at peace and ended my prayer with gratitude for the blessings of being a father. I then continued my projects, anxiously awaiting Camilla's return late that afternoon.

When Camilla returned home, she cheerfully reported that she had gotten to play! Her team was down, one to three, with fifteen minutes left, when the coaches traded out many of the players and put her in. They ended up tying, four to four, with their final goal being made only ten seconds before the game ended. Camilla was thrilled! She had been a part of the turn-around. I asked her what time it had been when she was put into the game. It was just after I had prayed for her. She said that the assistant coach insisted on playing her. I knew that the Lord had found in that assistant coach a heart He could touch.

I am grateful for a loving Heavenly Father who even cares about teen-age soccer players. A sparrow "shall not fall on the ground without your Father [knowing it]. . . . Fear ye not therefore, ye are of more value than many sparrows" (Matthew 10:29, 31).

THE PRAYERS OF COVENANT PEOPLE

The above three stories are treasures to my family. They give modern-day examples of inspired prayers. Such occasions are not very common, but when they do occur, they are significant. They demonstrate that the faith and prayers of God's covenant people on earth have power, and that these prayers are often needed in combination with the powers of heaven in order to work miracles. By involving us in such miracles, the Lord strengthens our faith as we strive to follow Jesus Christ.

When we make and keep our covenants with God, He blesses us. Guidance in what to pray for is one of these blessings. Prayer is an important tool that we should use frequently as we follow the covenant path. We are blessed to have the book of Enos that instructs us on prayer. Through prayer, the Spirit will guide us as we follow the covenant path back to God's presence.

CHAPTER 6

JAROM:
FAMILY HISTORY RESEARCH

The underlying story of the Small Plates of Nephi is that of a family. It is a family history document. This is apparent in the first verse of 1 Nephi: "I, Nephi, having been born of goodly parents" (1Nephi 1:1). Even before this verse, Nephi wrote a summary heading that includes a brief description of his family: "An account of Lehi and his wife Sariah, and his four sons, being called, (beginning at the eldest) Laman, Lemuel, Sam, and Nephi" (1 Nephi heading). Nephi's heart was clearly focused on his family.

Jacob was also focused on his family. In the first verse of his book, Jacob mentioned both his father, Lehi, and his brother, Nephi. Likewise, Enos wrote of his father in the first verse of his book. All of these prophet record-keepers made a connection between themselves and their families, reminding us repeatedly of the importance of family ties and the connection between children and their parents.

Jarom did this as well, beginning his book with, "Now behold, I, Jarom, write a few words according to the commandment of my father, Enos" (Jarom 1:1). Then Jarom continued by using a word in his introductory verse that his predecessors had not used in their opening verses, adding, "that our *genealogy* may be kept" (Jarom 1:1; emphasis added).

Jarom's use of the word *genealogy* in the first verse of his book marks a shift in the narrative on the Small Plates. Jarom saw himself more distant from the first fathers, writing that "two hundred years had passed away" (Jarom 1:5) since Lehi had left Jerusalem. So, while Jarom did write about his own father, he would have only known the earlier Book of Mormon prophets through oral stories and the records they left. Yet, these other men were part of his genealogy—his family history.

One attribute that Jarom appears to have had in common with his ancestors was a testimony of the coming of the Savor. He wrote, "Wherefore, the prophets, and the priests, and the teachers, did labor diligently, exhorting with all long-suffering the people to diligence; teaching the law of Moses, and the intent for which it was given; persuading them to look forward unto the Messiah, and believe in him to come as though he already was" (Jarom 1:11). There is little else that stands out in the book of Jarom. At the onset, he declared, "I shall not write the things of my prophesying, nor of my revelations. For what could I write more than my fathers have written? For have not they revealed the plan of salvation? I say unto you, Yea; and this sufficeth me" (Jarom 1:2). In spite of this, Jarom did add, "And there are many among us who have many revelations. . . . And as many as are not stiff-necked and have faith, have communion with the Holy Spirit" (Jarom 1:4), but he gave no details about these spiritual matters. In fact, a unique characteristic of Jarom's record is that it says so little.

Perhaps the most important thing that emerges from the book of Jarom is that it documents that Jarom lived. The record is brief, and it appears that Jarom's life was not as remarkable as his direct ancestors, but his life obviously mattered to his son, Omni, and to others he lived with. His life also mattered to God. The key message apparent in Jarom's short book is that every member of our family tree matters to God, and each should also matter to us, their descendants. We should search them out in our family history and see that their temple work is done. The covenant path theme for the book of Jarom is family history research.

Connecting the Hearts of Fathers and Children

The final words recorded by the Prophet Malachi are "Behold, I will send you Elijah the prophet before the coming of the great and dreadful day of the Lord: And he shall turn the heart of the fathers to the children, and the heart of the children to their fathers, lest I come and smite the earth with a curse" (Malachi 4:5–6). Referring to this prophecy, the Prophet Joseph Smith wrote, "It is sufficient to know, in this case, that the earth will be smitten with a curse unless there is a welding link of some kind or other between the fathers and the children, upon some subject or other—and behold what is that subject? It is the baptism for the dead. For we without them cannot be made perfect; neither can they without us be made perfect" (D&C 128:18). Of course, we know that this applies not only to baptism but also to all temple work for the dead.

The writings of Jarom demonstrate that the hearts of fathers and children are connected. This same theme seems to extend into the first half of the book of Omni as well, where Omni, Amaron, Chemish, and Abinadom all write briefly about their family connections. In fact, in his first sentence, Omni used the same family history word his father used—genealogy. He wrote, "Behold, it came to pass that I, Omni, being commanded by my father, Jarom, that I should write somewhat upon these plates, to preserve our genealogy . . ." (Omni 1:1).

The brief records of the final writers of the Small Plates of Nephi are unique in all of scripture. It is easy to wonder what value these writers add to the canon; however, each one acknowledges his family ties. It appears that the Lord wants us to recognize that every family story includes lesser figures along with the prominent ones, and that the name of each is to be acknowledged in the eternal chain linking families together by covenant. Each person plays a role in his or her own family heritage. Each one is a precious child of God who will not be forgotten.

Concern for the Lamanites: Cousin Lines

Jarom was schooled in the prophecies and revelations of his fathers, and he knew that these prophecies included the eventual destruction of the Nephites, for he wrote of his people, "Behold, it is expedient that much should be done among this people, because of the hardness of their hearts, and the deafness of their ears, and the blindness of their minds, and the stiffness of their necks; nevertheless, God is exceedingly merciful unto them, and has *not as yet* swept them off from the face of the land" (Jarom 1:3; emphasis added).

Knowing that the Nephites would eventually be destroyed and that the record he was adding to would ultimately come forth to the Lamanites, Jarom wrote, "And as these plates are small, and as these things are written for the intent of the benefit of our brethren the Lamanites, wherefore, it must needs be that I write a little" (Jarom 1:2). It appears that Jarom was concerned about his future cousins. He knew that his own direct family line would eventually end, but he also knew that his broader family lines—through the Lamanites—would continue into the last days. He wanted these future cousins to enjoy the blessings of gospel covenants.

Just as Jarom was concerned for the spiritual well-being of his future cousins, we ought to be concerned for the spiritual well-being of our cousin ancestors and do family history research and temple work for them. Elder Neil A. Anderson taught about this kind of research, explaining, "When our [family history] chart appears complete, we help others find those in their lines and we find those closely related to those on our family tree. We call it 'finding our cousins.' "[93] Jarom's concern for the Lamanites validates this instruction.

Each Person Has a Story

When we do family history research, we often find very little information about a person. Sometimes we only have a few dates and locations. Other times, we might find a letter, obituary, or newspaper article that provides additional details. However brief, each document is treasured as a glimpse into the personality or experiences of an ancestor. Sometimes just a date can tell a story. If we see that a woman died young and that she had a baby on the same day as her death, we know she died in childbirth, and we mourn for her and her family.

This type of detective work can be demonstrated by analyzing the writings of the final authors of the Small Plates of Nephi. These men— Jarom, Omni, Amaron, Chemish, Abinadom, and Amaleki—each inscribed only brief statements, leaving very little information about who they were and what they were like. Yet, clues are there, half-hidden in the style of their writings.

Dr. Robert K. Thomas was an exceptional literary scholar and English professor at Brigham Young University for over thirty years. He wrote an article analyzing the different literary styles of writers in the Book of Mormon, including special mention of the final seven authors of the Small Plates of Nephi. His ability to see differences in the personalities of these writers based on their words is fascinating. He didn't have much to go on—barely over seven pages for these seven authors. In fact, some of these record-keepers wrote only one or two verses, yet the style of each is distinctive and tells its own story.

Dr. Thomas described Enos as an impetuous man, full of vitality, who used "imprecise, fragmentary" language. He wrote, "Enos simply

can't wait for logic to catch up with him. His words roll forth in an irre-
sistible flood. . . . His sentences all have a spoken quality, and their length
seems determined only by a need for breath."⁹⁴ Dr. Thomas then gave a
glimpse into the personalities of the six authors of the books of Jarom and
Omni:

> From Enos to his son Jarom is the shortest of genealogical steps but
> a gigantic shift in style. . . . [He writes] with such crispness . . . in coher-
> ent, beautifully modulated sentences. His diction too is precise. . . . the
> general denunciations of Enos are focused in Jarom. . . .
>
> From calm, exacting Jarom we come to Omni. At once we are struck
> by a focus on the first person. There are seven "I"s in two verses. Omni is
> a soldier, dutifully carrying out the command of his father but not a bit
> averse to identifying himself as a wicked man. . . . [His] reference to "serious
> war" . . . suggests the concern of a man to whom war is neither incon-
> sequential nor detestable. It's simply a vocation. Omni is forthright, not
> very reflective, and his sentences march briskly but to no great end.
>
> Amaron, Omni's son, is more like his grandfather, Jarom. He is care-
> ful, organized, and in a few verses manages to turn our attention from
> personalities to issues. Yet Amaron lacks Jarom's linguistic sensitivity.
> His sentences, unlike Omni's, are neatly balanced, but it is a mechanical
> neatness. Here is a style that tries to synthesize the no-nonsense approach
> of his father with the carefully controlled cadence of his grandfather.
>
> If Amaron is not quite successful, what shall we say of Chemish?
> Poor, dear Chemish! Possibly he didn't expect to have to take his turn at
> the records, since they usually went from father to son, but [he seems]
> overwhelmed by the responsibility that is suddenly his. . . . How clearly
> Chemish is given to us. Not in what is said about him, but in what he
> says about himself through his style. Just one verse, but in it the whole
> history of inadequacy. . . .
>
> It's a relief to pass on to Abinadom. But in reading his account I
> seem to detect a bit of insecurity. I suspect he's looked back to see what
> others have written. There are echoes of Omni and Jarom, but nothing
> else. At this point we have had four men write in a total of eleven verses.
> This is all we know of them, yet I feel I might recognize them on the
> street.
>
> The final nineteen, rather long verses are the breezy contribution of
> Amaleki. He just loves to write. He mixes exhortation with history in
> about equal amounts and stops only when he's used up all the space
> that remained on the plates.⁹⁵

Dr. Thomas was able to extract more information about the personalities of these seven men than is immediately obvious from the brief records they left behind. He describes these people from the Nephite family history in such a way that they become more genuine to us. We sense that they were real people with strengths and weaknesses who lived real lives. What's more, we recognize that each person in this family mattered. Even though the records they left behind are brief, they are all God's children, and He cares about each one.

We will be blessed if we look at our own family history research in the same light. Each person matters, and we can come to know our ancestors through minor clues in the few details we find about them. My wife has experienced this. By piecing together names and dates on several different census records for one ancestral line, she discovered a family where the wife had died, leaving her husband a widower with four children. He then fathered another child with a woman who had been listed previously as the family maid, after which he also died. This maid then married another man, and they adopted all of the orphans of the first family. These, of course, were half-siblings of the maid's first child, but no relation to the adoptive parents. What an interesting story found only from names and dates in census, marriage, and death records! We honor this maid and her husband for welcoming the orphans into their family, and we felt a connection to them as we did temple work for them all.

Elder Neil A. Anderson said, "There is something powerful in searching out someone who needs temple ordinances, learning who they are, and then being part of their receiving these sacred ordinances. This is how you become 'saviors on Mount Zion.' There is a joy and satisfaction that is only understood through spiritual feelings. We are linked to them forever."[96] Doing temple and family history work will connect us to our roots. Seeing what our ancestors faced will inspire us and give us strength to better face our own challenges. At some future time, they will thank us for giving them the opportunity to be a part of an eternal covenant family. This work will "turn the heart of the fathers to the children, and the heart of the children to their fathers" (Malachi 4:6).

HEALING FAMILIES

The analysis of Dr. Thomas helps us see some intergenerational differences in the authors of the books of Jarom and Omni. Omni was obedient to the command of his righteous father, Jarom, to maintain the family record, but he confessed, "I of myself am a wicked man, and I have not kept the statues and the commandment of the Lord as I ought to have done" (Omni 1:2). Yet, even though Omni considered himself to be wicked, his father's words show little compassion for the wicked. As noted earlier, Jarom wrote that there was much work to be done among his people because of their stiff necks, adding, "Nevertheless, God is exceedingly merciful unto them, and has not as yet swept them off from the face of the land" (Jarom 1:3). Jarom's statement sounds like he was disappointed that God had not yet punished the Nephites for their sins. Could an inflexible and abrupt nature in the father have contributed to the rebellion and self-proclaimed wickedness of the son? We don't really know, but if so, we hope that they reconciled, either in this life or the next, and we do proxy temple work for such people without judgment.

Many of us have ancestors who, because of the circumstances of their lives, had struggles with sin, but we still search them out and do temple work for them. We hope that they have accepted the gospel in the Spirit World and are able to make changes through the power of the Atonement of Jesus Christ while living in their third estate. Others lived good, respectable lives, following the light that was available to them during the time in which they lived. Regardless of their life stories, our duty is to give them each an opportunity to enter into covenants with God by providing saving ordinances for them in the temple.

Healing can come to those who take the brave step of doing temple work for a family member who died estranged from them. Such acts of service can result in deeply spiritual experiences filled with love and reconciliation. Sister Becky Beus shared an experience she had while serving as an assistant to the matron of the Boise temple:

> One day, while working in the temple, I noticed a young man sitting alone in the lobby, close to the matron's office. I saw that he had a family name slip. I went over and asked him if it was for someone from his own family. He said that it was for his father. I replied, "Oh, that will be wonderful!"
>
> He looked at me with a very sad face and said, "Well, he wasn't a very nice man, but I need to do the work." I tried to look supportive and nodded, but I imagined all kinds of things about this father.
>
> Later, after his session, I saw the young man again as he was leaving, but this time he seemed so happy. I looked at him in surprise and asked if it went well. He said, with big smile, "Oh yes. I don't know if he will accept it, but now I know I can forgive him."[97]

Doing temple work for his estranged father helped this young man to forgive and heal. It demonstrates faith in this passage from President Joseph F. Smith's vision of the Redemption of the dead:

> Thus was the gospel preached to those who had died in their sins, without a knowledge of the truth, or in transgression, having rejected the prophets. These were taught faith in God, repentance from sin, vicarious baptism for the remission of sins, the gift of the Holy Ghost by the laying on of hands, and all other principles of the gospel that were necessary for them to know in order to qualify themselves that they might be judged according to men in the flesh, but live according to God in the spirit. (D&C 138:32–34)

Not only can temple and family history work heal wounds caused by deceased family members, but it can also heal relationships among the living. Elder Dale G. Renlund related the story of a rift that had developed between two brothers who were Apostles, Orson and Parley Pratt. Engaging in work for their ancestors reunited them. Elder Renlund taught,

> Family history and temple work is not only for the dead but blesses the living as well. For Orson and Parley, it turned their hearts to each other. Family history and temple work provided the power to heal that which needed healing. . . . As we participate in family history and temple work today, we . . . lay claim to "healing" blessings promised by prophets and apostles. . . . The blessings of the temple . . . have a stunning capacity to heal. Temple blessings can heal hearts and lives and families.[98]

In reference to work for the dead, the prophet Joseph Smith wrote, "For we without them cannot be made perfect; neither can they without us be made perfect" (D&C 128:18). Temple and family history work helps with healing and perfection on both sides of the veil.

THE COVENANT PATH IS A FAMILY PATH

The covenant path themes for the first four books in the Small Plates of Nephi are topics that correspond directly to temple covenants and rituals. They correspond to steps that we need to take as we progress along the covenant path to God. The book of Jarom diverts us from that pattern briefly to remind us that we do not travel this path alone. We are connected to those who came before us and to those who will come after us. We take this path as families—families that need to be sealed together for eternity. The book of Jarom reminds us of the need to search out all who are in our family chain and then link them in through temple work. This is important because the covenant path is a path for establishing and strengthening families.

The time period spanned by the books of Jarom and Omni is about 270 years, yet we only have the names of the six record-keepers from that period. Similarly, as we research the names of our ancestors, the records for some will not be found. However, that is the reason God has planned for the Millennium when open communication between the spirit world and this earth will occur so that proxy temple work can be done for those who did not leave written records behind.[99] As Nephi wrote, "The Lord . . . inviteth them all to come unto him and partake of his goodness; and he denieth none that come unto him, black and white, bond and free, male and female; and he remembereth the heathen; and all are alike unto God" (2 Nephi 26:33).

The book of Jarom teaches us that every member of our family tree is important. The brief inscriptions by Jarom and those who followed him to the end of the Small Plates remind us that doing family history research and temple work for our ancestors is an important part of our journey along the covenant path to return to God's presence.

CHAPTER 7

OMNI AND KING BENJAMIN: CONSECRATION

At the end of the book of Omni, its final author, Amaleki, extended this invitation:

> And now, my beloved brethren, I would that ye should *come unto Christ*, who is the Holy One of Israel, and partake of his salvation, and the power of his redemption. Yea, come unto him, *and offer your whole souls as an offering unto him*, and continue in fasting and prayer, and endure to the end; and as the Lord liveth ye will be saved. (Omni 1:26; emphasis added)

What a beautiful description of consecration: "Come unto Christ . . . and offer your whole souls as an offering unto him." Even if we could find nothing more on the topic, this statement alone would be sufficient evidence to declare consecration as a subtheme of the short book of Omni. However, Amaleki gave us some clues of where to look for more on this topic—in the life and teachings of the most prominent leader of his day, King Benjamin.

The brief writings of Amaleki in the book of Omni include a short summary of the reign of two kings, King Mosiah I and King Benjamin, and Amaleki had personal interactions with the latter. He wrote, "And it came to pass that I began to be old; and, having no seed, and knowing king Benjamin to be a just man before the Lord, wherefore, I shall deliver up these plates unto him" (Omni 1:25). This transfer of the Small Plates probably occurred before the king gave his farewell speech. However, Amaleki had likely heard King Benjamin teach similar principles on other occasions and had been influenced by him, for in the next verse, Amaleki extended his invitation to offer our souls to Christ, and this invitation summarizes the essence of the life and teachings of King Benjamin.

Note these similar words that Mormon used to summarize the life work of this noble king: "King Benjamin, *by laboring with all the might of his body and the faculty of his whole soul,* and also the prophets, did once more establish peace in the land" (Words of Mormon 1:18; emphasis added). King Benjamin himself used a similar phrase in his famous speech to his people, saying, "Ye are eternally indebted to your heavenly Father, *to render to him all that you have and are*" (Mosiah 2:34; emphasis added). Both statements echo Amaleki's call to offer our whole souls unto Christ.

In addition, the life of King Benjamin and the things he taught in his final sermon teach much about the principle of consecration. Elder Neal A. Maxwell wrote,

> Benjamin is such a superb example of consecration. He did things with the "faculty of his whole soul" (Words of Mormon 1:18). . . . No wonder Benjamin urged us to be sufficiently consecrated to give all that we "have and are" (Mosiah 2:34). How appropriate that his sermon was given near a temple. . . . In King Benjamin's consecration, there was no holding back, and it must become the same with us.
>
> The spirit of consecration pervades the lines of King Benjamin's speech as he urges followers, for instance, "to render to [God] all that you have and are" (Mosiah 2:34), thus touching a raw and reminding nerve in each of us insofar as we hold back some of ourselves. . . .
>
> No wonder we are instructed by the Savior to lose ourselves (see Luke 9:24). He is only asking us to lose the old self in order to find the new self. This is part of what Benjamin's sermon is all about—to put off the natural man in order to come into our spiritual inheritance. So, it is not a question of losing one's identity but of finding it.[100]

The setting and outcome of King Benjamin's speech provide other clues that he was discussing a holy, covenant topic. Not only was it presented on temple grounds, but an angel dictated a large portion of the speech as well (see Mosiah 3:2). Also, it resulted in the people entering into a covenant with God (see Mosiah 5:5). This speech was sacred.

In addition, King Benjamin's sermon is framed by two references to consecration. At the beginning of his speech, King Benjamin said, "I have been chosen by this people, and *consecrated by my father,* and was suffered by the hand of the Lord that I should be a ruler and a king over this people" (Mosiah 2:11; emphasis added). And after the speech, the record states, "And again, it came to pass that when king Benjamin had made an end of all these things, and had *consecrated his son Mosiah* to be a ruler and a king over his people . . . they returned, every one, according to their families, to their own houses" (Mosiah 6:3; emphasis added). The placement of these two bookend references to consecration help us recognize that consecration is an important theme of King Benjamin's sermon.

If we take as a definition of consecration Amaleki's phrase, "Come unto Christ . . . and offer your whole souls as an offering unto him" (Omni 1:26) and then review King Benjamin's speech through that lens, we will discover many teachings that will enhance our understanding of consecration. We will see that consecration is the covenant path theme of the combined writings of Amaleki in the book of Omni and King Benjamin in the first six chapters of the book of Mosiah.

Preparing to Be Taught

King Benjamin instructed his son, Mosiah, to send out a proclamation so that the people would gather to hear their king. He said that his purpose was two-fold. The first purpose was to have the people witness the consecration and coronation of Mosiah as their new king. Second, he said, "I shall give this people a name" (Mosiah 1:10), and we later learn that this involved a covenant of taking upon them the name of Christ (see Mosiah 5:5–12). King Benjamin's speech was designed not only to motivate his people to take upon themselves the name of Christ, but also to take upon themselves the nature of Christ. Notably, when the people gathered, they were organized as families, in tents that faced the temple, and their king spoke from a tower erected on the temple grounds.

King Benjamin began his speech by instructing his people on how they could gain the most from what he was going to say. He declared, "I have not commanded you to come up hither to trifle with the words which I shall speak, but that you should hearken unto me, and open your ears that ye may hear, and your hearts that ye may understand, and your minds that the mysteries of God may be unfolded to your view" (Mosiah 2:9).

The Lord gave similar instruction to Oliver Cowdery: "Yea, behold, I will tell you in your mind and in your heart, by the Holy Ghost, which shall come upon you and which shall dwell in your heart" (D&C 8:2). King Benjamin's three-fold formula—open your ears, your hearts, and your minds—should be a guide for us each time we sit at the feet of the Lord's servants for instruction and each time we go to the temple. If we follow this formula, "the mysteries of God may be unfolded to [our] view."

King Benjamin added, "I have not commanded you to come up hither that ye should fear me, or that ye should think that I of myself am more than a mortal man. But I am like as yourselves, subject to all manner of infirmities in body and mind" (Mosiah 2:10–11). He wanted his people to feel comfortable in his presence and not make him out to be any better than any of them—he just had a different role. President Gordon B. Hinckley stated something similar after being ordained as prophet: "Your obligation is as serious in your sphere of responsibility as is my obligation in my sphere."[101] The humility of such leaders helps us to be receptive to instruction from the Spirit as we listen with our ears, our hearts, and our minds.

THE CONSECRATED GIVE SERVICE

King Benjamin reminded the people that many years earlier he had "been chosen by this people, and consecrated by my father . . . that I should be a ruler and a king over this people" (Mosiah 2:11). Immediately after this reference to his royal consecration, he began speaking of the service he had given, saying that he had been kept and preserved by the Lord "to serve you with all the might, mind and strength which the Lord hath granted unto me" (Mosiah 2:11). Clearly, he saw that his consecration brought with it an obligation to serve his people, but he did not stop there. He drew a connection between his service and the need for his people to serve one another. Starting with verse 11 of chapter 2, he used a form of the word *serve* fourteen times in eleven verses. In this portion of his speech, King Benjamin taught the following points about consecrated service.

Those who give consecrated service:

1. Serve without receiving payment for their service (see Mosiah 2:12).

2. Serve without being compelled to serve (see Mosiah 2:13).

3. Serve others while supporting themselves (see Mosiah 2:14).

4. Serve without concern for class distinctions (see Mosiah 2:14, 18).

5. Serve without being proud or boastful (see Mosiah 2:15–16, 25).

6. Serve God by serving others (see Mosiah 2:17).

7. Serve with gratitude for their own blessings (see Mosiah 2:19–20).

8. Serve while keeping the commandments (see Mosiah 2:13, 22).

9. Serve while recognizing God's support and blessings (see Mosiah 2:21, 24).

10. Serve to the end of their lives (see Mosiah 2:26).

Giving service to others is the essence of a consecrated life. This was made clear in King Benjamin's famous declaration, "When you are in the service of your fellow beings, you are only in the service of your God" (Mosiah 2:17). This is a remarkable statement. It is perhaps the most memorable, succinct, and inspirational statement on service in all of scripture. It was inspired by the Lord, who later taught the same principle when He said, "Inasmuch as ye have done it unto one of the least of these my brethren, ye have done it unto me" (Matthew 25:40). How can we better demonstrate to God that we have consecrated our life to Him than by serving His children? If God's work and glory is "to bring to pass the immortality and eternal life of man" (Moses 1:39), then the best way to show that we have consecrated our lives to Him is by helping Him achieve that work through serving our fellowmen.

President Marion G. Romney taught, "We lose our life by serving and lifting others. By so doing we experience the only true and lasting happiness. Service is not something we endure on this earth so we can earn the right to live in the celestial kingdom. Service is the very fiber of which an exalted life in the celestial kingdom is made."[102] With that understanding, it makes sense that a covenant of consecration would be included along the pathway to enter that kingdom, for giving service is one of the best ways to fulfill that covenant.

The fascinating thing about consecrated service is that it often benefits the person giving the service as much as it benefits those being served—sometimes even more. This is often the case with Church callings, as I came to learn for myself. When I was called as the leader over my ward's first-year scout patrol, I felt very inadequate. I had grown up in a small branch with limited scouting exposure, so I knew very little about scouting and was not excited about this new calling. But true to my covenant of consecration, I determined to do my best. I learned a new skill each week and then taught it to the boys. I also enrolled in BSA training—something rare in my stake at the time. I came to love the program, and new callings in scouting followed, each bringing more and more involvement. I found that my service not only blessed the young men I served, but it also filled a personal need through the relationships I developed with other adults in the program. Scouting has changed a lot since then, but I greatly benefited from the program when I agreed to serve others in spite of little experience.

WE ARE ALWAYS INDEBTED TO GOD

The fact that consecrated service blesses the server is a witness that we can never do enough to pay back God for all His blessings. King Benjamin taught that no matter how much you give, you are still indebted to God, for He "has created you from the beginning, and is preserving you from day to day, by lending you breath, that ye may live and move and do according to your own will. . . . And behold, all that he requires of you is to keep his commandments" (Mosiah 2:21–22). Yet, when you do, "He doth immediately bless you; and therefore he hath paid you. And ye are still indebted unto him, and are, and will be, forever and ever" (Mosiah 2:24).

The concept of unprofitable servants is pertinent today. In the economics of the modern world, if you don't produce, you won't remain employed for long. If an engineer isn't performing at a productive rate, he will soon find himself looking for a new job. Lawyers are under constant pressure to have sufficient billable hours. Service workers who don't perform are often quickly replaced. Each employee costs his company a lot of money, so each needs to bring more value to the employer than the cost of his or her salary and benefits. I learned this in my own professional career. I was employed in corporate America for only two years when the company I worked for announced a downsizing. Fortunately, I survived, but as I watched others who were not so fortunate lose their jobs, I determined that I needed to make sure I was always a profitable servant.

However, with God, we can never do enough to equal the value of what He gives us, which includes our lives and this earth with all its bounty. King Benjamin taught that even "if ye should serve him with all your whole souls yet ye would be unprofitable servants" (Mosiah 2:21). Yet that is precisely what he wants us to do. He wants us to give our "whole souls" in His service. He wants us to "to render to him all that you have and are" (Mosiah 2:34). He wants each of us to consecrate to Him our heart and our personal will. Elder Neal A Maxwell said,

> The submission of one's will is really the only uniquely personal thing we have to place on God's altar. The many other things we "give," brothers and sisters, are actually the things He has already given or loaned to us. However, when you and I finally submit ourselves, by letting our individual wills be swallowed up in God's will, then we are really giving something to Him! It is the only possession which is truly ours to give! Consecration thus constitutes the only unconditional surrender which is also a total victory![103]

Consecration is the greatest offering we can give to God. In fact, it is such a sacred covenant that it should not be entered into lightly. After teaching about service and our indebtedness to God, King Benjamin gave this warning:

> And now, I say unto you, my brethren, that after ye have known and have been taught all these things, if ye should transgress and go contrary to that which has been spoken, that ye do withdraw yourselves from the Spirit of the Lord, . . . the same cometh out in open rebellion against God. . . . Therefore if that man repenteth not, and remaineth and dieth an enemy to God, the demands of divine justice . . . doth fill his breast with guilt, and pain, and anguish, which is like an unquenchable fire, whose flame ascendeth up forever and ever. And now I say unto you, that mercy hath no claim on that man; therefore his final doom is to endure a never-ending torment. (Mosiah 2:36–39)

The Lord obviously has serious penalties for those who do not live up to the sacred truths and covenants they have been taught; however, notice that these consequences are for those who come out "in open rebellion" and who "repenteth not." They are not for those who sometimes fall short but keep trying.

On the other hand, King Benjamin taught, "And moreover, I would desire that ye should consider on the blessed and happy state of those that keep the commandments of God. For behold, they are blessed in all things, both temporal and spiritual; and if they hold out faithful to the end they are received into heaven, that thereby they may dwell with God in a state of never-ending happiness" (Mosiah 2:41). Consecration is designed to help us achieve that happiness. As Elder Neil L. Anderson has said, "The surrender of our will to God's will is, in fact, not surrender at all but the beginning of a glorious victory."[104]

Paying tithing is one of the commandments that help us demonstrate that we have consecrated both our personal will and our material means to God. Tithing requires faith when finances are tight, but those who keep this commandment "are blessed in all things, both temporal and spiritual." Paying fast offerings and contributing to worthy charities such as the Church's Humanitarian Aid Fund are additional ways we can show our consecration.

My own parents were never financially rich, but they loved the Lord and always paid their tithing. For most of my growing-up years, my father operated fast food drive-in restaurants—not a high-paying career. After all eight of us kids were in school, my mother got a job as a secretary at a hospital. Even with both of them working, my parents often had to juggle which bills they would not pay in a given month. I remember the first time my mother asked me if she could use some of the money I earned from mowing lawns to help buy groceries. We all had to help contribute to the family finances.

In spite of the financial hardships in our family, my parents continued to pay their tithing and fast offerings, and they never hesitated to help others in need. Somehow we got by, but we never really had any extra. Still, we felt blessed, even though the blessings were not financial. The most visible tithing blessings for my parents showed up in the lives of their children, who have always been faithful in the Church, earned college degrees, and became more financially secure in the next generation.

Elder Robert L. Simpson said, "The main purpose of tithing is not to build hundreds of buildings all over this world this year. The main reason for the payment of tithing is what happens inside the individual—what happens as the soul is sanctified, what happens as the blessings of heaven unfold upon one as those windows are opened wide."[105] My parents experienced this. Their example of always paying tithes and offerings with an attitude of consecration made their souls more Christlike.

JESUS CHRIST: OUR MOTIVATION FOR CONSECRATION

After speaking about service, King Benjamin declared a prophecy of the coming of Jesus Christ, foretelling of His life, mission, Resurrection, and Atonement. The words of this prophecy had been given to

King Benjamin by an angel who told him, "Behold, I am come to declare unto you the glad tidings of great joy" (Mosiah 3:3). The prophecy revealed many beautiful details about Christ to these Saints who lived about 124 years before His birth. King Benjamin declared,

> The Lord . . . shall go forth amongst men, working mighty miracles, such as healing the sick, raising the dead, causing the lame to walk, the blind to receive their sight, and the deaf to hear, and curing all manner of diseases. And he shall cast out devils, or the evil spirits which dwell in the hearts of the children of men. And lo, he shall suffer temptations, and pain of body, hunger, thirst, and fatigue, even more than man can suffer, except it be unto death; for behold, blood cometh from every pore, so great shall be his anguish for the wickedness and the abominations of his people. And he shall be called Jesus Christ, the Son of God, the Father of heaven and earth, the Creator of all things from the beginning; and his mother shall be called Mary. (Mosiah 3:5–8)

For us who have always had the New Testament with its four gospels documenting the life and mission of Jesus Christ, it might be hard to imagine the joy felt by the Nephites when they heard these details about Christ. No wonder the angel who gave these words to King Benjamin said, "The Lord . . . hath sent me to declare unto thee that thou mayest rejoice; and that thou mayest declare unto thy people, that they may also be filled with joy" (Mosiah 3:4). He later added that prophets were sent to teach these truths "that thereby whosoever should believe that Christ should come, the same might receive remission of their sins, and rejoice with exceedingly great joy, even as though he had already come among them" (Mosiah 3:13).

The revealed details of Christ's suffering, including the fact that blood would come from every pore as He took upon Him the "anguish for the wickedness and the abominations of his people," must have struck the people with awe and wonder. It probably also impressed Joseph Smith and Oliver Cowdery as they translated this, for these verses confirmed as reality a detail that Luke's record leaves vague—that Christ really did sweat drops of blood (see Luke 22:44). Later, Joseph and Oliver heard Jesus Christ himself confirm this same detail when He appeared to them in the Kirtland Temple (see D&C 19:18). King Benjamin's sermon provides one of three scriptural witnesses that Christ bled from every pore, each witness recorded in a separate book of scripture.

King Benjamin continued his prophecy of Christ by teaching his people about the Crucifixion and Atonement of Jesus Christ:

> And lo, he cometh unto his own, that salvation might come unto the children of men even through faith on his name; and even after all this they shall . . . scourge him, and shall crucify him. And he shall rise the third day from the dead; and behold, he standeth to judge the world. . . . For behold, and also his blood atoneth for the sins of those who have fallen by the transgression of Adam. . . . For salvation cometh to none such except it be through repentance and faith on the Lord Jesus Christ. (Mosiah 3:9–12)

King Benjamin continued his focus on the Atonement by explaining that the Israelites "were a stiffnecked people, and . . . hardened their hearts, and understood not that the law of Moses availeth nothing except it were through the Atonement of his blood." (Mosiah 3:14–15). In addition to these two instances, King Benjamin spoke of the Atonement of Jesus Christ three more times in this portion of his sermon, and he taught something new with each mention:

- "And even if it were possible that little children could sin they could not be saved; but I say unto you they are blessed; for behold, as in Adam, or by nature, they fall, even so the blood of Christ atoneth for their sins" (Mosiah 3:16).

- "Salvation was, and is, and is to come, in and through the atoning blood of Christ, the Lord Omnipotent" (Mosiah 3:18).

- "For the natural man is an enemy to God . . . unless he yields to the enticings of the Holy Spirit, and putteth off the natural man and becometh a saint through the Atonement of Christ the Lord" (Mosiah 3:19).

The king ended this portion of his sermon by speaking more about judgment, and he gave the following prophecy, again witnessing of the power of the Atonement of Jesus Christ: "The time shall come when the knowledge of a Savior shall spread throughout every nation, kindred, tongue, and people. And behold, when that time cometh, none shall be found blameless before God, except it be little children, only through repentance and faith *on the name of the Lord God Omnipotent*" (Mosiah 3:20–21; emphasis added). There is power in the name of Jesus Christ. King Benjamin was preparing his people to take His name upon them and to consecrate their hearts and souls to Him. He did this by centering his sermon on Christ and His Atonement.

The definition of consecration taken from Amaleki is very Christ-centered: "Come unto Christ . . . and offer your whole souls as an offering unto him" (Omni 1:26). However, Elder Bruce R. McConkie gave a different definition: "The law of consecration is that we consecrate our time, our talents, and our money and property to the cause of the Church: such are to be available to the extent they are needed to further the Lord's interests on earth."[106] Since the Church is Christ's kingdom on the earth, Elder McConkie's definition could be considered a practical application of the words of Amaleki. However, it does not remove Jesus Christ as the center of our motivation for consecration. His Church is just the vehicle of that commitment. Jesus said, "For where your treasure is, there will your heart be also" (Matthew 6:21; 3 Nephi 13:21). When our hearts are with Christ, it is no burden to consecrate our time, our talents, and all we possess to His Church and His purposes.

The people of King Benjamin were ready to turn their hearts and souls to Christ. They were motivated to do this because of the love they felt for their Savior when they learned of His life, His mission, and His Atonement. As covenant people, we likely feel the same: We are willing to enter into a covenant of consecration because we love our Savior, Jesus Christ. It is to Him that we offer our whole souls, including our time, talents, and everything we possess for the building up of His kingdom on the earth.

Put Off the Natural Man

King Benjamin's invitation to use the power of the Atonement to put off the natural man within each of us teaches more about consecration. King Benjamin declared,

> For the natural man is an enemy to God, and has been from the fall of Adam, and will be, forever and ever, unless he yields to the enticings

of the Holy Spirit, and putteth off the natural man and becometh a saint through the Atonement of Christ the Lord, and becometh as a child, submissive, meek, humble, patient, full of love, willing to submit to all things which the Lord seeth fit to inflict upon him, even as a child doth submit to his father. (Mosiah 3:19)

King Benjamin's statement is an appeal for each of us to surrender our agency to the Lord by becoming as submissive, meek, and humble as a small child. This is surely consecration. About two centuries later, Paul gave the Corinthians similar counsel, writing, "The natural man receiveth not the things of the Spirit of God: for they are foolishness unto him: neither can he know them, because they are spiritually discerned" (1 Corinthians 9:14). In words that sound like he had studied both King Benjamin and Paul, the author C. S. Lewis wrote,

> Christ says "Give me All. I don't want so much of your time and so much of your money and so much of your work: I want You. I have not come to torment your natural self, but to kill it. No half-measures are any good. . . . Hand over the whole natural self, all the desires which you think innocent as well as the ones you think wicked—the whole outfit. I will give you a new self instead. In fact, I will give you Myself: my own will shall become yours."[107]

That is what Christ wants. He wants us to give up the natural man and consecrate our all to Him. If we will do so with all our hearts, then our hearts will change and we will become like Christ. After hearing King Benjamin's speech, his people declared, "The Spirit of the Lord Omnipotent . . . has wrought a mighty change in us, or in our hearts, that we have no more disposition to do evil, but to do good continually" (Mosiah 5:2). They had truly put off the natural man and had become saints.

Becoming a saint has more than one level to it. At the first level, we become a saint when we become members of His Church through baptism. At this level, our status of being a saint refers to the community we have joined and the direction we are headed. However, the word *saint* also means to be *sanctified*—to be made holy. Achieving this higher level occurs when we put off the natural man or woman and consecrate our lives to Christ. And how is this achieved? King Benjamin said it: "Through the Atonement of Christ the Lord" (Mosiah 3:19). That is the power behind this mighty change of heart.

Consecration is the process of putting off the natural man. For King Benjamin's people, this apparently happened quickly. They were so moved by King Benjamin's speech and so motivated by the Spirit that their hearts were changed while in the presence of this Christlike king. However, for most of us, this process takes longer.

King Benjamin outlined some of the attributes that will help us put off the natural man and becoming a saint. He said that we must become "as a child, submissive, meek, humble, patient, full of love, willing to submit to all things which the Lord seeth fit to inflict upon him, even as a child doth submit to his father" (Mosiah 3:19). These six attributes (with triple mention of submissiveness) are all of the same tenor—they are synonyms to a degree. Yet, by stating each one in sequence, King Benjamin encourages us to consider different dimensions of what it means to consecrate ourselves to God. Elder Neal A. Maxwell was an avid scholar of consecration and delivered entire sermons on each of these characteristics. Included here are quotes by him about each.

As a Child

No wonder the divine direction is for each of us to "becometh as a child" (Mosiah 3:19). Such saintliness will sustain us as we cross our Sinai, including in those moments when we must "be still, and know that I am God" (Ps. 46:10). Such submissive stillness is necessary, because the process of consecration is not one of explanation. Only "after the trial of [our] faith" does the full witness come; meanwhile, often "a little child shall lead [us]" (Ether 12:6; Isa. 11:6).[108]

Submissive

Submissiveness . . . checks our tendency to demand advance explanations of the Lord as a perplexed yet trusting Nephi understood: "I know that [God] loveth his children; nevertheless, I do not know the meaning of all things" (1 Ne. 11:17). So did a wondering but submissive Mary: "And Mary said, Behold the handmaid of the Lord; be it unto me according to thy word" (Luke 1:38). Just as the capacity to defer gratification is a sign of real maturity, likewise the willingness to wait for deferred explanation is a sign of real faith and of trust spread over time.[109]

Meek

Meekness . . . is more than self-restraint; it is the presentation of self in a posture of kindness and gentleness, reflecting certitude, strength, serenity, and a healthy self-esteem and self-control. . . . Among the meek there is usually more listening and less talking. . . . The meek think of more clever things to say than are said. And it's just as well, for there is so much more cleverness in the world than wisdom, so much more sarcasm than idealism. . . . Meekness permits us to be prompted as to whether to speak out or, as Jesus once did, be silent. But even when the meek speak up, they do so without speaking down.[110]

Humble

Is there not deep humility in the omnicompetent Christ, the majestic Miracle Worker, who acknowledged, "I can of mine own self do nothing" (John 5:30)? Jesus neither misused nor doubted his power, but he was never confused about its source, either. Instead, we mortals—perhaps even when otherwise modest—are sometimes quite willing to display our accumulated accomplishments, as if we had done it all by ourselves.[111]

Patient

Patience is a willingness, in a sense, to watch the unfolding purposes of God with a sense of wonder and awe, rather than pacing up and down within the cell of our circumstance. . . . Patience permits us to cling to our faith in the Lord when we are tossed about by suffering as if by surf. When the undertow grasps us, we will realize that even as we tumble we are somehow being carried forward; we are actually being helped even as we cry for help. . . . Patience is . . . clearly not fatalistic, shoulder-shrugging resignation. It is the acceptance of a divine rhythm to life; it is obedience prolonged. Patience stoutly resists pulling up the daisies to see how the roots are doing.[112]

Full of Love

A fascinating thing about joy and love, with which you are surely familiar, is that when we enlarge our capacity to love, other people become real individuals, not merely functions. Gospel duties cease to be mere routine and become, instead, doors to delight. . . . Hear what [Brigham Young] says about love: "There is one virtue, attribute, or principle, which, if cherished and practiced by the Saints, would prove salvation to thousands upon thousands. I allude to charity, or love, from which proceed forgiveness, long-suffering, kindness, and patience" [*Journal of Discourses* 7:133–34]. A marvelous insight! Charity initiates and sustains all the other spiritual qualities in much the same way that courage sustains these qualities at the testing point.[113]

These characteristics, revealed to King Benjamin by an angel, serve as instructions to help us put off the natural man and become a saint, and they also describe attributes required for true consecration. If a person is going to be willing to do whatever the Lord asks of him, he must be "as a child, submissive, meek, humble, patient, full of love, willing to submit to all things which the Lord seeth fit to inflict upon him, even as a child doth submit to his father" (Mosiah 3:19). These are the opposite of pride. An attitude of consecration cannot exist in the presence of pride—they are incompatible. Abandoning pride and embracing these characteristics of saintliness will help us fulfill our commitment to consecrate our whole souls unto Christ.

President Ezra Taft Benson described what can happen if we turn our lives over to the Lord this way: "Men and women who turn their lives over to God will discover that He can make a lot more out of their lives than they can. He will deepen their joys, expand their vision, quicken their minds, strengthen their muscles, lift their spirits, multiply their blessings, increase their opportunities, comfort their souls, raise up friends, and pour out peace."[114] Such are the blessings of consecration.

A MIGHTY CHANGE OF HEART

King Benjamin's focus on the Atonement and putting off the natural man had a dramatic effect on his people. Initially, they were struck with fear at the thought of judgment and the consequences of their sins, but then they realized that they could be saved from those consequences through Jesus Christ:

> And they all cried aloud with one voice, saying: O have mercy, and apply the atoning blood of Christ that we may receive forgiveness of our sins, and our hearts may be purified; for we believe in Jesus Christ, the Son of God, . . . And it came to pass that after they had spoken these words the Spirit of the Lord came upon them, and they were filled with joy, having received a remission of their sins, and having peace of conscience, because of the exceeding faith which they had in Jesus Christ who should come. (Mosiah 4:2–3)

These ancient Nephites understood and embraced King Benjamin's message. Their focus on the atoning blood of Christ changed them. At the end of their king's speech, they declared,

> Yea, we believe all the words which thou hast spoken unto us; and also, we know of their surety and truth, because of the Spirit of the Lord Omnipotent, which has wrought *a mighty change in us, or in our hearts,* that we have no more disposition to do evil, but to do good continually. . . . And we are willing to enter into a covenant with our God to do his will, and to be obedient to his commandments in all things that he shall command us, all the remainder of our days. (Mosiah 5:2, 5; emphasis added)

These people wanted a covenant relationship with God. They promised to be obedient to His will for the remainder of their lives, but their changed hearts suggest they offered even more: It appears that they gave their whole souls to Jesus Christ. They would never be the same. King Benjamin responded, "Ye shall be called the children of Christ, his sons, and his daughters; for behold, this day he hath spiritually begotten you; for ye say that your hearts are changed through faith on his name; therefore, ye are born of him" (Mosiah 5:7).

Their covenant[q] came with a name—the name of Christ. "There is no other name given whereby salvation cometh; therefore, I would that ye should take upon you the name of Christ, all you that have entered into the covenant with God" (Mosiah 5:8), their righteous king said. He added, "I would that ye should remember to retain the name written always in your hearts, . . . that ye hear and know the voice by which ye shall be called, and also, the name by which he shall call you. For how knoweth a man the master whom he has not served, and who is a stranger unto him, and is far from the thoughts and intents of his heart?" (Mosiah 5:12–13). If we know our Master, then the desire of our hearts will be to serve Him. Covenanting to consecrate our souls to Him will then be an honor, not an obligation. When he calls, we will answer.

C. S. Lewis borrowed a parable from George MacDonald that describes this sort of change a person goes through when he offers his whole soul to God:

> Imagine yourself as a living house. God comes in to rebuild that house. At first, perhaps, you can understand what He is doing. He is getting the drains right and stopping the leaks in the roof and so on; you knew that those jobs needed doing and so you are not surprised. But presently He starts knocking the house about in a way that hurts abominably and does not seem to make any sense. What on earth is He up to? The explanation is that He is building quite a different house from the one you thought of—throwing out a new wing here, putting on an extra floor there, running up towers, making courtyards. You thought you were being made into a decent little cottage: but He is building a palace. He intends to come and live in it Himself.[115]

It seems that this is what had happened to the people of King Benjamin. They had turned over their whole souls to the Lord so that He could dwell therein. They were motivated to do this because they experienced a mighty change in their hearts when they truly comprehended the Atonement of Jesus Christ, repented of their sins, and entered into a covenant relationship with Him.

---

q Others have written about the covenant-making process demonstrated in King Benjamin's speech and parallels found in ancient Israelite covenants. A good summary by Taylor Halverson is "Mosiah 4–6: Children of Christ," *Interpreter: A Journal of Latter-day Saint Faith and Scholarship*, Apr. 12, 2016. See interpreterfoundation.org/res-mosiah-4-6-children-of-christ/.

We can likewise experience a mighty change of heart and cry out, "O have mercy, and apply the atoning blood of Christ that we may receive forgiveness of our sins, and our hearts may be purified" (Mosiah 4:2). We will then desire to form covenants with God, starting with obedience and culminating in a covenant of consecration: We will offer our whole souls unto Christ. When we do this we will likely experience the knocking out of walls and the throwing up of new wings and towers in our own lives. We cannot experience changes like this and not feel deep gratitude for and commitment to the Carpenter of Galilee. Our souls will then become places where Christ might dwell, and we will be like Him. As Elder Gerrit W. Gong has said, "When we covenant all that we are, we can become more than we are."[116]

COUNSEL FOR THE CONSECRATED

After King Benjamin's people had cried out, "O have mercy, and apply the atoning blood of Christ" (Mosiah 4:2), then "the Spirit of the Lord came upon them, and they were filled with joy, having received a remission of their sins, and having peace of conscience" (Mosiah 4:3). These people were humble and teachable, and King Benjamin knew they were ready to learn more. He loved them and wanted to prepare them for life ahead so that they would not lose the sense of commitment they felt that day. He addressed them as "My friends and my brethren, my kindred and my people" (Mosiah 4:4) and began to instruct them on steps they should take to ensure that they would remain faithful, saying, "This is the man who receiveth salvation through the Atonement" (Mosiah 4:7; see also verses 5–6). King Benjamin then elaborated and expanded on his counsel, declaring, "If ye do this ye shall always rejoice, and be filled with the love of God, and always retain a remission of your sins (Mosiah 4:12; see also verses 8–11).

King Benjamin's counsel is similar to principles taught by Amaleki. His invitation to offer our whole souls unto Christ is part of a larger description of what he said should be done in order to be saved (see Omni 1:25–26).

The teachings from King Benjamin and Amaleki can be combined into one overall formula which, if followed, will help us retain a remission of our sins so that we can be filled with the love of God and receive salvation—or, as we might say today, exaltation. These instructions could be called counsel for the consecrated:

1. Obtain a remission of your sins in the first place:

    a. "As ye . . . have received a remission of your sins, which causeth such exceedingly great joy in your souls . . ." (Mosiah 4:11).

    b. This implies being baptized and receiving the gift of the Holy Ghost, for these are necessary prerequisites to receiving a remission of sins (see 2 Nephi 31:17).

2. Come to know God and always remember Him:

    a. "If ye have come to a knowledge of the goodness of God, and his matchless power, and his wisdom, and his patience, and his long-suffering towards the children of men . . ." (Mosiah 4:6).

    b. "Believe in God; believe that he is, and that he created all things, both in heaven and in earth; believe that he has all wisdom, and all power, both in heaven and in earth; believe that man doth not comprehend all the things which the Lord can comprehend" (Mosiah 4:9).

    c. "As ye have come to the knowledge of the glory of God, or if ye have known of his goodness and have tasted of his love, . . . ye should remember, and always retain in remembrance, the greatness of God . . . and his goodness and long-suffering towards you" (Mosiah 4:11).

    d. "Come unto God, the Holy One of Israel" (Omni 1:25).

3. Engage the power of the Atonement in your life:

    a. "And also, [if ye have come to a knowledge of] the Atonement which has been prepared from the foundation of the world, that thereby salvation might come to him that should put his trust in the Lord . . ." (Mosiah 4:6).

    b. "I say, that this is the man who receiveth salvation, through the Atonement which was prepared from the foundation of the world for all mankind" (Mosiah 4:7).

    c. "Come unto Christ, who is the Holy One of Israel, and partake of his salvation, and the power of his redemption" (Omni 1:26).

4. Be humble and repent:

   a. "If the knowledge of the goodness of God at this time has awakened you to a sense of your nothingness, and your worthless and fallen state . . ." (Mosiah 4:5).

   b. "And again, believe that ye must repent of your sins and forsake them, and humble yourselves before God; and ask in sincerity of heart that he would forgive you" (Mosiah 4:10).

   c. "And [remember] your own nothingness, . . . unworthy creatures, . . . and humble yourselves even in the depths of humility" (Mosiah 4:11).

5. Keep the commandments:

   a. "And [if ye] should be diligent in keeping his commandments . . ." (Mosiah 4:6).

6. Develop the gifts of the spirit:

   a. "Believe in prophesying, and in revelations, and in the ministering of angels, and in the gift of speaking with tongues, and in the gift of interpreting languages, and in all things which are good" (Omni 1:26).

   b. See also 1 Corinthians 12 and D&C 46.

7. Pray daily and continue in fasting and prayer:

   a. "Calling on the name of the Lord daily . . ." (Mosiah 4:11).

   b. "Continue in fasting and praying" (Omni 1:26).

8. Steadfastly endure to the end:

   a. "And [if ye] continue in the faith even unto the end of his life, I mean the life of the mortal body . . ." (Mosiah 4:6).

   b. "And standing steadfastly in the faith of that which is to come, which was spoken by the mouth of the angel . . ." (Mosiah 4:11).

   c. "And endure to the end" (Omni 1:26).

King Benjamin continued by adding two more points that focus on our families and serving others (see Mosiah 4:14–26). The second of these he explicitly stated was required "for the sake of retaining a remission of your sins from day to day" (Mosiah 4:26).

9. Meet the needs of your family and teach them:

   a. "And ye will not suffer your children that they go hungry, or naked; neither will ye suffer that they transgress the laws of God, and fight and quarrel one with another" (Mosiah 4:14).

   b. "But ye will teach them to walk in the ways of truth and soberness; ye will teach them to love one another, and to serve one another" (Mosiah 4:15).

10. Be kind and serve those in need:

   a. "And ye will not have a mind to injure one another, but to live peaceably, and to render to every man according to that which is his due" (Mosiah 4:13).

   b. "Ye yourselves will succor those that stand in need of your succor; ye will administer of your substance unto him that standeth in need" (Mosiah 4:16).

   c. "I would that ye should impart of your substance to the poor . . . feeding the hungry, clothing the naked, visiting the sick and administering to their relief, both spiritually and temporally, according to their wants" (Mosiah 4:26).

It is important to realize whom King Benjamin was talking about when he said that his people should "come to the knowledge of the glory of God . . . [and] remember, and always retain in remembrance, the greatness of God" (Mosiah 4:11). He earlier described God as "the Lord Omnipotent who reigneth, who was, and is from all eternity to all eternity, shall come down from heaven among the children of men, and shall dwell in a tabernacle of clay" (Mosiah 3:5). So while it is always good to remember God the Father, it is Jesus Christ whom we are specifically commanded to always remember. The sacrament, scripture reading, and prayer help us remember Them both.

Although enduring to the end is one of the ten points, it can also be considered as the umbrella doctrine under which all the other points combine. In fact, there are many similarities between these points and the process of enduring to the end as outlined in 2 Nephi. Both sets of counsel align with the sacrament, scriptures, and prayer. However, the counsel of King Benjamin and Amaleki expands on what Nephi taught. We should not only have faith in Jesus Christ, but we should also engage the power of His Atonement in our lives. We should not only follow the guidance of the Holy Ghost, but we should also develop the gifts of the Spirit. We should not only pray, but we should combine it with fasting. We should not only help our fellow Saints according to the law of the gospel, but we should also succor any around us who are in need and teach our families to do the same.

King Benjamin and Amaleki seem to be saying that consecration requires that we walk in a higher level of spirituality. It appears that the principles taught in 2 Nephi as part of the law of the gospel teach us how to qualify for salvation in the next life, and the principles taught by King Benjamin and Amaleki as part of the law of consecration add to that instruction by teaching how to achieve sanctification in this life while preparing for exaltation as families in the next.

We can see that the Lord has two levels of instruction. The first is preparatory for the second, much like the Aaronic Priesthood is preparatory for the Melchizedek. In fact, the law of obedience and sacrifice and the law of the gospel could be said to pertain to the Aaronic Priesthood and the keys of salvation, while the law of chastity and the law of consecration, along with eternal marriage, could be said to pertain to the Melchizedek Priesthood and the keys of exaltation (see D&C 132:15–17). Indeed, the ritual sacrifices performed before Christ, and the sacrament after Christ are both administered through the Aaronic Priesthood, and the Melchizedek Priesthood is required for temple marriage, which is part of exaltation.

We are blessed to have the ordinance of the sacrament to help us stay on the path toward both salvation and exaltation. The sacrament is not only a renewal of the law of the gospel; it is also a renewal of the law of consecration, because it recommits our souls to Christ. It also helps us renew our commitment to the law of sacrifice by remembering Christ's sacrifice, and it renews the laws of obedience and chastity when we promise to keep the commandments. As Elder Delbert L. Stapley said, "By partaking of the sacrament, we renew all covenants entered into with the

Lord."[117] The instructions of Amaleki and King Benjamin align with this. They are wise counsel for those who seek to live the law of consecration as a culmination of the other commitments along the covenant path. King Benjamin would likely say to us, as he said to his people, "And now, if you believe all these things see that ye do them" (Mosiah 4:10).

Consecration and Families

As already noted, King Benjamin described those who would retain a remission of their sins as having the following characteristics of righteous parenting. His statement is both a description and a directive, giving guidance to consecrated parents of the covenant:

> And ye will not suffer your children that they go hungry, or naked; neither will ye suffer that they transgress the laws of God, and fight and quarrel one with another, and serve the devil, who is the master of sin, or who is the evil spirit which hath been spoken of by our fathers, he being an enemy to all righteousness. But ye will teach them to walk in the ways of truth and soberness; ye will teach them to love one another, and to serve one another. (Mosiah 4:14–15)

At first, this seems like good, basic advice on parenting fundamentals: Parents have a responsibility to provide for the physical and spiritual needs of their children, training them up in righteousness. However, considering the context of King Benjamin's speech, perhaps he was also saying, "Don't let your new found zeal lead you to neglect your families."

King Benjamin was speaking to people who were so overcome by his spiritual message that "they had fallen to the earth, for the fear of the Lord had come upon them" (Mosiah 4:1). They had experienced a significant spiritual awakening and a mighty change of heart. All of these feelings and desires are right and good, but they come with a risk for those who are not spiritually mature. The risk is that a person might begin to focus so much on building the kingdom of God that he neglects his own family. Doing so would negate the whole purpose of the covenant of consecration. We commit to the law of consecration because it is one of the steps along the covenant path leading to the celestial kingdom, but what good would it be to attain that without our loved ones beside us? The celestial kingdom is meant for families.

Sometimes members of the Church are so committed to their callings and to building the kingdom of God that they inadvertently neglect their families. This is not the proper order of things. King Benjamin said, "And see that all these things are done in wisdom and order; for it is not requisite that a man should run faster than he has strength. And again, it is expedient that he should be diligent, that thereby he might win the prize; therefore, all things must be done in order" (Mosiah 4:27).

Finding a proper balance is important. If many people were to refuse callings because they wanted to focus only on their families, their own spiritual growth would be curtailed, their children's testimonies would be weakened, and the kingdom of God would not grow. On the other hand, a person must not give so much time and effort to callings that he or she neglects both spouse and children. It is good to remember that caring for our families is an important part of building the kingdom. We must use the Holy Ghost to guide us in these matters.

My own personality is such that I frequently have to remind myself of this need for balance. Early in my marriage, I was called to serve as a stake missionary. At the time, stake missionaries were encouraged to spend twenty hours a week in missionary work on top of meeting the needs of our family and employment. I loved missionary work and was diligent in my duties, usually doing missionary work one or two evenings a week plus weekends. My calling included being secretary in our stake mission presidency, so I attended a monthly stake mission coordination meeting with our stake presidency, the stake mission presidency, the full-time mission president, his assistants, and the zone leaders for our stake.

Each month, I prepared a report of the work of all the stake missionaries in our fifteen-unit stake and presented it at this meeting. This was in the days before email, and it took a lot of time, but I was honored to be involved with so many good leaders whom I respected. They appreciated my work, and I have to admit that I became more than a little caught up in the validation I received as I diligently put my entire consecrated soul into my calling.

One evening, as I hurried to change clothes and eat a quick supper before heading out to another stake coordination meeting, I could sense that my wife was upset. She needed to talk, and now was the time. I took off my suit coat and sat down beside her. She explained that she didn't resent that I was going to go do this service, but she resented how much I *wanted* to go. She didn't see any regret on my part when I had to leave my family. I realized that she was right—I was so caught up in the validation of these brethren that my heart was not in the right place. My service for the Lord had turned into service *for me*. The experience was a wake-up call, and I recommitted my heart to my wife and our family. Before long, she was encouraging me to get going to my meeting. I was probably only twenty minutes late that evening, but it was the most consecrated time I ever spent not doing my presumed duty.

That experience greatly impacted me and helped me remember to strive to be aware of the needs of my family while continuing to serve diligently in my callings. Perhaps this is what King Benjamin desired when he admonished his people to not neglect their families in the midst of his talk that emphasized service: "And see that all these things are done in wisdom and order" (Mosiah 4:27).

SUCCOR THOSE THAT STAND IN NEED OF SUCCOR

King Benjamin also taught how his people should treat one another. Again, he was addressing a group of Saints at the temple, so his counsel was directed to the consecrated. He said, "And ye will not have a mind to injure one another, but to live peaceably, and to render to every man according to that which is his due" (Mosiah 4:13). If our souls are consecrated to God, we will be honest in all of our dealings with others and will not say hurtful things or otherwise injure one another.

As noted earlier, King Benjamin also said that those who wish to retain a remission of their sins should help and serve those in need. He admonished,

> And also, ye yourselves will succor those that stand in need of your succor; ye will administer of your substance unto him that standeth in need; and ye will not suffer that the beggar putteth up his petition to you in vain, and turn him out to perish. . . .
>
> And now, . . . for the sake of retaining a remission of your sins from day to day, that ye may walk guiltless before God—I would that ye should impart of your substance to the poor, every man according to that which he hath, such as feeding the hungry, clothing the naked, visiting the sick and administering to their relief, both spiritually and temporally, according to their wants. (Mosiah 4:16, 26)

It is no wonder that under President Thomas S. Monson the Church added "caring for the poor and needy" to the description of its mission or purpose.[118] It is an essential characteristic of those who will attain exaltation.

In a talk about personal conversion, Elder Robert J. Whetten quoted Mosiah 4:26 and asked, "Do you administer spiritual or temporal relief to those who need it? Do you reach out and strengthen the faith of those coming into the fold, as asked by the prophets of our day? Conversion means consecrating your life to caring for and serving others who need your help and sharing your gifts and blessings."[119] Consecration through serving others was where King Benjamin had begun his sermon, and he returned to it at the end.

King Benjamin recognized that his audience included both rich and poor Saints, so he gave customized counsel for each group. After instructing them all to succor the needy, he said to the rich:

> Perhaps thou shalt say: The man has brought upon himself his misery; therefore I will stay my hand, and will not give unto him of my food, nor impart unto him of my substance that he may not suffer, for his punishments are just—But I say unto you, O man, whosoever doeth this the same hath great cause to repent. . . . For behold, are we not all beggars? Do we not all depend upon the same Being, even God, for all the substance which we have? (Mosiah 4:17–19)

That might hit close to home. Many of us have sometimes felt this way toward those in need—that they brought their misery upon themselves, and if they would just be a little more ambitious, maybe they could obtain what they need. However, remembering the counsel of King Benjamin will help us respond in a more generous manner.

King Benjamin had separate counsel for the poor. To them, he admonished,

> And again, I say unto the poor, ye who have not and yet have sufficient, that ye remain from day to day; I mean all you who deny the beggar, because ye have not; I would that ye say in your hearts that: I give not because I have not, but if I had I would give. And now, if ye say this in your hearts ye remain guiltless, otherwise ye are condemned; and your condemnation is just for ye covet that which ye have not received. (Mosiah 4:24–25)

This is wise counsel for those "who have not and yet have sufficient" or who have a sense of entitlement that leads them to "covet that which ye have not received." However, problems arise when the rich tell the poor what they need to do, and the poor tell the rich what they need to do. Each should follow the counsel that applies to himself or herself and not tell others how to behave. Only a bishop has the appropriate keys to give specific direction to others on such matters.

King Benjamin tempered his instruction to succor others with these words, which were applied earlier to families but apply even more directly here: "And see that all these things are done in wisdom and order; for it is not requisite that a man should run faster than he has strength. And again, it is expedient that he should be diligent, that thereby he might win the prize; therefore, all things must be done in order" (Mosiah 4:27). Consecration does not mean we should give away all we possess and live in poverty. We are to share and to serve, but living the law of consecration requires wisdom and guidance from the Holy Ghost.

Consecration Is Related to Other Laws

Because consecration so often involves succoring, serving, and giving, it is apparent that the law of consecration is closely related to the law of sacrifice. The difference is in the timing of the offering. Sacrifice often occurs in response to an unexpected and difficult need—something we didn't plan for but are willing to do because it achieves some greater good. But when something is consecrated, it is set aside as an offering to the Lord before it is asked for. So when He calls upon us to give that which we have already consecrated, it is not considered a sacrifice, for it was already appropriated for the Lord's purposes. With consecration, there is often little sense of sacrifice felt at the moment of need because what is required has already been promised. Sacrifice is reactive, whereas consecration is proactive.

However, sometimes a consecrated offering is so immense that a sacrifice is still required at the time the offering is called for. The Savior's Atonement and Crucifixion fall into this category. His commitment to suffer for our sins and give His innocent life so that we can be resurrected was a consecration that began in the early councils before the world was created, when He declared, "Here am I, send me" (Moses 4:1). This is one reason why King Benjamin's people and others who lived before Christ could access the power of His Atonement before it occurred. The premortal Christ had already consecrated His life, by covenant, for their salvation—a covenant whose fulfillment was certain. But this does not mean His offering was not a sacrifice. When His consecrated offering was called for, it was still the greatest sacrifice the world has ever known. Likewise, we might experience feelings of sacrifice when the Lord calls for something from us that we have already consecrated to Him. If so, this can be an opportunity to think upon the consecrated life of our Savior and the sacrifice He experienced through His Atonement and Crucifixion.

The law of consecration is also related to the law of the gospel. The law of the gospel requires that we help our fellow Saints. We do this by serving them, offering emotional support, and sharing our consecrated means with them as needed. So the law of consecration has a connection to both the law of the gospel and the law of sacrifice.

A Consecration Story

Classic literature often teaches Christian principles in creative ways. By creating realistic characters and an interesting plot, a skilled and inspired author can teach gospel truths in such a way that many people may not recognize that they are being taught about Jesus Christ and the principles He taught. However, the astute, faithful reader will see parallels that teach and edify.

Uncle Tom's Cabin is an anti-slavery novel written by Harriet Beecher Stowe and first published in 1852. The novel had a huge impact on nineteenth century America, strengthening the anti-slavery sentiment in the years leading up to the Civil War. Its social characterizations and style are now considered somewhat outdated, causing the novel to fall out of favor in many circles today. Its many Biblical references and strong Christian influence have probably also contributed to its fall from grace in the modern world, but in the mid-1800s, when those values were widely espoused in America, the novel raised social awareness about the evils of slavery and its impact on families.

The novel includes a segment in which Tom, the lead character, beautifully demonstrates an attitude of consecration and enduring to the end. He was able to show kindness in the face of hardship by focusing on the sacrifice and Atonement of Jesus Christ.

Tom was a slave who came under the evil command of a wicked master, Simon Legree. Mr. Legree managed to debase Tom to a point of almost breaking him, but then Tom had a sacred experience wherein he had a vision of the Lord. It changed him. Harriet Beecher Stowe told the story as follows:

Tom sat, like one stunned, at the fire. Suddenly everything around him seemed to fade, and a vision rose before him of one crowned with thorns, buffeted and bleeding. Tom gazed, in awe and wonder, at the majestic patience of the face; the deep, pathetic eyes thrilled him to his inmost heart; his soul woke, as, with floods of emotion, he stretched out his hands and fell upon his knees,—when, gradually, the vision changed: the sharp thorns became rays of glory; and, in splendor inconceivable, he saw that same face bending compassionately towards him, and a voice said, "He that over-cometh shall sit down with me on my throne, even as I also overcame, and am set down with my Father on his throne."

How long Tom lay there, he knew not. When he came to himself, the fire was gone out, his clothes were wet with the chill and drenching dews; but the dread soul-crisis was past, and, in the joy that filled him, he no longer felt hunger, cold, degradation, disappointment, wretchedness. From his deepest soul, he that hour loosed and parted from every hope in the life that now is, and offered his own will an unquestioning sacrifice to the Infinite.[120]

Tom "offered his own will an unquestioning sacrifice to the Infinite." That sounds very much like Amaleki's invitation to "offer your whole souls as an offering unto [Christ]" (Omni 1:26). Tom, a slave, had nothing to give his Savior but his heart, his soul, his will—and those he freely gave. He fulfilled Elder Neal A. Maxwell's description of consecration: "The submission of one's will . . . is the only possession which is truly ours to give! Consecration thus constitutes the only unconditional surrender which is also a total victory!"[121]

The effect that came upon Tom from this focus on Jesus Christ was just such a victory. It was transformative. Mrs. Stowe wrote of Tom:

When the dim gray of dawn woke the slumberers to go forth to the field, there was among those tattered and shivering wretches one who walked with an exultant tread; for firmer than the ground he trod on was his strong faith in Almighty, eternal love. Ah, Legree, try all your forces now! Utmost agony, woe, degradation, want, and loss of all things, shall only hasten on the process by which he shall be made a king and a priest unto God!

From this time, an inviolable sphere of peace encompassed the lowly heart of the oppressed one,—an ever-present Saviour hallowed it as a temple. Past now the bleeding of earthly regrets; past its fluctuations of hope, and fear, and desire; the human will, bent, and bleeding, and struggling long, was now entirely merged in the Divine. So short now seemed the remaining voyage of life,—so near, so vivid, seemed eternal blessedness,—that life's uttermost woes fell from him unharming.

All noticed the change in his appearance. Cheerfulness and alertness seemed to return to him, and a quietness which no insult or injury could ruffle seemed to possess him.[122]

Consecration had changed Tom. It prepared him to be made a king and a priest unto God (see Rev 1:6). Legree became bothered by Tom's attitude and suspicious of his motives. He went to the slave quarters one night and, upon hearing Tom sing an old Methodist Hymn, Legree beat Tom again. "But the blows fell now only on the outer man, and not, as before, on the heart. Tom stood perfectly submissive; and yet Legree could not hide from himself that his power over his bond thrall was somehow gone."[123]

Tom's submissiveness was like Christ's example of submissiveness when He was beaten and mocked (see Matthew 27:26–31). Tom had been changed: He was a new creature. And what was the effect of the transformation? He used his new, lighter heart to lift those around him who were burdened. It seems that the Spirit taught him the same principle that King Benjamin had taught when he said, "When ye are in the service of your fellow men, ye are only in the service of your God" (Mosiah 2:17). Harriet Beecher Stowe described the effect on Tom in these words:

> Tom's whole soul overflowed with compassion and sympathy for the poor wretches by whom he was surrounded. To him it seemed as if his life-sorrows were now over, and as if, out of that strange treasury of peace and joy, with which he had been endowed from above, he longed to pour out something for the relief of their woes. It is true, opportunities were scanty; but, on the way to the fields, and back again, and during the hours of labor, chances fell in his way of extending a helping-hand to the weary, the disheartened and discouraged. The poor, worn-down, brutalized creatures, at first, could scarce comprehend this; but, when it was continued week after week, and month after month, it began to awaken long-silent chords in their benumbed hearts. Gradually and imperceptibly the strange, silent, patient man, *who was ready to bear every one's burden*, and sought help from none,— who stood aside for all, and came last, and took least, yet was foremost to share his little all with any who needed,—the man who, in cold

nights, would give up his tattered blanket to add to the comfort of some woman who shivered with sickness, and who filled the baskets of the weaker ones in the field, at the terrible risk of coming short in his own measure,—and who, though pursued with unrelenting cruelty by their common tyrant, never joined in uttering a word of reviling or cursing,—this man, at last, began to have a strange power over them; and, when . . . they were allowed again their Sundays for their own use, many would gather together to hear from him of Jesus.[124]

Like Uncle Tom, if we give our whole souls to God through a covenant of consecration, then we, too, can be filled with joy and peace in spite of the difficult circumstances of our lives. In His great intercessory prayer, Jesus said, "And this is life eternal, that they might know thee the only true God, and Jesus Christ, whom thou hast sent" (John 17:3). Tom experienced this. He exemplified the following statement by Elder Neal A. Maxwell:

> One of the last, subtle strongholds of selfishness is the natural feeling that we "own" ourselves. Of course we are free to choose and are personally accountable. Yes, we have individuality. But those who have chosen to "come unto Christ" soon realize that they do not "own" themselves. Instead, they belong to Him. We are to become consecrated along with our gifts, our appointed days, and our very selves. Hence, there is a stark difference between stubbornly "owning" oneself and submissively belonging to God. Clinging to the old self is not a mark of independence, but of indulgence![125]

Consecration: An Important Step in the Covenant Path

King Benjamin taught much about the law of consecration. He taught the importance of giving service, and he emphasized our perpetual indebtedness. He taught his people about the life, mission, and Atonement of Jesus Christ so that they would be motivated to consecrate their lives to Him through obedience. He encouraged them and us to put off the natural man by acquiring the characteristics of saintliness. He taught principles that help us, as consecrated members of the Church, make sure we will always retain a remission of our sins and receive exaltation. He also taught that we should meet the needs of our own families and succor the poor. These are all important aspects of consecrating our souls to Christ and to the building up of His kingdom.

Of course, King Benjamin's speech is not exclusively about consecration. Nevertheless, studying his speech along with the admonition of Amaleki through the lens of consecration can increase our understanding of this covenant principle and teach us how to live it. Consecration is an important step in the covenant path to return to God's presence. It will help us fulfill the following plea given by King Benjamin:

> I say unto you, I would that ye should remember to retain the name written always in your hearts, that ye are not found on the left hand of God, but that ye hear and know the voice by which ye shall be called, and also, the name by which he shall call you. For how knoweth a man the master whom he has not served, and who is a stranger unto him, and is far from the thoughts and intents of his heart? . . .
>
> Therefore, I would that ye should be steadfast and immovable, always abounding in good works, that Christ, the Lord God Omnipotent, may seal you his, that you may be brought to heaven, that ye may have everlasting salvation and eternal life, through the wisdom, and power, and justice, and mercy of him who created all things, in heaven and in earth, who is God above all. Amen. (Mosiah 5:12–13, 15)

May this be the desire of us all—to be sealed as one of Christ's own with His name always written in our hearts. This is what King Benjamin's people achieved. They not only took upon themselves the name of Christ, but they also acquired the nature of Christ after experiencing a mighty change in their hearts. This is also what Amaleki taught in the book of Omni when he invited all to "Come unto Christ . . . and offer your whole souls as an offering unto him" (Omni 1:26). This is consecration. It is an important step on the covenant path to God.

CHAPTER 8

CHRIST AND COVENANTS

W hen I was a young man, I was shown an illustration of an old, haggled, toothless woman with a broad hook nose, her coat pulled up to her chin, and her head covered with a scarf. At least, that is what I thought it was a picture of. It was shown as part of an object lesson in my seminary class, and others in the class saw something different. They saw the profile of a pretty, young woman, with a slender face and a choker necklace, looking like she was dressed up for some fancy event. I could not see the younger woman. I could only see the old woman. It wasn't until others pointed out to me the specific features of the young woman that I could finally see her clearly. Now, whenever I see this picture, I can see both women in the same illustration. In fact, some days the second perspective stands out over the first.

Young Girl-Old Woman Illusion[126]

The same is true with my perspective of the Small Plates of Nephi. I once saw it as the story of Nephi and his family and their descendants, along with inspired revelations, sermons, and prophecies that could guide me in my life and lead me to Christ. I knew it was scripture, and I knew it was true. But now I see an additional level of complexity and spiritual instruction that I never before knew was there. I now see it also as a manual for understanding the covenants of the temple and a witness that these covenants are designed to lead me to Christ. As Elder Jeffrey R. Holland said regarding the substitution of the Small Plates of Nephi for the lost manuscript portion of Nephi's first record, "We got back more than we lost."[127]

In the revealed prayer given at the dedication of the Kirtland Temple, Joseph Smith pled, "And do thou grant, Holy Father, that all those who shall worship in this house may be taught words of wisdom out of the best books, and that they may seek learning even by study, and also by faith, as thou hast said" (D&C 109:14). The Book of Mormon is the best of all possible books that could be used to teach us words of wisdom related to worship in the Lord's House.

I am in awe at the wisdom and intelligence and majesty of God who designed a link to temple doctrines and principles within the Book of Mormon. Even the order in which the covenant topics are presented is aligned with the temple. These features were sitting there, right in front of my eyes, and I did not see them, but now a witness of the ingenuity of God has come into full view, and I am amazed to see the intricacy of God's design and the way in which He offers multiple witnesses of His truths. I feel like Joseph Smith, who wrote after one heavenly visit, "Our minds being now enlightened, we began to have the scriptures laid open to our understandings, and the true meaning and intention of their more mysterious passages revealed unto us in a manner which we never could attain to previously, nor ever before had thought of" (JS—H 1:74). Like many people in the Book of Mormon, I am "astonished exceedingly" (Jacob 7:21, et. al).

With this new perspective, we can see that the Book of Mormon bears witness of the temple and the temple bears witness of the Book of Mormon. Not even Joseph Smith pointed this out. Joseph is credited as the originator of both, yet, if he had been, one would think that he would have brought attention to the connection. He did not; he attributed both to God, who is the Master Designer. These two unique icons of Latter-day Saint theology, the Book of Mormon and the temple, validate one another, and the link confirms that they come from God.

THE BOOK OF MORMON AND ELIJAH

On September 21, 1823, while his siblings were asleep in their shared bedroom loft, seventeen-year-old Joseph Smith "betook [himself] to prayer and supplication to Almighty God" (JS—H 1:29), seeking forgiveness and guidance. The angel Moroni appeared to him and told him about an ancient record that he would translate as the Book of Mormon. "He also said that the fulness of the everlasting Gospel was contained in it, as delivered by the Savior to the ancient inhabitants" (JS—H 1:34).

Moroni described the ancient record and the translation stones that were buried with it, and then he quoted the third and fourth chapters of Malachi, which end with the famous prophecy of the coming of Elijah that we associate with temple work. Of course, Joseph did not know about temple work at that time, but looking back, it appears that Moroni was linking it to the Book of Mormon. Apparently, before temple work could be restored, it was necessary to bring forth the Book of Mormon, which contains "the fulness of the everlasting gospel," including the laws and principles upon which the covenants of the temple were to be based.

Some people have questioned how it can be claimed that the Book of Mormon contains the fulness of the gospel when the book says nothing about temple rites. This concern is usually addressed by explaining that the Lord's definition of the gospel is limited and that it is fully taught in the Book of Mormon,[128, 129] as we saw in 2 Nephi. However, in addition we now see that the Book of Mormon teaches the principles taught in the temple—and the clear presence of these covenant teachings bears witness to all aspects of temple worship. Other people have questioned why some elements of the temple ceremonies are similar to Masonry.[r] However, it should now be obvious that the covenants of the endowment were received by revelation. When the covenants become the primary focus of our temple worship, questions regarding the origins of the ceremony or changes to it melt away.

King Benjamin told his son, Mosiah, to send out a proclamation that the people "might go up to the temple to hear the words which king Benjamin should speak unto them" (Mosiah 2:1). He did so, "And it came to pass that when they came up to the temple, they pitched their tents round

---

r For more information, see the Church History Topics article "Masonry," churchofjesuschrist.org/study/history/topics/masonry?lang=eng.

about, every man according to his family, . . . every man having his tent with the door thereof towards the temple" (Mosiah 2:6). King Benjamin then addressed his people, saying, "Hearken unto me, and open your ears that ye may hear, and your hearts that ye may understand, and your minds that the mysteries of God may be unfolded to your view" (Mosiah 2:9).

We are also blessed when we gather our families and face the temple. We can gather our living family members in person, and we can gather our deceased family members through family history research. We can take both groups to the temple and there open our ears and minds so that the mysteries of God may be unfolded to our view. The insights discussed in this book have been presented with the hope that they will help in this process and will motivate readers to seek additional insights as they go to the temple with these perspectives in mind.

THE SMALL PLATES TESTIFY OF CHRIST AND COVENANTS

Nephi said that he created the Small Plates record according to the commandment of the Lord and so "that the more sacred things may be kept for the knowledge of my people" (1 Nephi 19:5). He later added, "And if my people are pleased with *the things of God* they will be pleased with mine engravings *which are upon these plates*" (2 Nephi 5:32; emphasis added). So Nephi equated the sacred engravings on the Small Plates with the things of God. No wonder Joseph Smith said of the Book of Mormon that "a man would get nearer to God by abiding by its precepts, than by any other book."[130] The Small Plates portion of the Book of Mormon, in particular, plays a special role in helping us draw near to God because it teaches us about our temple covenants. This record contains the fulness of the gospel including everything we need to know to be a covenant people and return to God's presence.

Referring to the Small Plates of Nephi, Mormon wrote, "For there are great things written upon them, out of which my people and their brethren shall be judged at the great and last day, according to the word of God which is written" (Words of Mormon 1:11). Could it be possible that one way in which we will be judged out of the things that are written on the Small Plates of Nephi is by how well we have kept our temple covenants that are described therein?

Lehi quoted the Lord, who told Joseph of Egypt:

> That which shall be written by the fruit of thy loins, and also that which shall be written by the fruit of the loins of Judah, shall grow together, unto the confounding of false doctrines and laying down of contentions, and establishing peace among the fruit of thy loins, and bringing them to the knowledge of their fathers in the latter days, and also *to the knowledge of my covenants*, saith the Lord. (2 Nephi 3:12; emphasis added)

This prophecy says that the Bible and the Book of Mormon together will bring the latter-day seed of Israel to a knowledge of God's covenants. The previous chapters of this book show how literally this prophecy has been fulfilled. The teachings about our covenants found in the Book of Mormon elucidate similar teachings found in the Bible in order to bring us to a knowledge of these covenants. Nephi described the things he wrote on his Small Plates, saying, "Wherefore, the things which are pleasing unto the world I do not write, but the things which are pleasing unto God and unto those who are not of the world" (1 Nephi 6:5). Clearly, this includes instructions about our temple covenants.

The title page of the Book of Mormon says that the book was prepared in order that the remnant of the house of Israel who will read it "may know the covenants of the Lord . . . And also to the convincing of the Jew and Gentile that Jesus is the Christ, the Eternal God" (Title Page of the Book of Mormon). These purposes of the Book of Mormon are strongly evident in the Small Plates of Nephi. They assure that modern-day remnants of Israel who have been gathered as covenant people may know the covenants of the Lord and be convinced that Jesus is the Christ.

With these purposes stated at the onset of the Book of Mormon, it should not be surprising to us that the Lord would include in these inspired pages specific instructions about the covenants we make as we come unto Him. These instructions include examples of obedience and sacrifice from Nephi and his family. They include guidance to help us understand and live the law of the gospel from 2 Nephi and lessons on the law of chastity from the teachings of Jacob. They include direction on consecrating our whole souls to Christ, as Amaleki and King Benjamin taught. They also include an example of prayer from Enos and insights on the importance of family history research from Jarom and the other minor record keepers. By following these examples and instructions, we will be able to fulfill our covenants more fully. They will help us come unto Christ and prepare to enter into God's presence.

As the previous chapters have shown, the Small Plates of Nephi are packed with covenant teachings. No wonder Nephi exclaimed, "My soul delighteth in the covenants of the Lord" (2 Nephi 11:5), and his brother, Jacob, similarly declared, "And behold how great the covenants of the Lord" (2 Nephi 9:53).

Nephi described a vision he saw of our day: "And it came to pass that I, Nephi, beheld the power of the Lamb of God, that it descended upon *the saints of the church of the Lamb, and upon the covenant people of the Lord*, who were scattered upon all the face of the earth; and they *were armed with righteousness and with the power of God in great glory*" (1 Nephi 14:14; emphasis added). As the covenant people of the Lord who are today scattered upon all the face of the earth, we become armed with righteousness and with the power of God in great glory when we go to the temple and enter into covenants with Him and then keep those covenants. We are further strengthened when we return to the temple and remember our covenants while performing saving ordinances on behalf of our ancestors and others who have gone before us. We are blessed to live in an era when the Lord's holy houses are scattered upon all the face of the earth as broadly as the Lord's covenant people are.

WHY COVENANT WITH US UNWORTHY CREATURES?

It is amazing that God chooses to make covenants with us. A covenant is a contractual agreement between two or more parties. It implies reciprocity and therefore equality on some level. Yet, we are not equals with God; we are His creations. King Benjamin said, "Ye cannot say that ye are even as much as the dust of the earth" (Mosiah 2:25), later adding that we should remember our "own nothingness, and his goodness and long-suffering towards you, unworthy creatures" (Mosiah 4:11).

It seems that God should not have to ask us to enter into any sort of reciprocal agreements with Him. He should simply command and we should obey. Since we are His subjects and His creations, why didn't He just create us in such a way that obedience was programmed in us? Or, at least He could have established a world where consequences were so immediate and swift that we would want to behave no matter what. But wait—that was Satan's plan. He wanted forced compliance.

God does not compel us to obey. Instead, He gave us our agency (see Moses 7:32). He created an environment where we would be free to choose, and one of the things we can choose is whether or not to enter into covenants with Him—righteous agreements whose terms have been set by God and whose purposes are to bless and lift us to become like Him. That is where the reciprocity comes in—not in any current equality with God, but in our potential to become like Him if we keep our covenants. He uses covenants to lift us to His level. We are His children and He wants us to return to His presence and receive all that He has. All faithful covenant keepers are promised, "All that my Father hath shall be given unto him [or her]" (D&C 84:38). That is one reason why the endowment culminates with entrance into the celestial room, symbolizing a return to God's presence. Covenants are required to attain that reward.

God wants us to return to live with Him eternally because He loves us. His work and glory is "to bring to pass the immortality and eternal life of man" (Moses 1:39), and He said that "men are that they might have joy" (2 Nephi 2:25). God loves us so much that He realizes His greatest glory when He sees us experience joy. Isn't that just like any good parent? God knows we only experience true joy when we are on the path to eternal life. Covenants keep us on that path.

God not only loves us, but He also respects us. He respects us as individual beings created from intelligences that existed eternally (see D&C 93:29). He respects us so much that He wants us to receive all that He has. He is not threatened by the thought of lifting us to His level—He is further glorified by it. His covenants are designed to help achieve this. Maybe that is why He has so often called us His friends (see D&C 84:77; 88:3, 62; 94:1; 97:1; 98:1; 103:1). President Russell M. Nelson wrote, "Our Heavenly Father wants us to come home, but He gives us the dignity of choosing to come home."[131] That dignity is a sign of His love and respect for us, and these are manifest through His covenants.

Our covenants are designed to bless us. Every covenant is associated with a saving ordinance, and the Lord has said that in the ordinances of the priesthood "the power of godliness is manifest" (see D&C 84:19–20). This occurs in at least two ways. First, each of the saving ordinances comes with a covenant promise of godly power: Baptism and confirmation come with the promise of power from the Holy Ghost, ordination to the priesthood brings the promise of God's authoritative power, and the endowment and temple marriage include promises of eternal divine power. Second, every ordinance of the priesthood includes the pronouncement of blessings: If we keep our covenants, God will bless us, and these blessing are another manifestation of His power. Elder Marcus B. Nash wrote, "It is through the priesthood ordinances that the power of godliness is manifest in our lives—but only to the extent that we keep the associated covenants. The covenant activates, or gives life to, the ordinance, just as an engine activates a car and enables it to transport its occupants from one place to another."[132]

God also uses covenants as a test to see who will follow in His path. Who will rise above the influences of the world and keep their covenants in spite of the natural man? Who has it in them to stick to the commitments made by covenant? We might even enter into these commitments before we fully understand them, but maybe that is part of the test. Do we have enough faith in God and in the goodness of His covenants that we will accept them, in spite of our limited understanding, and see what God will make of us through these covenants? If so, we are on the path to becoming like Him.

President Boyd K. Packer wrote,

> We are a covenant people, and the temple is the center of our covenants. It is the source of the covenant. Come to the temple. . . . Be faithful to the covenants and ordinances of the gospel. . . . Do this and you will be happy. Your lives will then be in order—all things lined up in proper sequence, in proper ranks, in proper rows. Your family will be linked in an order that can never be broken.
>
> In the covenants and ordinances center the blessings that you may claim in the holy temple. Surely the Lord is pleased when we are worthy of the title: A keeper of the covenants. . . . If we will . . . enter into our covenants without reservation or apology, the Lord will protect us. We will receive inspiration sufficient for the challenges of life. . . . So come to the temple—come and claim your blessings. It is a sacred work.[133]

ALL COVENANTS CENTER ON CHRIST

Nephi taught, "For the Lord covenanteth with none save it be with them that repent and believe in his Son, who is the Holy One of Israel" (2 Nephi 30:2). Every one of the covenant steps presented in this review of the Small Plates of Nephi has included a focus on Jesus Christ. The following are section headings in previous chapters that point directly to Jesus Christ and His Atonement:

1 Nephi: The Law of Obedience and Sacrifice

Obedience and Sacrifice Point to Jesus Christ and Covenants

2 Nephi: The Law of the Gospel

The Creation, the Fall, and the Atonement
Resurrection and Judgment Complete the Atonement
The Doctrine of the Atonement
Isaiah and Nephi: We Talk of Christ, We Rejoice in Christ
The Doctrine of Christ: Nephi's Closing Sermon on the Gospel

Jacob: The Law of Chastity

Spiritual Power from Christ

Enos: Prayer

Because of Thy Faith in Christ

Omni/King Benjamin: The Law of Consecration

Jesus Christ: Our Motivation for Consecration

This list shows one of the great insights that come from searching the scriptures for the meaning of our covenants: They are designed to help us come unto Christ. Elder Robert D. Hales said, "Temple ordinances guide us to our Savior and give us the blessings that come to us through the Atonement of Jesus Christ."[134] Elder David A. Bednar said, "The temple is the house of the Lord. Everything in the temple points us to our Savior, Jesus Christ."[135]

In the final words Moroni inscribed in the Book of Mormon, he wrote,

> And again I would exhort you that ye would *come unto Christ*, and lay hold upon every good gift, and touch not the evil gift, nor the unclean thing. And awake, and arise from the dust, O Jerusalem; yea, and put on thy beautiful garments, O daughter of Zion; and strengthen thy stakes and enlarge thy borders forever, that thou mayest no more be confounded, *that the covenants of the Eternal Father which he hath made*

unto thee, O house of Israel, may be fulfilled. Yea, come unto Christ, and be perfected in him, and deny yourselves of all ungodliness. (Moroni 10:30–32; emphasis added)

We are invited to come unto Christ so that covenants may be fulfilled. Not only will our coming unto Christ fulfill the covenants that God made to Israel, but it is also through our covenants that we come unto Christ. This is like the old chicken and egg question: Which came first? The answer is that Christ and covenants go together. They are part of one eternal round. We cannot fully have one without the other. When we combine the power of the Atonement of Jesus Christ with the power of our covenants, together they will help us overcome all ungodliness so that we become perfected and sanctified. Moroni added this promise:

> And if ye shall deny yourselves of all ungodliness, and love God with all your might, mind and strength, then is his grace sufficient for you, that by his grace ye may be perfect in Christ; . . . then are ye sanctified in Christ by the grace of God, through the shedding of the blood of Christ, which is in the covenant of the Father unto the remission of your sins, that ye become holy, without spot. (Moroni 10:32–33)

This is what all covenant keepers desire. We want to become holy, without spot. We want to become perfect in Christ. We want to become like Him, and the promise of the Father is that we can be—through Christ and by keeping our covenants.

In his inaugural address as an Apostle, Elder Gerrit W. Gong said,

> This Easter Sabbath, I joyfully sing, "Alleluia." The song of our risen Savior's redeeming love celebrates the harmony of covenants (that connect us to God and to each other) and the Atonement of Jesus Christ (that helps us put off the natural man and woman and yield to the enticings of the Holy Spirit). Together, our covenants and our Savior's Atonement enable and ennoble. Together, they help us hold on and let go. Together, they sweeten, preserve, sanctify, redeem.[136]

The combination of our covenants and the Atonement of Jesus Christ can overcome anything. It is by making and keeping sacred covenants that we access the power of the Atonement of Jesus Christ, and together they guide us back to God.

ESCAPING CONDEMNATION

Those of us who lived while President Benson was prophet did not wonder what topic he would speak on at general conference. We knew we would be instructed more about the Book of Mormon. Over and over again, he emphasized the need to read, study, follow, and share the Book of Mormon. He taught us to come unto Christ through the Book of Mormon. He emphasized the statement by Joseph Smith that the Book of Mormon is "the keystone of our religion, and a man would get nearer to God by abiding by its precepts, than by any other book."[137]

President Benson frequently referred to Doctrine and Covenants 84, wherein the Lord said that the entire Church was under condemnation because they treated lightly the things they had received. Verse 57 says, "And they shall remain under this condemnation until they repent and remember the new covenant, even the Book of Mormon and the former commandments which I have given them, not only to say, but to do according to that which I have written."

How has the Book of Mormon been neglected? Near the end of President Benson's life, President Dallin H. Oaks, then a member of the Quorum of the Twelve Apostles, answered this question. He summarized all of President Benson's sermons and writings about the Book of Mormon and concluded, "The subject I believe we have neglected is the Book of Mormon's witness of the divinity and mission of Jesus Christ and our covenant relationship to him."[138] President Oaks also explained,

> The covenant described in these scriptures, made new by its renewal and confirmation in these latter days, refers to our covenant relationship with Jesus Christ.
> . . . The new covenant contained in the Book of Mormon and the former commandments is that central promise of the gospel, rooted in the atonement and resurrection of Jesus Christ, which gives us the assurance of immortality and the opportunity for eternal life if we will repent of our sins and make and keep the gospel covenant with our Savior.
> . . . In order to escape condemnation, we must come unto Christ and enter into the gospel covenant, not only "to say" but also "to do according to that which [the Lord has] written." We must "give diligent heed to the words of eternal life" and "live by every word that proceedeth forth from the mouth of God" (D&C 84:43–44).[139]

So, to escape condemnation, we need to come unto Christ and enter into and keep all our covenants with diligence. The Book of Mormon will help us do this. One way it does this is by teaching the principles included in our sacred temple covenants. That is why we must not neglect this book. By using it to help us understand and keep our covenants, we will come unto Christ. We will draw nearer to God and escape His condemnation. We will be guided through life's challenges, because we will be on His covenant path.

STAY ON THE COVENANT PATH

The Lord encouraged us to stay on the covenant path when he decreed, "I will prove you in all things, whether you will abide in my covenant, even unto death, that you may be found worthy. For if ye will not abide in my covenant ye are not worthy of me" (D&C 98:14–15). To abide in the Lord's covenant means to keep the covenant promises we have made with Him.

This need to keep our covenants has been emphasized by modern prophets. In his first public address as President of the Church, President Russell M. Nelson spoke in a live broadcast from the entry room of the Salt Lake Temple. In that sacred covenant space he admonished,

> To each member of the Church I say, keep on the covenant path. Your commitment to follow the Savior by making covenants with Him and then keeping those covenants will open the door to every spiritual blessing and privilege available to men, women and children everywhere.
> . . . The end for which each of us strives is to be endowed with power in a house of the Lord, sealed as families, faithful to covenants made in a temple that qualify us for the greatest gift of God—that of eternal life. The ordinances of the temple and the covenants you make there are key to strengthening your life, your marriage and family, and your ability to resist the attacks of the adversary. Your worship in the temple and your service there for your ancestors will bless you with increased personal revelation and peace and will fortify your commitment to stay on the covenant path.
> Now, if you have stepped off the path, may I invite you with all the hope in my heart to please come back. Whatever your concerns, whatever your challenges, there is a place for you in this, the Lord's Church.

You and generations yet unborn will be blessed by your actions now to return to the covenant path.[140]

"Keep on the covenant path. . . . Stay on the covenant path. . . . Return to the covenant path." These are the pleas of a prophet of God. The same message arises from the writings of the early prophets of the Book of Mormon, from Nephi to King Benjamin. They left us sacred instructions to help us understand and keep each covenant along that path.

What a blessing the marvelous Book of Mormon is! What a blessing it is to see the link between this holy book and our temple covenants. What a blessing it is to have the sacred portion called the Small Plates of Nephi to guide us along the covenant path as we seek to return to God and enter into His presence. I pray, along with President Benson, that we will utilize the Book of Mormon more, and I pray, along with President Nelson, that we will all stay on the covenant path.

WORKS CITED

Publications of The Church of Jesus Christ of Latter-day Saints, Salt Lake City, Utah, USA

A Parent's Guide, 1985, churchofjesuschrist.org/manual/a-parents
　　-guide?lang=eng.

Bible Dictionary, 2013, churchofjesuschrist.org/scriptures/bd?lang=eng.

Book of Mormon, 2013, churchofjesuschrist.org/scriptures/bofm?lang=eng.

Book of Mormon Student Manual, 2009, churchofjesuschrist.org/manual/book
　　-of-mormon-student-manual?lang=eng.

Children's Songbook, 1989, churchofjesuschrist.org/music/library/childrens
　　-songbook?lang=eng.

Church History Topics, 2019, churchofjesuschrist.org/study/topics?lang=eng.

Conference Reports, archive.org/details/conferencereport.

Doctrine and Covenants, 2013, churchofjesuschrist.org/scriptures/
　　dc-testament?lang=eng.

Ensign, churchofjesuschrist.org/ensign?lang=eng.

Family Home Evening Resource Book, 1983, churchofjesuschrist.org/manual/
　　family-home-evening-resource-book?lang=eng.

For the Strength of Youth, 2011, churchofjesuschrist.org/youth/for-the-strength
　　-of-youth?lang=eng.

Friend, churchofjesuschrist.org/friend?lang=eng.

Gospel Principles, 2011, churchofjesuschrist.org/manual/gospel
　　-principles?lang=eng.

Handbook 2: Administering the Church, 2018, churchofjesuschrist.org/ handbook/handbook-2-administering-the-church?lang=eng.

Holy Bible, 2013, churchofjesuschrist.org/study/scriptures/ot/title -page?lang=eng.

Hymns, 1985, churchofjesuschrist.org/music/library/hymns?lang=eng.

Liahona, churchofjesuschrist.org/liahona?lang=eng.

Millett, Joseph Sr., Diary of Joseph Millett Sr., Journal and papers typescript 1852–1919, Joseph Millet journal and papers 1852–1932, Church History Library, The Church of Jesus Christ of Latter-day Saints, Salt Lake City, Utah.

New Era, www.churchofjesuschrist.org/new-era?lang=eng.

Packer, Boyd K., *Preparing to Enter the Holy Temple*, 2002, churchofjesuschrist. org/manual/preparing-to-enter-the-holy-temple/preparing-to-enter-the -holy-temple?lang=eng.

Pearl of Great Price, 2013, churchofjesuschrist.org/scriptures/pgp?lang=eng.

Preach My Gospel: A Guide to Missionary Service, 2019, churchofjesuschrist.org/ manual/preach-my-gospel-a-guide-to-missionary-service?lang=eng.

Teachings of Presidents of the Church: Joseph Fielding Smith, 2013, churchofjesuschrist.org/manual/teachings-of-presidents-of-the-church -joseph-fielding-smith?lang=eng.

Teachings of Presidents of the Church: Joseph Smith, 2007, churchofjesuschrist.org/ manual/teachings-joseph-smith?lang=eng.

LDS Leader Video Broadcasts, churchofjesuschrist.org/broadcasts?lang =eng&_r=1.

Nelson, Russell M., Facebook post, Apr. 17, 2018, facebook.com/ russell.m.nelson/.

Church-Related Publications

Benson, Ezra Taft, *The Teachings of Ezra Taft Benson*, Bookcraft, Salt Lake City, UT, 1988.

BYU Speeches, Brigham Young University, Provo, UT, speeches.byu.edu/.

BYU Studies, Brigham Young University, Provo, UT, byustudies.byu.edu/.

Encyclopedia of Mormonism, Macmillan Publishing, New York, 1992, eom .byu.edu/.

Hinckley, Gordon B., *Teachings of Gordon B. Hinckley*, Deseret Book, Salt Lake City, UT, 1997.

Holland, Jeffrey R., *Christ and the New Covenant*, Deseret Book, Salt Lake City, UT, 1997.

Halverson, Taylor, "Mosiah 4–6: Children of Christ," *Interpreter: A Journal of Latter-day Saint Faith and Scholarship*, The Interpreter Foundation, Orem, UT, 2016, interpreterfoundation.org/res-mosiah-4-6-children-of-christ/.

Journal of Discourses, vol. XVI, Latter-Day Saints Book Depot, London, 1874.

McConkie, Bruce R., *Promised Messiah*, Deseret Book, Salt Lake City, UT, 1978.

Smith, Joseph Jr., *Teachings of the Prophet Joseph Smith*, editor Joseph Fielding Smith, Deseret Book, Salt Lake City, UT, 1974, scriptures.byu.edu/tpjs/STPJS.pdf.

Smith, Joseph Jr., *Lectures on Faith*, 6:7, lecturesonfaith.com/6/. See also oneClimbs.com.

Smith, Joseph Jr., *History of The Church of Jesus Christ of Latter-day Saints,* vol. 4, Deseret Book, Salt Lake City, UT, 1954.

Talmage, James E., *The House of the Lord*, rev. ed., Deseret Book, Salt Lake City, UT, 1979.

Thomas, Robert K., "A Literary Critic Looks at the Book of Mormon," *To the Glory of God*, ed. Charles D. Tate and Truman G. Madsen, Deseret Book, 1972.

Maxwell, Neal A., "King Benjamin's Sermon: A Manual for Discipleship," *King Benjamin's Speech "That Ye May Learn Wisdom,"* ed. John W. Welch and Stephen D. Ricks, FARMS, 1998.

Widtsoe, John A., "Temple Worship," *The Utah Genealogical and Historical Magazine*, Deseret News Press, Apr. 1921, archive.org/details/utahgenealogical1921gene.

Other Publications

Biography.com, 2019.

Frankl, Viktor, *Man's Search for Meaning*, 4th ed., Beacon Press, 1992, 115, edisciplinas.usp.br/pluginfile.php/3403095/mod_resource/content/1/56ViktorFrankl_Mans%20Search.pdf.

Lewis, C. S., *Mere Christianity*, Samizdat, Feb. 2014 (public domain under Canadian copyright law), 68, samizdat.qc.ca/vc/pdfs/MereChristianity _CSL.pdf.

Stowe, Harriet Beecher, *Uncle Tom's Cabin*, 1852, 340, books.google.com/ books?id=rlDaAAAAIAAJ&pg=PA320&source=gbs _toc_r&cad=4#v=onepage&q&f=false. See also gutenberg.org/ ebooks/203.

Wikipedia, The Free Encyclopedia, 2019, wikipedia.org/wiki/Main_Page.

Notes

Chapter 1—Introduction

1   Jeffrey R. Holland, "For a Wise Purpose," *Ensign*, Jan. 1996, churchofjesuschrist.org/study/ensign/1996/01/for-a-wise-purpose?lang=eng.

2   David A. Bednar, "Prepared to Obtain Every Needful Thing," *Ensign*, May 2019, churchofjesuschrist.org/study/ensign/2019/05/prepared-to-obtain-every-needful-thing?lang=eng. Formatting modified.

3   Ezra Taft Benson, "A Vision and a Hope for the Youth of Zion," Brigham Young University devotional, Apr. 12, 1977, speeches.byu.edu/talks/ezra-taft-benson_vision-hope-youth-zion/.

4   John A. Widtsoe, "Temple Worship," *The Utah Genealogical and Historical Magazine*, Apr. 1921, 60–63, archive.org/details/utahgenealogical1921gene.

5   "Gaining Knowledge of Eternal Truths," Chapter 22, *Teachings of Presidents of the Church: Joseph Smith*, 2011, churchofjesuschrist.org/manual/teachings-joseph-smith/chapter-22?lang=eng.

6   Lance B. Wickman, "Of Compasses and Covenants," *Ensign*, June 1996, churchofjesuschrist.org/study/ensign/1996/06/of-compasses-and-covenants?lang=eng.

7   N. Eldon Tanner, "The Administration of the Church," *Ensign*, Nov. 1979, churchofjesuschrist.org/study/ensign/1979/11/the-administration-of-the-church?lang=eng.

8   George S. Tate, "Prayer Circle," *Encyclopedia of Mormonism*, 1992, eom.byu.edu/index.php/Prayer_Circle.

9   D. Michael Quinn, "Latter-day Saint Prayer Circles," BYU Studies, 19, no. 1, 1978, byustudies.byu.edu/content/latter-day-saint-prayer-circles.

10 Thomas S. Monson, "Consider the Blessings," *Ensign*, Nov. 2012, churchofjesuschrist.org/study/ensign/2012/11/sunday-morning-session/ consider-the-blessings?lang=eng.

11 "House of the Lord," *Friend*, Mar. 2002, churchofjesuschrist.org/study/ friend/2002/03/house-of-the-lord?lang=eng.

12 Russell M. Nelson, "As We Go Forward Together," *Ensign*, Apr. 2018, churchofjesuschrist.org/study/ensign/2018/04/as-we-go-forward -together?lang=eng.

13 James E. Talmage, *The House of the Lord* (Salt Lake City: Bookcraft, 1962), 100. Quoted by Boyd K. Packer in *Preparing to Enter the Holy Temple*, 2002, churchofjesuschrist.org/study/manual/preparing-to-enter -the-holy-temple/preparing-to-enter-the-holy-temple?lang=eng.

14 Gordon B. Hinckley, *Teachings of Gordon B. Hinckley* (Salt Lake City: Deseret Book, 1997), 146–47. Quoted by Keith B. McMullin, "An Invitation with a Promise," *Ensign*, May 2001, churchofjesuschrist.org/ study/ensign/2001/05/an-invitation-with-promise?lang=eng.

15 Bruce R. McConkie, "Obedience, Consecration, and Sacrifice," *Ensign*, May 1975, churchofjesuschrist.org/study/ensign/1975/05/obedience -consecration-and-sacrifice?lang=eng.

16 Robert D. Hales, "Coming to Ourselves: The Sacrament, the Temple, and Sacrifice in Service," *Ensign*, May 2012, churchofjesuschrist.org/study/ ensign/2012/05/saturday-afternoon-session/coming-to-ourselves-the -sacrament-the-temple-and-sacrifice-in-service?lang=eng. Capitalization modified.

17 Jeffrey R. Holland, "Keeping Covenants: A Message for Those Who Will Serve a Mission," *New Era*, Jan. 2012, churchofjesuschrist.org/study/ new-era/2012/01/keeping-covenants-a-message-for-those-who-will-serve -a-mission?lang=eng.

18 James E. Faust, "Who Shall Ascend into the Hill of the Lord?" *Ensign*, Aug. 2001, churchofjesuschrist.org/study/ensign/2001/08/who-shall -ascend-into-the-hill-of-the-lord?lang=eng.

19 Boyd K. Packer, "Sacred Covenants," *Preparing to Enter the Holy Temple*, 2002, churchofjesuschrist.org/manual/preparing-to-enter-the-holy-temple/ preparing-to-enter-the-holy-temple?lang=eng.

20 D. Todd Christofferson, "Come to Zion," *Ensign*, Nov. 2008, churchofjesuschrist.org/study/ensign/2008/11/come-to-zion?lang=eng.

21 Bonnie D. Parkin, "Celebrating Covenants," *Ensign*, May 1995, churchofjesuschrist.org/study/ensign/1995/05/celebrating -covenants?lang=eng.

22   Dallin H. Oaks, "Our Strengths Can Become Our Downfall," Brigham
      Young University devotional, June 7, 1992, speeches.byu.edu/talks/
      dallin-h-oaks_strengths-can-become-downfall/, and *Ensign*, Oct. 1994,
      churchofjesuschrist.org/study/ensign/1994/10/our-strengths-can-become
      -our-downfall?lang=eng.

23   "Understanding Our Covenants with God," *Ensign*, July 2012,
      churchofjesuschrist.org/study/ensign/2012/07/understanding-our
      -covenants-with-god?lang=eng.

24   Wouter Van Beek, "Covenants," *Encyclopedia of Mormonism*, 1992,
      eom.byu.edu/index.php/Covenants. Capitalization modified.

Chapter 2—1 Nephi

25   Joseph F. Smith, *Journal of Discourses*, 16:248, scriptures.byu
      .edu/#:t27123:j16.

26   Ezra Taft Benson, "A Vision and a Hope for the Youth of Zion," Brigham
      Young University devotional, Apr. 12, 1977, speeches.byu.edu/talks/ezra
      -taft-benson_vision-hope-youth-zion/.

27   Bill N. Hansen Jr. and Lisa T. Hansen, "Nephi's Courage," *Children's
      Songbook* (Salt Lake City: The Church of Jesus Christ of Latter-day Saints,
      1989), 120, churchofjesuschrist.org/music/library/childrens-songbook/
      nephis-courage?lang=eng.

28   Jeffrey R. Holland, "The Will of the Father in All Things," Brigham
      Young University devotional, Jan. 17, 1989, speeches.byu.edu/talks/
      jeffrey-r-holland_will-father/.

29   Russell M. Nelson, "Lessons from Eve," *Ensign*, Nov. 1987,
      churchofjesuschrist.org/study/ensign/1987/11/lessons-from-eve?lang=eng.

30   Joseph Smith Jr., *Lectures on Faith* 6:7, lecturesonfaith.com/6/.

31   Lance B. Wickman, "Of Compasses and Covenants," *Ensign*, June
      1996, churchofjesuschrist.org/study/ensign/1996/06/of-compasses-and-
      covenants?lang=eng. Emphasis added.

32   Ballard, M. Russell, "The Law of Sacrifice," *Ensign*, Oct. 1998,
      churchofjesuschrist.org/study/ensign/1998/10/the-law-of
      -sacrifice?lang=eng.

33   James Montgomery, "A Poor Wayfaring Man of Grief," *Hymns of
      The Church of Jesus Christ of Latter-day Saints* (Salt Lake City: The
      Church of Jesus Christ of Latter-day Saints, 1985), no. 29, verse 7,
      churchofjesuschrist.org/music/library/hymns/a-poor-wayfaring-man-of
      -grief?lang=eng.

34 As quoted by Donald L. Staheli in "Obedience—Life's Great Challenge," *Ensign*, May 1998, churchofjesuschrist.org/study/ensign/1998/05/ obedience-lifes-great-challenge?lang=eng.

Chapter 3—2 Nephi

35 Joseph Smith Jr., *Teachings of the Prophet Joseph Smith*, ed. Joseph Fielding Smith (Salt Lake City: Deseret Book, 1976), 149. Quoted by Robert J. Matthews, "Resurrection," *Ensign*, Apr. 1994, churchofjesuschrist.org/ study/ensign/1991/04/resurrection?lang=eng.

36 Dieter F. Uchtdorf, "O How Great the Plan of Our God!" *Ensign*, Nov. 2016, churchofjesuschrist.org/study/ensign/2016/11/saturday-morning -session/o-how-great-the-plan-of-our-god?lang=eng.

37 "What Is My Purpose as a Missionary?" *Preach My Gospel: A Guide to Missionary Service*, 2019, online version. See churchofjesuschrist.org/ manual/preach-my-gospel-a-guide-to-missionary-service/what-is-my -purpose-as-a-missionary?lang=eng.

38 "Gospels," Bible Dictionary, 2013, churchofjesuschrist.org/scriptures/bd/ gospels?lang=eng.

39 Bruce R. McConkie, *Promised Messiah* (Salt Lake City: Deseret Book, 1978), 421.

40 Bruce R. McConkie, "Christ and the Creation," *Ensign*, June 1982, churchofjesuschrist.org/study/ensign/1982/06/christ-and-the -creation?lang=eng.

41 Russell M. Nelson, "Joy and Spiritual Survival," *Ensign*, Nov. 2016, churchofjesuschrist.org/study/ensign/2016/11/sunday-morning-session/ joy-and-spiritual-survival?lang=eng.

42 Wikipedia contributors, "Stephen Hawking," Wikipedia, The Free Encyclopedia, accessed Sept. 14, 2018, en.wikipedia.org/wiki/Stephen _Hawking.

43 Biography.com editors, "Stephen Hawking Biography," Biography.com, accessed Sept. 14, 2018, biography.com/people/stephen-hawking-9331710.

44 Viktor Frankl, *Man's Search for Meaning*, 4th ed. (Boston: Beacon, 1992), 115, edisciplinas.usp.br/pluginfile.php/3403095/mod_resource/ content/1/56ViktorFrankl_Mans%20Search.pdf.

45 Frankl, *Man's Search for Meaning*, 116–17.

46 M. Russell Ballard, "Pure Testimony," *Ensign*, Nov. 2004, churchofjesuschrist.org/study/ensign/2004/11/pure-testimony?lang=eng.

47 Bruce R. McConkie, "This Final Glorious Gospel Dispensation," *Ensign*, Apr. 1980, churchofjesuschrist.org/study/ensign/1980/04/this-final -glorious-gospel-dispensation?lang=eng.

48 Holland, "For a Wise Purpose." See also Jeffrey R. Holland, *Christ and the New Covenant* (Salt Lake City: Desert Book, 1997), 33–36.

49 Bruce R. McConkie, "Ten Keys to Understanding Isaiah," *Ensign*, Oct. 1973, churchofjesuschrist.org/study/ensign/1973/10/ten-keys-to -understanding-isaiah?lang=eng.

50 Dieter F. Uchtdorf, "Are You Sleeping through the Restoration?" *Ensign*, May 2014, churchofjesuschrist.org/study/ensign/2014/05/priesthood -session/are-you-sleeping-through-the-restoration?lang=eng.

51 Joseph Smith Jr., *History of the Church of Jesus Christ of Latter-day Saints*, ed. B. H. Roberts, 7 vols. (Salt Lake City: The Church of Jesus Christ of Latter-day Saints, 1932–51), 4:609–10. Quoted by Joseph B. Wirthlin in "The Restoration and Faith," *Ensign*, Jan. 2006, churchofjesuschrist .org/study/ensign/2006/01/the-restoration-and-faith?lang=eng. Emphasis added.

52 David A. Bednar, "Ask in Faith," *Ensign*, May 2008, churchofjesuschrist .org/study/ensign/2008/05/ask-in-faith?lang=eng.

53 Boyd K. Packer, "The Plan of Happiness," *Ensign*, May 2015, churchofjesuschrist.org/study/ensign/2015/05/saturday-morning-session/ the-plan-of-happiness?lang=eng.

54 Chapter 7, "Baptism and the Gift of the Holy Ghost," *Teachings of Presidents of the Church: Joseph Smith*, 2011, churchofjesuschrist.org/ manual/teachings-joseph-smith/chapter-7?lang=eng.

55 Russell M. Nelson, "Hope of Israel," Worldwide Youth Devotional, June 3, 2018, churchofjesuschrist.org/languages/eng/content/broadcasts/ worldwide-devotional-for-young-adults/2018/06/hope-of-israel.

56 L. Tom Perry, "The Gospel of Jesus Christ," *Ensign*, May 2008, churchofjesuschrist.org/study/ensign/2008/05/the-gospel-of-jesus -christ?lang=eng.

57 Dale G. Renlund, "Latter-day Saints Keep on Trying," *Ensign*, May 2015, churchofjesuschrist.org/study/ensign/2015/05/saturday-afternoon-session/ latter-day-saints-keep-on-trying?lang=eng, emphasis added.

58 Ezra Taft Benson, *Teachings of Ezra Taft Benson* (Salt Lake City: Bookcraft, 1988), 337.

59 Ronald A. Rasband, "Standing by Our Promises and Covenants," *Ensign*, Nov. 2019, churchofjesuschrist.org/study/ensign/2019/11/standing-by-our- promises-and-covenants/?lang=eng.

60 Spencer W. Kimball, "Small Acts of Service," *Ensign*, Dec. 1974, churchofjesuschrist.org/study/ensign/1974/12/small-acts-of -service?lang=eng.

61 Joseph Millett Sr., Diary of Joseph Millett Sr., journal and papers typescript 1852–1919, Joseph Millet journal and papers 1852–1932, Church History Library, The Church of Jesus Christ of Latter-day Saints, Salt Lake City, Utah, dcms.churchofjesuschrist.org/delivery/ DeliveryManagerServlet?dps_pid=IE11452259, file 72; minor edits included. Quoted by Boyd K. Packer in "A Tribute to the Rank and File of the Church," *Ensign*, May 1980, churchofjesuschrist.org/study/ ensign/1980/05/a-tribute-to-the-rank-and-file-of-the-church?lang=eng.

62 James E. Faust, "The Surety of a Better Testament," *Ensign*, Sept. 2003, churchofjesuschrist.org/study/ensign/2003/09/the-surety-of-a-better -testament?lang=eng.

63 Larry E. Dahl, "The Higher Law," *Ensign*, Feb. 1991, churchofjesuschrist .org/study/ensign/1991/02/the-higher-law?lang=eng.

64 Monte S. Nyman, "How are we to look at the Beatitudes and make them useful in our lives?" *Ensign*, Dec. 1974, churchofjesuschrist.org/study/ ensign/1974/12/i-have-a-question/how-are-we-to-look-at-the-beatitudes -and-make-them-useful-in-our-lives?lang=eng.

Chapter 4—Jacob

65 "Teaching about Procreation and Chastity," *Family Home Evening Resource Book*, 1983, churchofjesuschrist.org/manual/family-home-evening -resource-book/building-a-strong-family/teaching-about-procreation-and -chastity?lang=eng.

66 "Introduction," *A Parent's Guide*, 1985, churchofjesuschrist.org/manual/a -parents-guide/introduction?lang=eng.

67 C. S. Lewis, *Mere Christianity* (New York City: Macmillan 1952), 68. See samizdat.qc.ca/vc/pdfs/MereChristianity_CSL.pdf for a Canadian public domain version of the text. Also quoted by Ezra T. Benson, "Beware of Pride," *Ensign*, May 1989, churchofjesuschrist.org/study/ensign/1989/05/ beware-of-pride?lang=eng.

68 "The Family: A Proclamation to the World," *Ensign*, Nov. 2010, churchofjesuschrist.org/study/ensign/2010/11/the-family-a-proclamation -to-the-world?lang=eng.

69 Dallin H. Oaks, "Pornography," *Ensign*, May 2005, churchofjesuschrist .org/study/ensign/2005/05/pornography?lang=eng.

70 Steve Gilliland, "Chastity," *Ensign*, June 1980, churchofjesuschrist.org/study/ensign/1980/06/chastity-a-principle-of-power?lang=eng.

71 Gordon B. Hinckley, "Some Thoughts on Temples, Retention of Converts, and Missionary Service," *Ensign*, Nov. 1997, churchofjesuschrist.org/study/ensign/1997/11/some-thoughts-on-temples-retention-of-converts-and-missionary-service?lang=eng.

72 Dallin H. Oaks, "Recovering from the Trap of Pornography," *Ensign*, Oct. 2015, churchofjesuschrist.org/study/ensign/2015/10/recovering-from-the-trap-of-pornography?lang=eng.

73 See fightthenewdrug.org/.

74 Hinckley, "Some Thoughts."

75 "Sexual Purity," *For the Strength of Youth*, 2011, churchofjesuschrist.org/youth/for-the-strength-of-youth/sexual-purity?lang=eng.

76 Richard L. Evans in Conference Report, Oct. 1964, 135–36, archive.org/details/conferencereport1964sa/page/n135. Quoted by Jeffrey R. Holland in "A Prayer for the Children," *Ensign*, May 2003, churchofjesuschrist.org/study/ensign/2003/05/a-prayer-for-the-children?lang=eng. Emphasis added.

77 Vaughn J. Featherstone, "One Link Still Holds," *Ensign*, Nov. 1999, churchofjesuschrist.org/study/ensign/1999/11/one-link-still-holds?lang=eng.

78 "The Family: A Proclamation to the World."

79 "The Family: A Proclamation to the World."

80 M. Russell Ballard, "The Lord Needs You Now!" *Ensign*, Sept. 2015, churchofjesuschrist.org/study/ensign/2015/09/the-lord-needs-you-now?lang=eng.

81 "The Family: A Proclamation to the World."

82 Jeffrey R. Holland, "Personal Purity," *Ensign*, Nov. 1998, churchofjesuschrist.org/study/ensign/1998/11/personal-purity?lang=eng.

Chapter 5—Enos

83 N. Eldon Tanner, "The Administration of the Church," *Ensign*, Nov. 1979, churchofjesuschrist.org/study/ensign/1979/11/the-administration-of-the-church?lang=eng.

84 Tate, "Prayer Circle," *Encyclopedia of Mormonism*.

85 "House of the Lord," *Friend*, Mar. 2002, churchofjesuschrist.org/study/friend/2002/03/house-of-the-lord?lang=eng.

86 Truman G. Madsen, Know Your Religion lectures, 1972–73. Quoted by Gerald R. Schiefer in "Where Two or Three are Gathered," *Ensign*, Jan. 1976, churchofjesuschrist.org/study/ensign/1976/01/where-two-or-three-are-gathered?lang=eng. Formatting modified.

87 Chapter 17, "Enos—Words of Mormon," *Book of Mormon Student Manual*, 2009, churchofjesuschrist.org/manual/book-of-mormon-student-manual/chapter-17-enos-words-of-mormon?lang=eng.

88 "Prayer," Bible Dictionary, 2013, churchofjesuschrist.org/scriptures/bd/prayer?lang=eng.

89 Russell M. Nelson, "Sweet Power of Prayer," *Ensign*, May 2003, churchofjesuschrist.org/study/ensign/2003/05/sweet-power-of-prayer?lang=eng.

90 "Prayer," Bible Dictionary.

91 Melvin L. Jones, "Bud's Story," from tape recordings done Mar. 2000, transcribed and edited by Rosemary W. Jones. Unpublished family records in possession of the author.

92 Anne Jones Sloat, "An Answered Prayer," *Stories and Experiences from the Merlyn Paul Jones Family Lineage*, editor Wesley C. Jones, July 1992. Unpublished family records in possession of the author.

Chapter 6—Jarom

93 Neil A. Anderson, "Find Our Cousins!" Family Discovery Day Devotional for Youth (held in conjunction with the RootsTech Family History Conference in Salt Lake City, Utah), Feb. 8, 2014, churchofjesuschrist.org/prophets-and-apostles/unto-all-the-world/find-our-cousins?lang=eng.

94 Robert K. Thomas, "A Literary Critic Looks at the Book of Mormon," *To the Glory of God*, ed. Charles D. Tate and Truman G. Madsen (Salt Lake City: Deseret Book, 1972), 156. Formatting modified.

95 Thomas, "A Literary Critic," 156–59.

96 Anderson, "Find Our Cousins!"

97 Becky Beus, personal communication, Sept. 25, 2018.

98 Dale G. Renlund, "Family History and Temple Work: Sealing and Healing," *Ensign*, May 2018, churchofjesuschrist.org/study/ensign/2018/05/saturday-afternoon-session/family-history-and-temple-work-sealing-and-healing?lang=eng.

99 Chapter 45, "The Millennium," *Gospel Principles* (2011), 265, churchofjesuschrist.org/manual/gospel-principles/chapter-45-the-millennium?lang=eng.

Chapter 7—Omni & King Benjamin

100 Neal A. Maxwell, "King Benjamin's Sermon: A Manual for Discipleship," *King Benjamin's Speech "That Ye May Learn Wisdom,"* ed. John W. Welch and Stephen D. Ricks, 1998, publications.mi.byu.edu/fullscreen/?pub=1087&index=1.

101 Gordon B. Hinckley, "This Is the Work of the Master," *Ensign*, May 1995, churchofjesuschrist.org/study/ensign/1995/05/this-is-the-work-of-the-master?lang=eng.

102 Marion G. Romney, "The Celestial Nature of Self-reliance," *Ensign*, Nov. 1982, churchofjesuschrist.org/study/ensign/1982/11/the-celestial-nature-of-self-reliance?lang=eng.

103 Neal A. Maxwell, "Swallowed Up in the Will of the Father," *Ensign*, Nov. 1995, churchofjesuschrist.org/study/ensign/1995/11/swallowed-up-in-the-will-of-the-father?lang=eng.

104 Neil L. Anderson, "The Prophet of God," *Ensign*, May 2018, churchofjesuschrist.org/study/ensign/2018/05/saturday-morning-session/the-prophet-of-god?lang=eng.

105 Robert L. Simpson, "Tithing: A Law of Peace and Security," Brigham Young University devotional, Dec. 2, 1979, speeches.byu.edu/talks/robert-l-simpson_tithing-law-peace-security/.

106 Bruce R. McConkie, "Obedience, Consecration, and Sacrifice," *Ensign*, May 1975, churchofjesuschrist.org/study/ensign/1975/05/obedience-consecration-and-sacrifice?lang=eng.

107 C. S. Lewis, *Mere Christianity* (New York City: Macmillan 1952), 105. See samizdat.qc.ca/vc/pdfs/MereChristianity_CSL.pdf for a Canadian public domain version of the text. Also quoted by Robert L. Backman in "Jesus the Christ," *Ensign*, Nov. 1991, churchofjesuschrist.org/study/ensign/1991/11/jesus-the-christ?lang=eng.

108 Neal A. Maxwell, "Becometh As a Child," *Ensign*, May 1986, churchofjesuschrist.org/study/ensign/1996/05/becometh-as-a -child?lang=eng.

109 Neal A. Maxwell, "Willing to Submit," *Ensign*, May 1985, churchofjesuschrist.org/study/ensign/1985/05/willing-to -submit?lang=eng.

110 Neal A. Maxwell, "Meekness—A Dimension of True Discipleship," *Ensign*, Mar. 1983, churchofjesuschrist.org/study/ensign/1983/03/ meekness-a-dimension-of-true-discipleship?lang=eng.

111 Neal A. Maxwell, "Meek and Lowly," Brigham Young University devotional, Oct. 21, 1986, speeches.byu.edu/talks/neal-a-maxwell _meek-lowly/.

112 Neal A. Maxwell, "Patience," Brigham Young University devotional, Nov. 27, 1979, speeches.byu.edu/talks/neal-a-maxwell_patience/.

113 Neal A. Maxwell, "Brim with Joy," Brigham Young University devotional, Jan. 23, 1996, speeches.byu.edu/talks/neal-a-maxwell _brim-joy/.

114 Ezra Taft Benson, "Jesus Christ—Gifts and Expectations," *Ensign*, Dec. 1988, churchofjesuschrist.org/study/ensign/1988/12/jesus-christ-gifts -and-expectations?lang=eng.

115 C. S. Lewis, *Mere Christianity* (New York City: Macmillan 1952), 109–10. See samizdat.qc.ca/vc/pdfs/MereChristianity_CSL.pdf for a Canadian public domain version of the text. Also quoted by Marvin J. Ashton, "Progress through Change," *Ensign*, Nov. 1979, churchofjesuschrist.org/study/ensign/1979/11/progress-through -change?lang=eng.

116 Gerrit W. Gong, "Covenant Belonging," *Ensign*, Nov. 2019, churchofjesuschrist.org/study/ensign/2019/11/covenant -belonging/?lang=eng.

117 Delbert L. Stapley in Conference Report, Oct. 1965, 14, archive.org/ details/conferencereport1965sa/page/n15.

118 *Handbook 2: Administering the Church*, 2018 edition, section 2.2, "The Purpose of the Church," churchofjesuschrist.org/study/manual/ handbook-2-administering-the-church/priesthood-principles/priesthood -principles?lang=eng.

119 Robert J. Whetten, "Strengthen Thy Brethren," *Ensign*, May 2005, churchofjesuschrist.org/study/ensign/2005/05/strengthen-thy -brethren?lang=eng.

120 Harriet Beecher Stowe, *Uncle Tom's Cabin* (New York City: Harper-Collins, 1852), 340. For a public domain version of the text, see books.google.com/books?id=rlDaAAAAIAAJ&printsec=frontcover& source=gbs_ge_summary_r&cad=0#v=onepage&q&f=false. See also gutenberg.org/files/203/203-h/203-h.htm.

121 Maxwell, "Swallowed Up in the Will of the Father."

122 Stowe, *Uncle Tom*, 341.

123 Stowe, *Uncle Tom*, 343.

124 Stowe, *Uncle Tom*, 343; emphasis added.

125 Neal A. Maxwell, "Put Off the Natural Man, and Come Off Conqueror," *Ensign*, Nov. 1990, churchofjesuschrist.org/study/ ensign/1990/11/put-off-the-natural-man-and-come-off -conqueror?lang=eng.

Chapter 8—Christ & Covenants

126 The history of this public domain picture is discussed by Eric W. Weisstein in "Young Girl-Old Woman Illusion." See *MathWorld*—A Wolfram Web Resource, July 31, 2018, at mathworld.wolfram.com/ YoungGirl-OldWomanIllusion.html.

127 Holland, "For a Wise Purpose."

128 Monte S. Nyman, "Question: Since the Book of Mormon contains the fulness of the gospel, why is there no mention of temples or temple work?" *Liahona*, July 1984, churchofjesuschrist.org/study/ liahona/1984/07/questions-and-answers/why-is-there-no-mention-of -temples-or-temple-work-in-the-book-of-mormon?lang=eng.

129 Daniel H. Ludlow, "Why do we say that the Book of Mormon contains 'the fulness of the gospel' (D&C 20:9) when it doesn't contain some of the basic teachings of the Church?" *Ensign*, Sept. 1985, churchofjesuschrist.org/study/ensign/1985/09/i-have-a-question/i-have-a- question?lang=eng.

130 Joseph Smith Jr., quoted in the introduction to the Book of Mormon, ix. See churchofjesuschrist.org/scriptures/bofm/introduction?lang=eng.

131 Russell M. Nelson, Facebook post, Apr. 17, 2018, facebook.com/ lds.russell.m.nelson/photos/pcb.1704606872940075/ 1704605372940225/?type=3.

132 Elder Marcus B. Nash, "The New and Everlasting Covenant," *Ensign*, Dec. 2015, churchofjesuschrist.org/study/ensign/2015/12/the-new-and -everlasting-covenant?lang=eng.

133 Packer, *Preparing to Enter the Holy Temple*, 35, 37. Formatting modified.

134 Robert D. Hales, "Temple Blessings," Brigham Young University devotional, Nov. 15, 2005, speeches.byu.edu/talks/robert-d-hales _temple-blessings/.

135 David A. Bednar, "Prepared to Obtain Every Needful Thing," *Ensign*, May 2019, churchofjesuschrist.org/study/ensign/2019/05/prepared-to -obtain-every-needful-thing?lang=eng.

136 Gerrit W. Gong, "Christ the Lord Is Risen Today," *Ensign*, May 2018, churchofjesuschrist.org/study/ensign/2018/05/sunday-afternoon-session/ christ-the-lord-is-risen-today?lang=eng.

137 Smith, introduction to the Book of Mormon, ix.

138 Dallin H. Oaks, " 'Another Testament of Jesus Christ,' " *Ensign*, Mar. 1994, churchofjesuschrist.org/study/ensign/1994/03/another-testament- of-jesus-christ?lang=eng.

139 Oaks, " 'Another Testament of Jesus Christ.' "

140 Russell M. Nelson, "As We Go Forward Together," *Ensign*, Apr. 2018, churchofjesuschrist.org/study/ensign/2018/04/as-we-go-forward -together?lang=eng.

About the Author

Valiant K. Jones grew up in Utah, Indiana, and Idaho, and he attended Brigham Young University where he received a BS degree, summa cum laude with honors, followed by an MS degree, both in chemical engineering.

He worked for over thirty-two years in the chemical industry, primarily in the areas of new process development and computerized process automation, and he authored many research and technology reports during his career.

Brother Jones enjoys using his analytical skills in the study of Latter-day Saint scripture and doctrine. He has served in a variety of callings in The Church of Jesus Christ of Latter-day Saints, including serving a mission in the Cordoba Argentina Mission and serving as a temple worker, a branch president, and a high councilor. He has also served in civic and community roles including extensive BSA volunteer positions where he received the Silver Beaver Award.

Brother Jones resides in central Michigan where he enjoys the beautiful outdoors, camping, biking, and snow skiing. He and his wife, the former Lori Ransom, are the proud parents of five children and have a growing number of grandchildren.

Scan to visit

valiantjones.com